She Calls Herself Betsey Stockton

—— The Illustrated Odyssey of a Princeton Slave ——

Constance K. Escher

FOREWORD BY
John J. Baxter

RESOURCE *Publications* · Eugene, Oregon

SHE CALLS HERSELF BETSEY STOCKTON
The Illustrated Odyssey of a Princeton Slave

Resource Publications
An Imprint of Wipf and Stock Publishers
199 W. 8th Ave., Suite 3
Eugene, OR 97401

www.wipfandstock.com

PAPERBACK ISBN: 978-1-7252-7544-7
HARDCOVER ISBN: 978-1-7252-7545-4
EBOOK ISBN: 978-1-7252-7546-1

01/21/22

Cover image: Betsey Stockton. "Daguerreotype portrait, studio of Augustus Moran (Brooklyn, NY), May or June 1863. Original carte de visite, N-0774, photograph collection of Hawaiian Children's Mission Society Library, Used with permission of the Mission Houses Historic Site and Archives, Honolulu.

Cover image: *Cleopatra's Barge.* Watercolor on paper 17 ⅞ x 22 ⅞", by George Ropes (American, 1788–1819), 1818. Gift of Mrs. Francis B. Crowninshield, 1953, M8255. Used with permission of Peabody Essex Museum, Salem, MA. Photograph by Mark Sexton.

This book is dedicated to teachers of literacy,
wherever they may be.

They that do business in the great waters,
these see the works of God,
and his wonders in the deep.

    —Louisa Everest Ely, missionary sister of Betsey Stockton,
      Atlantic Ocean, Ship *Thames*, December 2, 1822

Contents

List of Illustrations

Foreword

IN APRIL 2017, CONSTANCE Escher received a letter from Princeton University officials asking about the complete name of the woman of color for whom a new public garden near Firestone Library was to be named. Escher's reply was "She Calls Herself Betsey Stockton," the title of her 1991 seminal work, a thirty-page biographical sketch of Stockton. Princeton Theological Seminary followed the university's lead, naming the Betsey Stockton Research Center within Speer Library and pledging $27.5 million dollars to research the past relationship with slavery. Betsey Stockton was beginning to receive the recognition she deserved from her hometown and the institutions to which her story is tied.

The life of Betsey Stockton is a story of literacy. Her life spanned roughly seventy years, from the presidency of John Adams to the final year of the Civil War. She lived at a time when the American Revolution—founded on the lofty proposition that all men are created equal—was confronted with the hypocrisy of what it had produced: a slaveholding republic. Literacy was a crucial front during the antebellum fight over slavery. As Frederick Douglass observes, "education and slavery are incompatible with each other."[1]

Anti-literacy laws—laws which criminalized the education of slaves—were born out of the fears that literacy among the slave population would lead to the forgery of manumission documents, awareness of abolitionist efforts, increased runaways, and organization of rebellion.

Betsey Stockton was born into bondage, owned by Robert Stockton of Princeton, New Jersey—a state without an anti-literacy law. In fact, a 1788 law required every slave under the age of twenty-one be taught to read by their owner. At an early age, Betsey was given to Robert's daughter Elizabeth and her husband Ashbel Green. In the Green household, Betsey learned to read.

While Betsey benefitted from the law of 1788, New Jersey's Gradual Abolition Law of 1804 passed her by. That law put children born to slave mothers on the path to freedom if born after July 4, 1804. Betsey was roughly eight years old when the law was passed. Under the law, she would remain a slave for life if not manumitted.

---

1. Douglass, as cited in Blight, *Frederick Douglass*, 35.

Freedom for Betsey, however, would come through literacy. It un-
leashed her intellect, and, with the backing of Green, her brilliance brought
access to the world of missionary work. In 1823, Betsey began her teaching
career in the Sandwich Islands. She exhibited an extraordinary talent for
learning indigenous languages. With that, she developed a keen understanding for the importance of teaching literacy and spreading Christianity
in the native tongue of her students, called scholars.

By the time she returned to the United States in 1826, Betsey Stockton
had circumnavigated the globe, and the country was increasingly divided
over slavery. The Missouri Compromise had drawn a geographical line di-
viding free from slave territory, a line that Thomas Jefferson believed would
grow deeper and deeper, sounding the death knell of the country.

She was hired by a team of women to organize and become the head
teacher of the Infant School for the Coloured in Philadelphia. Meanwhile,
New York ended the process of gradual abolition with the emancipation
of all remaining slaves in 1827, and Betsey travelled to New York City to
observe the teaching of Joanna Bethune.

From Philadelphia, Betsey continued with her missionary calling in
Grape Island, Upper Canada, where she established schools among the
Ojibwa Indians. When she returned to the United States in the mid-1830s,
the country was further divided. The slave rebellion led by Nat Turner had
tightened enforcement of anti-literacy laws in the South. Northern abolitionists such as Lloyd Garrison were increasingly outspoken and calling for
immediate emancipation. Secession was being openly debated in the United
States Senate and threatened by South Carolina.

In New Jersey, under the Gradual Abolition Law, those African Americans born after July 4, 1804, had remained bound to servitude until age
twenty-one for females, age twenty-five for males. Their offspring were born
free. Betsey was returning to a growing free population in need of education
in her home town. Literacy still played a role in ending the institution of
slavery, but in the northern states, it was more essential to economic opportunity. She would rise to the occasion—and then some.

"Literacy is a bridge from misery to hope. . . . [and] is a platform
for democratization."[2] Kofi Annan's words mirror the history of struggle
for racial equality in the United States and why for two hundred years literacy was inextricably linked to that struggle. Anti-literacy laws defended
slavery until the Thirteenth Amendment of 1865, only to be followed by
so-called literacy tests to deny democracy to African Americans until the
Voting Rights Act of 1965.

It is an ugly irony indeed that African Americans' hard-won access to literacy, provided by champions such as Betsey Stockton during the antebellum

2. Annan, "Secretary-General Stresses Need."

period and feeble during the Jim Crow era of separate but equal, was used by white legislatures to bludgeon African Americans' voting rights. Literacy tests, despite the name, had nothing to do with literacy and everything to do with the color of the applicant's skin. Literacy, long prohibited and grudgingly conceded through the bloodshed of Civil War, was a potent word to be used as a weapon and a disingenuous mask for racial bigotry. Nevertheless, the seeds of equality had been sown by persons such as Betsey Stockton. Walking like a queen, this community matriarch shattered the chains of racism, gender, and poverty, a heroic example of Christian humanism, the teacher who embedded the immutable tool of literacy in each of her scholars.

John J. Baxter, Esquire

"This is to Certify that Miss Betsey Stockton has been Constituted by the Contributions of the Col 1 Sabbath School of the Witherspoon Chr. Princeton N. Jersey, An Honorary Life Member of the Board of Foreign Missions of the Presbyterian Church." W. W. Phillips, President; John C. Lowrie, Secretary. Used with permission of Speer Library, Princeton Theological Seminary

Acknowledgments

I THANK THE FOLLOWING individuals, who have assisted me with research and support: Wanda S. Gunning, Constance M. Greiff, John J. Baxter, Shirley Satterfield, Ray Ollwerther, Professor Sean Wilentz, Professor Richard Fenn, Kate Skebutends, Brian Shelter, William Harris, Kenneth Henke, Philip Lapansky, Eileen Moffatt, Lee Arnold, Louisa Watrous, William Johnson, Lynn Harkness, Lyn Nosker, Richard Woodbridge, Karen Woodbridge, Charles Green, John Delaney, Stephen Ferguson, Annalees Pauls, Joseph C. Felcone, Britt Bowen, Andrew Williams, Kate Duff, Britt Bowen, Erin Beasley, Dorianne Perrucci.

From the Princeton Public Library: Janie Hermann, Hannah Schmidl, Kim Dorman, Timothy Quinn, Susan Conlon.

From Trinity Episcopal Church: Rev. Canon Dr. Kara S. Slade, Rev. Louise Kingston, Rev. Joan Fleming, Juliana McI. Fenn, Rob Frazier, Rev. Joanne Epply-Schmidt, Rector Paul Jeannes III, Nancy Hearne, Kay Mack, Margot Southerland, Thom Southerland, Henry Rulon-Miller, Susan Taylor, Susan McGregor, Rev. Frank and Carrie Strassburger.

From the United Church of Christ: Rev. Dr. Karen Georgia A. Thompson and Rev. Dr. Monica Dawkins-Smith.

From Hawaii: Kelsey Karson, Mission Houses Museum, Honolulu.

From Nantucket: Elizabeth Oldham, Marie Henke, Nantucket Historical Association.

From Whaling Research: Dan Hickey, NARA, Northeast Region, Boston, for the *Thames'* crew manifest documentation; Stuart M. Frank, New Bedford Whaling Museum, for inspiration and scholarship.

From the Connecticut Historical Society Museum and Library: Tasha Caswell, Andrea V. Rapacz.

Faithful friends and family: Amelie Scott Escher; Elsbeth House Escher; Professor Mark Wolfmeyer; Patricia Killian; Wally Killian; Susan Weatherley; Marilyn and Owen Shteir; Lianne S. Escher; Gustav E. Escher III; and my parents, Anita Scott Killian and Edgar W. Killian, who taught me to think and to dream.

And thanks to Christopher Eisgruber, Lorie A. Martin, and James Steward for words of inspiration and solace for us all.

Chapter 1: **Deconstructing an Icon**

"FACES ARE THE LEDGERS of our experience," writes photographer Ricard Avedon.[1]

Portrait photographs present the public face of the private life of the sitter. So a life portrait is an invaluable gift to the writer of an historical biography.

Betsey Stockton's apotheosis to Princeton celebrity has come in the last two years. Two institutions, Princeton University and Princeton Theological Seminary, claim her as their internationally famous teacher. In 2018, Princeton University named a garden for her on the college's campus. In October 2019, Princeton Theological Seminary announced the creation of the Betsey Stockton Research Center within its Speer Library.

My Betsey Stockton "Aha!" moment came in 1984. As I opened a biographical file in the upstairs library in Bainbridge House on Nassau Street, a period photograph labelled "Betsey Stockton" tumbled out. There, staring back at me, was a portrait with engaging eyes. It showed the intelligence, the nobility, and the authority of the sitter. Inquisitive by nature and training, I began by asking myself questions a historical biographer uses to ferret out basic facts. Who was Betsey Stockton? What was the life story behind the portrait of this former Princeton slave?

The facts behind the daguerreotype portrait eventually surfaced. Taken two years before her death in 1865, Stockton saved her teaching wages to pay for it. At the time, she was in shaky health and living in genteel poverty in her house on Witherspoon Street. Understanding this artifact and its provenance was essential for comprehending Betsey Stockton's self-proclaimed identity.

We know now where, when, how—and possibly why—this unique artifact was created, changing inaccurate or undocumented attributions. For modern viewers, as for this author, finding the authentic portrait was tantamount to finding Betsey Stockton herself.

By glimpsing the pose of the famous Frederick Douglass, I was prompted to compare two other period photographs. Douglass's was included in a

---

1. Richard Avedon, as cited by Quotely, https://quotely.org/quote/255054-faces-are-the-ledgers-of-our-experience./.

recently published catalogue, *Picturing Frederick Douglass: An Illustrated Biography of the Nineteenth Century's Most Photographed American.*[2] The pose jogged my memory.

I compared one of Douglass's poses to two portraits of Stockton's missionary brother, Reverend Charles Samuel Stewart, and one of Betsey Stockton herself, appearing together in *A Missionary Album*, published in Hawaii in 1966.[3] The vague attribution for each was "around 1863"—with no other information given in any archive. From her letters, Betsey Stockton was known to have maintained a lifelong friendship and correspondence with Stewart, a College of New Jersey graduate of 1815 and a Princeton Theological Seminary student in 1821. His portrait attribution was an integral clue to documenting Stockton's own.

I compared my former copies of Stewart's portrait, front and back, housed in the archives of Princeton Theological Seminary.

The clue to linking all three portraits was there. On the reverse of Stewart's *carte de visite*, a 3 x 5" photograph, was the unmistakable commercial stamp of the photographer, "Augustus Morand, 292 Fulton Street, on the corner of John Street Brooklyn." Stewart's portrait exactly matched the pose and positive attribution of the *carte de visite* of "Plate 20, catalogue #23" of Frederick Douglass.[4] Both Stewart's and Douglass's portraits were taken by Augustus Morand. But what about Betsey Stockton's? Was it taken at the same time and place as Stewart's or in the same daguerreotype studio as Douglass's?

The Douglass book's authors give a possible date for the Douglass portrait. They note the possibility that "Douglass probably sat for this photograph during a visit for him to give a lecture at the Brooklyn Academy of Music, on May 15, 1863."[5] Morand's daguerreotype studio was fairly near the academy, then located at 176–194 Montague Street, Brooklyn Heights.

Very likely, Betsey Stockton, her friend Stewart, and Frederick Douglass all visited Morand's studio during the summer of 1863. In fact, on June 18, 1863, Stewart was awarded an honorary doctorate of divinity from the University of the City of New York.[6]

Did Stewart, who was known for his published loathing of the transatlantic slave trade, travel with Betsey Stockton to hear Douglass, the Silver-Tongued Lion of Abolitionism, at the Brooklyn Academy of Music? Did

2. Stauffer et al., *Picturing Frederick Douglass*, 22.

3. Judd, Beatrice. Missionary Album, 184, 185, 186.

4. Stauffer et al., *Picturing Frederick Douglass*, 22.

5. Stauffer et al., *Picturing Frederick Douglass*, 22.

6. ———. Catalogue of the University of the City of New York, 1863.16.

they travel together by railroad and then take the ferry to the Fulton Street Terminal in Brooklyn and go on to Morand's studio?

Let us look at the evidence of those three sittings. All three daguerreo-type portraits show the floating half bust as posed by Morand. All three reveal the sitter's intensity by focusing a three-quarter view of each face. With a half shadow of the sitter's profile on the right or left of the viewer, the eyes, nose, hair, and shape of the sitter's face is revealed as no full-face image could do. Stewart's floating bust portrait by Morand faces to his right, while Stockton and Douglas both face to their left.

More than a symbol for his cause, Frederick Douglass knew how to dress as an actor for his part on the stage of public opinion. The texture of Douglass's goatee and his lion-mane hair, carefully combed back to reveal his face, emphasize his age. The formality of his heavily starched white shirt with its attached white collar, white vest, and black silk cravat, enveloped in his fashionable lapelled coat, present Douglass as heroic, as powerful, as eternal. Like Stockton, Frederick Douglass was born to an African American slave mother and a free White father. Like Stockton, he was a published author.

Stockton's portrait and its attribution is among the rarest of the rare. As Henry Louis Gates Jr. notes in his essay "The Face and Voice of Black-ness," "The rareness of existing portraits of prominent black figures is both a telling commentary on the singular numbers of these figures in the nineteenth century and early twentieth-century American society and an effective critique of the visual arts as a medium of constructing images of black identity."[7] In other words, few portraits of prominent individuals of color exist, either through the historical record's ignorant omissions or by its purposeful exclusion.

"Douglass believed that art was a terrain that was about emotional and imaginative, as well as intellectual and social, transformation," says Celeste-Marie Bernier, one of the authors of *Picturing Frederick Douglass*.[8] Newspa-per reporters noted "a colored lady or gentlemen sitting in the audience" at BAM. Surely, one of those could well have been Betsey Stockton. Douglass's topic that evening?—"What Shall Be Done with the Negro?" With great logic and forceful presentation, Douglass touched on the Negro voter's abil-ity to read—a subject close to Betsey Stockton's heart.[9]

---

7. Gates, *Face and Voice of Blackness*, xxix.

8. Bernier, Celeste-Marie. "Frederick Douglass the Destination." New York Times, Dec 1, 2019, 20.

9. Hamm, *Frederick Douglass in Brooklyn*, 54–81.

Historically, in contrast, American individuals of color were almost never identified as individuals but instead grouped as grotesque, comic, or subhuman figures by White painters, writers, or illustrators.

Because of Betsey Stockton's accurate portrait attribution, she joins the acknowledged pantheon of famous nineteenth-century African American women who rose above the negative stereotypes of portraiture: Isabella Van Wagener, who renamed herself "Sojourner Truth"; Harriet Tubman, the "Moses" of the Underground Railroad; and New Jersey preacher Jarena Lee, who self-published her autobiography with her engraved portrait as a frontispiece.[10]

Smiling for daguerreotype portraits was not possible. Exactly what was the process that Stockton, Stewart, and Douglass replicated as they sat for Morand's camera? The sitter bought a ticket, then passed it to the camera operator, who never left his equipment. A highly polished silver-covered glass plate made by the polisher was brought to Morand. He then posed the subject against a blank background. Stockton, Stewart, and Douglass had to cooperate with Morand, and each sat perfectly still for about a minute. If the sitter moved, the picture was ruined. Conversely, if the subjects could not compose themselves and appear at ease in the spirit of the moment, their anxiety would be visible, and the likeness would be forced and unnatural.[11] The portrait would be a failure.

Like everyone else, Betsey Stockton had the barest of moments to compose her face for posterity. Posed against a plain background with diffused light from a studio skylight or side window, the sitting for her daguerreotype was finished. Within fifteen minutes, she would have been on her way, the *carte de visite* in her hand, either within a velvet-lined folding case or within a cheaper version. The cost for a studio Morand daguerreotype was anywhere from twelve and a half cents to several dollars in 1863 currency.

Why would Stockton have wanted to have her daguerreotype taken? Scholar Henry Gates answers that question: "In the first decades of the nineteenth century, the few prominent blacks who obtained access to the middle and upper classes commissioned paintings and later—photographs—of themselves, so they could metaphorically enshrine and quite literally perpetuate the example of their own identities."[12]

Take a look at the curly wisp of graying hair that has escaped her cloth-covered head. Today, celebrated by Princeton University and Princeton

---

10. Escher and Gifford, "Jarena Lee," *Past and Promise*, 77–79.

11. Newhall, *History of Photography*, 30–39.

12. Gates, *Face and Voice of Blackness*, xxix.

Theological Seminary alike, no one would dare to label Stockton's hair stereotypically "kinky" or "nappy."

Also prominent in the portrait is Stockton's headgear. Apparently, Stockton chose to present her everyday self for her public likeness. Her friends recalled that she always wore a turban of simple white cotton cloth wound around her head. When I first noticed this reference, my guess was that the turban referred to her African American slave mother. However, after years of thought and research, another clearer answer presented itself through a British journal article. The journal published an account documenting Hawaiian King Kamehameha II and Queen Kahamalu's fatal London visit in 1824.[13] The article described in depth the fashionable neoclassical (Turkish-inspired) headgear of the Hawaiian queen and those who saw her in the Royal Opera box at the Drury Lane Theatre. Later, a published London engraving showed their majesties in formal dress, with the queen wearing that turban.

The origin of Betsey Stockton's turban was found not in the African American tradition but within the centuries of royal Hawaiian women's headdresses. The earliest recorded example of this indigenous headdress was a circlet of beads twisted into the wearer's hair. *A Young Woman of the Sandwich Islands*, a portrait engraved by English artist John Webber, depicts this pre-contact adornment.[14]

Gushed a London journalist: "The queen [Kahamalu] particularly felt gratified with that kind of urbanity of manners and which was an honor to herself . . . and moreover, . . . more than one [London] lady begged to have the pattern of Kahamalu's turban."[15]

By adopting the headdress—and with it, the style and authority of Hawaiian Queens—as a matriarch in Princeton, Betsey Stockton embodied culture convergence. "Her [Stockton's] word was law . . . and she walked like a queen," remembered Princeton friend Lewis W. Mudge, "[with] her turban as she always wore it."[16]

Was there a hidden reason why Betsey Stockton and Charles S. Stewart had their daguerreotypes made in 1863? Would visual evidence gleaned from her daguerreotype confirm or refute clues as to the identity of her unnamed White father?

---

13. Byron, *Voyage of H.M.S. Blonde*, 62–64.
14. Little and Ruthenberg, eds., *Life in the Pacific*, 38.
15. Byron, *Voyage of H.M.S. Blonde*, 64.
16. Woodhull and Mudge, "Betsey Stockton and Hawaiian School."

Chapter 2: **Early Life**

DISCOVERING THE LIFE AND writings of a Mulatto woman who was one of the most widely traveled, highly educated, and socially active beings of her time has been the focus of my research since 1984. A Children's Museum exhibit introduced Betsey Stockton, with her portrait, at the Historical Society of Princeton.[1] Primary sources document her identity, her travels, and her legacy. Betsey Stockton was an extraordinary agent of change during her lifetime and beyond.

Those sources allow a contemporary picture of Betsey Stockton and the emergence of the power of agency for newly freed slaves. Many, like Stockton, were individuals of color, born to one African American parent, usually a mother, and one White parent, usually a father.[2] Frederick Douglass and John Brown Russwurm are two famous examples. Marcus Marsh, born in slavery in Princeton thirty years before Betsey Stockton, is another example. Six decades before the Civil War, these individuals wrested their lives from lethal racism to reshape American thinking about the individuals held in the barbaric institution of slavery. In doing so, they laid the foundation for new—and enlightened—ways of changing their worlds.

In the prestigious slaveholding Stockton families of Princeton, two slaveowners followed the 1788 New Jersey law. Passed on November 16 in Princeton, this state law required slaveholders to teach their chattel slaves to read and write. Detailed in section 6 of the Acts of the General Assembly, the Act instructed "Persons owning slaves how and when to educate them."

> That every Person or Persons within this State, who shall be the owner or owners of any Negro or Mulatto Slave or Slaves, Servant or Servants for Life or Years, born after the Publication of this Act, shall cause every such Slave or Slaves, Servant or Servants, while under the Age of Twenty-one years to be taught and instructed to read . . . or shall forfeit and pay the Sum of Five Pounds . . . before any Justice of the Peace.[3]

---

1. Escher, "Being Themselves: Four Stars of Princeton: The Children's Museum Exhibit Guide," The Historical Society Princeton, 1984.

2. Blight, *Frederick Douglass*, xiv.

3. New Jersey General Assembly, *Acts of Thirteenth General Assembly*, 488.

Contradicting racially biased customs regarding slavery and literacy, this law and its application educated at least two Princeton children born into slavery. Poet Annis Boudinot Stockton breastfed "my poor Marcus"—later Marcus Marsh—after his slave mother's death in 1765.[4] Marsh was born into slavery on April 1, 1765, at Morven, the plantation of Annis and Richard, known as the Signer.[5] Literacy caught up with Marsh sometime in his early life.

Like Marsh, Betsey Stockton's life challenged hardwired racial views about the mental capacity and innate humanity of African Americans during the American Empire period. Thomas Jefferson "openly speculated that black people were inferior to white people."[6] Princeton College of New Jersey graduate Dr. Benjamin Rush published his essay "Observations Intended to Favour a Supposition That the Black Color (as It Is Called) Is Derived from Leprosy" in the prestigious American Philosophical Society in 1799 but was an abolitionist.[7]

Because they were born on American soil, neither Marcus March nor Betsey Stockton endured the lethal horrors of the Middle Passage. During the seventeenth and eighteenth centuries, American and European merchants of human flesh immorally transported millions of individuals. The watery route to bondage shipped thousands of slaves stolen from Sierra Leone and other communities in Africa to the Caribbean Sea islands. The triangular trade cargoes of kidnapped Africans were sold to sugar cane plantations for three years of "hardening off" before being resold to American slaveholders, mainly in the South, chiefly for growing cotton as a cash crop. On January 1, 1808, the United States law banning the international slave trade went into effect—to be continually violated.[8]

Marcus Marsh was formally manumitted by Annis Boudinot Stockton, "widow of the deceased Richard Stockton, Esq." on March 2, 1798, in Philadelphia, through a holograph manuscript by Stockton "who to this testimony sets her hand."[9] Earlier, the Stockton slave Marsh had become a medical assistant to Stockton's son-in-law Dr. Benjamin Rush—so much for leprosy—and probably saved his life during the 1793 yellow fever epidemic in Philadelphia.[10]

---

4. Greiff and Gunning, eds., *Morven*, 44, 78.

5. Grieff and Gunning, eds., *Morven*, 44, 78.

6. "A Powerful Letter," *NYTimes*, 1619 Project, April 18, 2019. 11.

7. Rush, "Observations Intended to Favour."

8. "Describing the Depravity," in Roper, "New York Times Magazine."

9. Dye, "Early American Merchant Seafarers," 352.

10. Morales, "Great Physician Had Help."

In the case of Betsey Stockton, born on Robert Stockton's Princeton farm, Constitution Hill, the child Bet was later given as an enslaved person to Elizabeth Stockton as part of her marriage dowry to Rev. Ashbel Green.[11] "Bet" became a child slave held by Green and his wife as Green assumed the co-pastorate of the Second Presbyterian Church in Philadelphia.[12]

As an educated elite, Betsey Stockton was an heir to the Scottish American (read *Presbyterian*) Enlightenment of the Princeton-Philadelphia axis, which the President of the College of New Jersey John Witherspoon bestrode like a modern colossus until his death in 1794. Ashbel Green followed Witherspoon, also a slaveholder, to became the eighth president of the College of New Jersey in 1812.

In 1989, Green's holograph diaries, four thousand pages in typescript, were purchased by Princeton University's Rare Books and Manuscripts department from his descendants.[13] This primary source provides irrefutable, if sketchy, details documenting Green's relationship with his slave Bet. Green functioned *in loco parentis*, as a surrogate father, and as a tutor while holding Betsey Stockton as an enslaved child in his household: first in the church manse in Philadelphia and later in the President's House (now Maclean House) adjacent to Nassau Hall.

In his will, written in 1848, Green described his mastery of the shorthand method of this "secret diary." He stipulated that "no part of this diary will be printed unless it be some short article for the purpose of ascertaining a fact or a date. Perhaps I may destroy the whole before I die . . . "[14] In retrospect, Green may have reconsidered the intimacy of his relationship with Bet. It stands at odds with the fact that, in 1848, he preached his last sermon in her Witherspoon Street Presbyterian Church. Green's faithful support and pride in Betsey Stockton's accomplishments lasted throughout his lifetime.[15]

Whether located in Princeton or Philadelphia, Green's household was in love with Christ and with the written and spoken word. Language was used for praising God, for healing prayer, for consolations after children's deaths, for treatment of the mentally ill. Letters, sermons, hymns, books, chapbooks (pamphlets sold by peddlers), magazines, and newspapers infused every aspect of daily life in the Green household. From 1787 to 1816, Green bought books from William Young in Philadelphia.

---

11. J. Jones, *Life of Ashbel Green*, 326.
12. McLachlan, "Ashbel Green," 407.
13. Escher, "She Calls Herself Betsey Stockton," 72.
14. Green, "Last Will and Testament."
15. McLachlan, "Ashbel Green," 419.

In 1785, Ashbel Green married into the Princeton aristocracy of land and influence, taking Elizabeth Stockton, daughter of Robert, known as the Quartermaster, as his wife. Four years after Witherspoon's death, in or about 1798, Betsey Stockton was born to an African American enslaved woman of color. No birth, marriage, or manumission documents have been found for this enslaved woman to date. This mother was the property of Robert Stockton, owner of Constitution Hill, a large farm near Princeton, no longer extant. The farm's single blurry photographic image shows the vertical silhouette, high basement, and segmental arched windows of the early Georgian period.[16]

There is a strong possibility that Betsey Stockton's mother was the woman born into slavery referred to as Sealy by Robert Stockton in an April 24, 1797, letter of appeal to son-in-law Green in Philadelphia. Only the merest—and rarest—wisp of a ghostly presence of Betsey Stockton's enslaved mother of color glides across the pages of the historical record. From internal evidence in the letter, we learn about a pregnant and terrified Black runaway woman, referred to as Sealy, with no family name appended by Robert Stockton, her owner. Stockton must have written his holograph missive in a hurry, because he crossed out the word *if* twice in his letter to Green on that April day. The slaveowner's demanding tone made it clear to the recipient that he wanted his valuable Black property secured and that information about his runaway was to be sent back immediately, "by first post."

> Princeton 24th April 27
>
> Mr. Richd Stockton informed me that you wanted a line from me Respecting Sealy coming to Princeton. You please to inform her [Sealy] that I wish her to return and that I shall treet [sic] her as usual looking over what has passed she conducting herself as she ought to [*if* crossed out] she will not Return I wish you to take such steps as is proper to secure her so that she cannot make her escape, and it Necessary I shall come to Philadelphia. My love to Betsey [his daughter: the only time her name was spelled this way] and [unreadable name].
>
> . . . . D Sire yours,
>
> Rob Stockton
>
> [*If* crossed out] Please to let me hear from you by first post—.[17]

---

16. Greiff et al., *Princeton Architecture*, 28.

17. Robert Stockton, "Letter to Ashbel Green."

Ashbel Green possessed some previous information about Sealy, whom he called Celia, according to an April 11, 1797, diary entry. "Got to Princeton about sundown. At night received a letter from Major Rodgers relative to Celia," he wrote.[18] On June 4, 1797, he noted that "Celia came here [to Green's house in Philadelphia] and agreed to go to Princeton."[19] Green had fulfilled his father-in-law's request to return his runaway slave to Constitution Hill. It is clear not only that Green knew this enslaved woman of color, but that Sealy/Celia placed trust and confidence in him—as did his father-in-law, Robert Stockton.

This mysterious letter raises as many questions as it does answers. Why did Ashbel Green rename this slave from Robert Stockton's Sealy to Celia, a more Anglicized name? Why would Celia run to Green in the city of Philadelphia? Had she sensed his forgiving nature, when she realized that she was pregnant, possibly for the first time in her life? Why did she assume that Green would protect her present life—and that of her unborn child—from her older and more powerful owner, Robert Stockton? So full of pathos and anguish on the part of Sealy, this letter is singularly rare. It is the authentic record of a named pregnant runaway who gave birth to a known daughter. Betsey Stockton's full biography is a testament to the endurance of her enslaved mother.

Seemingly, following Green's urging or help to return Sealy/Celia to Constitution Hill, her daughter was born into slavery there sometime around the year 1798. The year before, in 1797, Green wrote that he "wrote a letter to Mr. Stockton." In August of that year he moved his family from Philadelphia to his "father-in-law's farm at Constitution Hill."[20] "Fear and gloom at the farm" wrote Green in September of 1799, as reports of unhealthy conditions in Philadelphia continued.[21] Specifically, in 1798, Green and Elizabeth Stockton Green resided there with their sons, Robert, eleven; Jacob, eight; and James Sproat, six years old, as they sought refuge at Constitution Hill from yet another yellow fever epidemic in Philadelphia.[22]

Green's secret diary is the only primary source of the life of Celia's daughter, first known by the barest minimum of names, Bet. Perhaps this slave name was a reference to her first owner, Elizabeth Stockton Green, who was sometimes called Betsy. Notice the spelling. During 1799 to 1804, Green's entries

18. Green, *Diaries*, 595.
19. Green, *Diaries*, 778.
20. Green, *Diaries*, 778.
21. Green, *Diaries*, 802.
22. Green, *Diaries*, 1010.

are full of concern about his children, whom he sends out of Philadelphia to Princeton, Constitution Hill.[23] Was Bet sent there with his sons?

In 1802, Green a family member died, and, in 1803, he notes his baptism of a Black woman "by the name of Lettis."[24] This early date is surprising, considering that the Presbyterians questioned extending the sacrament of baptism to African Americans, whether slave or free at the time.

Bet, Celia's daughter, first makes her presence known in September 1804. Green's entry: "A six-year old Bet played the mischief." She had captured her busy owner's attention. What exactly was her playful act, such that Green "corrected" it the next day, as he recorded in his diary?[25]

Perhaps that correction took the form of corporal punishment; but knowing Green's temperament, his rigorous sense of duty and decorum, and his experience with his own three sons, fatherly Green probably did no more than his parental duty—a verbal reprimand—as any devoted Christian parent might do. Green's diary contains no evidence of massive whippings given to enslaved children of color—or none are recorded by him. Green fathered no daughters through his two marriages.

Terse diary references to Bet are all that exist of Bet's Philadelphia girlhood. Green's catechism of Bet can be interpreted as teaching lessons from the Bible itself or from Presbyterian lessons taken from it. This early question and response method shaped Betsey Stockton's mind. In the future, she would recall it.

Green had finished "A Catechism for Children" on a "new plan" in January 1806, then began to teach son James "to cipher." They all lived through the "Lightning Incident" in 1807. Green considered "manumitting negro George, which I find I cannot do," but changed his mind six months later and "wrote a manumission for George at Princeton."[26]

Since Elizabeth Stockton Green, called Betsy, had died in January 1807, the 1808 note "Betsey's mother here" is very intriguing. Green had moved to his house in Arch Street, Philadelphia, that same year.[27] Considering the spelling of the name, could this visit have been made by Celia to see her ten-year old slave daughter Bet? Diarist Green never wrote the mother's name.

During the years 1808 to 1809, Green was filled with concerns about his Woodbury relatives, with the execution of the will of his father-in-law, which might have legally transferred the ownership of Bet to him, through his now

23. Green, *Diaries*, 1010.

24. Green, *Diaries*, 1144.

25. Green, *Diaries*, 1145.

26. Green, *Diaries*, 1241.

27. McLachlan, "Ashbel Green," 409; Green, *Diaries*, 1405.

deceased wife. He recalled that a former tutor for his children, a Mr. John Ely, "talked with Bet" in August 1809.[28] A year later, he wrote, "Bett came to inform me that my mother-in-law is dying."[29] Green's conversations with his slave were to continue. In June 1811, he wrote, "in the evening I had a long conversation with Bett." In July he "catechized Bet," and on July 21, 1811, Green "wrote 3 long letters; one to Mr. Todd about Bett."[30] Green was deliberating about his young slave's future. Decision made: on July 29, "Mr. M[oses] Bradford came from Woodbury to take Bet. He stayed with us one day."[31] July 30, "Betty left us and went with Mr. Bradford to Woodbury."[32] With no local school available for young girls of color, Green chose what other educated and financially able parents did: he provided for Bet to be tutored by a master teacher in a school setting in Woodbury, New Jersey.

When Bet/Betty/Betsy was fifteen, three years of her work and time were sold by Green to his nephew, the Rev. Nathaniel Todd. June 24, 1813: "Mr. and Mrs. Todd also (visited) and left us June 24th. Sold to Mr. Todd 3 years of the time of Betty to commence from July 30th (1813)."[33] On July 12, 1813, "Betsy left us this morning."[34] Green never recorded an amount of money from selling the paid labor of Bet.

Reading Green's careful and repetitive diary entries, one is struck by the writer's fatherly care for his slave's safe physical transportation to the Todds through the trusted Moses Bradford. Ambivalence toward Bet/Betty/Betsy's departure rises from these pages of Green's diary. The almost plaintive "left us" shows that her departure was felt by Green's entire household. Years later, Green wrote that Bet lived with the Todds between four and five years.[35]

For Ashbel Green, to whom teaching came far more easily than preaching or college administration, Stockton's education was seen as Christian reclamation. It was in Green's character to nurture the spiritual and academic growth of the naughty and bright mulatta child in his household. He was keenly interested in the education of children, in the spiritual growth and education of African Americans, and in gradual emancipation, an enlightened view inherited from his father, Rev. Jacob Green, Harvard 1744.

28. Green, *Diaries*, 1521.

29. Green, *Diaries*, 1601.

30. Green, *Diaries*, 1654.

31. Green, *Diaries*, 1654.

32. Green, *Diaries*, 1654.

33. Green, *Diaries*, 1655.

34. Green, *Diaries*, 1741.

35. Green, as cited in Escher, "She Calls Herself," 77.

Green's parenting of Betsey Stockton was the perfect example of what some historians describe as the duality of Green's character. He possessed a stern, unyielding, even a repulsive public persona, and a singularly opposite private character. With Bet, his surrogate daughter, he was the exemplary private man "who was mild, pliable and peculiarly attractive . . . . And [by his followers] he was uncommonly beloved and regarded an oracle."[36]

36. McLachlan, "Ashbel Green," 404, 408.

Chapter 3: **From Childhood Slave to Adult Missionary**

IN PHILADELPHIA, ASHBEL GREEN had served as co-chaplain to Congress until 1800, when the capital was transferred to Washington. Green, a member of the American Philosophical Society, sat for his portrait by Charles Willson Peale in 1804. Green married into Princeton's landed aristocracy in 1785, through his marriage to Robert Stockton's daughter Elizabeth (sometimes called Betsy). At this father-in-law's farmstead, Constitution Hill (so named because the state constitution of New Jersey was written there), an African American slave mother gave birth to a daughter. Sealy or Celia's child, first known as Bet, was given to Elizabeth Stockton Green and Ashbel as a dower slave, part of a marriage settlement against the estate of Robert Stockton, who died in 1805. Elizabeth died two years later, in January 1807, leaving Green the sole owner of the child slave.[1]

In New Jersey, the Gradual Abolition Act stated that female children born to slave mothers *after July 4, 1804*, remained in bondage until they reached the age of twenty-one.[2] Green, however, followed his own timetable to decide when to educate and, later, to manumit Celia's child, Bet.

During the next five years, partially through Green's service and tenacity, Princeton became the epicenter of some branches of Presbyterian activism. In 1812, Green was saddled with a charge, that of assuming the presidency of the College of New Jersey and establishing a new institution—Princeton Theological Seminary—on a firm foundation. Housed in stoneclad Alexander Hall on Mercer Street, the new seminary and its founders looked to Green for leadership.[3] Both Green's presidency of the college and his fundraising efforts for the new seminary were to have profound effects on his young slave's life.

The founding of the Theological Seminary was followed by a great religious revival in 1815, of which Green happily wrote: "The house [college] is literally a house of prayer. Yet all is still and silent, no noise, no enthusiasm . . . . Surely there was scarcely ever so altered a place as our

1. MacLachlan, "Ashbel Green," 409.
2. Mitros, "Jacob Green and Slavery Debate," 33.
3. MacLachlan, "Ashbel Green," 411.

college . . . . We have nothing but meetings for religious conferences, and fervent social prayer," and he concluded that the presence of the seminary students was partially the reason.[4]

Betsey Stockton was the recipient of Green's belief partly inherited from his father, Jacob Green. It favored gradual emancipation for African Americans based on age and gender. Green practiced what he preached. Jacob Green's published plan called for freeing female slaves who were born under slavery, to be emancipated as they turned twenty-five years old.[5] Like his father, Ashbel sought training for his slaves in practical work in household tasks and trades beneficial for slaves, before emancipation. For Betsey Stockton, this meant practical lessons in cooking, cleaning, and nursing the sick, in addition to her early reading lessons taught by Green and his sons.

In his own right, Green was the principal author of an antislavery resolution of the General Assembly of 1818, which was the strongest condemnation of slavery that the undivided Presbyterian Church ever made:

> We consider the voluntary enslaving of one part of the human race by another . . . as utterly inconsistent with the law of God . . . and as totally irreconcilable with the spirit and the principles of the gospel of Christ.[6]

Writing about the complexity of the Presbyterian Church's views on slavery, Sean Wilentz portrays Princeton's Old School theologians as holding "conservative views about anti-slavery."[7] In 1816, Rev. Robert Finley, a 1787 College of New Jersey graduate, founded the American Colonization Society in Washington, DC. Its stated goal was to support the migration of free African Americans to the continent of Africa. Controversary followed this organization's goals, as reports of the death rate of immigrant free Blacks in the colony of Liberia surfaced in the United States. By the 1820s, many African American leaders such as Frederick Douglass, Sojourner Truth, and David Walker were opposed to the goals of the society. They were individuals of color who, like Betsey Stockton, were born to racially mixed parents.

In the eighteenth century and early decades of the nineteenth, admission to the educational institutions followed strict rules of gender prejudice: boys only were to be admitted to grammar schools. These were the next schools beyond the rudimentary literacy taught to both genders in English schools or through family tutors. For example, Nassau Hall Grammar

---

4. MacLachlan, "Ashbel Green," 410, 414.

5. Mitros, "Slavery Debate," 43.

6. Link, ed., *First Presbyterian Church*, 692; J. Jones, *Life of Ashbel Green*, 323.

7. Wilentz, "Princeton and Controversies," 105.

School, initially kept in the basement of Nassau Hall, prepared boys for college admission by teaching Greek and Latin (and perhaps Hebrew) grammar. Girls were never admitted to grammar schools, as they were excluded from the professions which necessitated this preparation. Women were never lawyers, clerics, or professors in the eighteenth century.

Busy as he was, Ashbel Green needed to find a way to continue his mulatta slave's education beyond his own household. His recognition of his young slave's unique skills and interest guided him to further her education. Bound by his own professional duties, Green looked to extended family members for additional schooling for his slave Bet.

When Stockton was fifteen, in June 1813, three years of her work and time were sold by Green to his nephew, the Rev. Nathaniel Todd, with whom she was well acquainted, for an unspecified amount of money.[8] One wonders whether or not Stockton wore or needed to show a slave badge identifying her as Green's property. Stockton's years with Todd and his wife were spent in Woodbury, New Jersey, a few miles northeast of Philadelphia. Todd was a lifelong teacher who also served as pastor of the Presbyterian Church in Woodbury and headmaster of the Woodbury Academy associated with it.[9]

Fondly remembered as "Father Todd," he was later the principal of the renowned Mifflinburg (Pennsylvania) Academy, among other classical schools, and trained future physicians, lawyers, teachers, and ministers. Near the end of a long and varied career, Todd was composer Stephen Foster's private tutor. If Stockton did not attend the all-male classes at Woodbury Academy, she surely enjoyed tutelage in between her paid household chores. She may have attended the Deptford School, run by Quakers but open to children of all faiths.

These years with the Todds in Woodbury were ones of important intellectual growth for the adolescent Stockton. What had been called an apprenticeship in medieval times was, by the early nineteenth century, invaluable hands-on vocational training for many future young laborers and/or professionals, whether slave or free, Black or White. Stockton was no exception. No doubt her acknowledged skills as an excellent nurse, cook, and housekeeper were honed during these years and afterwards.

With Stockton's years of residence in Woodbury in mind, surrounded as she was by master teachers and a myriad of schools, what prompted Ashbel Green's boast that Stockton "has made all of these attainments by improving her time and privileges in my family, without ever going to

---

8. Green, *Diaries*, 1741.
9. Cushing and Sheppard, *History of Counties*, 169.

school at all"?[10] Green's fatherly pride in overseeing Bet's education by his sons was unmistakable.

Returning to Princeton to live with Green in 1816, in what is now Maclean House, Stockton applied for admission to communion at the Presbyterian Church facing Nassau Street, whose manuscript records describe her as "a coloured woman living in the family of the Revd. Dr. Green."[11] She was not described as a slave or female servant as others on the list were, although "thirty-one were colored persons, some free and some slaves."[12] Already her singular status was evident. Evidently, Green and his wife had discussed giving Bet her freedom before Elizabeth's death.[13]

Revealing the warmth of his private persona, Green attracted students to his newly established Bible Society at Nassau Hall.[14] One such member of the society was to become Stockton's lifelong friend. He was Charles Samuel Stewart, a native of Flemington and an 1815 graduate of the College of New Jersey.[15] Stewart, also taken under Green's patriarchal wing, attended Princeton Theological Seminary, finishing in 1821. Stockton attended informal classes there, possibly on Sundays, an unusual opportunity for a young Mulatto woman. No doubt, as one raised in seminary founder Green's household, she received that special privilege. Stockton's advanced reading during those tutorials was to prove invaluable.

By the fall of 1821, plans were afoot for Stewart's missionary service for the Sandwich Island (now the Hawaiian Islands). As Stockton's spiritual and educational mentor, Green wrote a letter for Stockton at the request of Stewart. It was sent to the American Board of Commissioners for Foreign Mission. Founded in 1811 in Boston by New England Congregationalists and Middle States Presbyterians, the ABCFM had previously sent only married couples to the coveted foreign mission posts.

The board's consideration of Stockton for a foreign mission was unique. As a single woman of color, Stockton seemed disqualified on two counts. But she had four factors in her favor: her education; her confirmed Christian experience; her church baptism; and her prestigious mentor, Ashbel Green. But what weighed most strongly in Stockton's favor was her growing friendship with Charles and Harriet Bradford Tiffany Stewart, his newly pregnant bride. Merely having a desire to go on a mission to spread

10. Green, "Letter to Jeremiah Evarts."

11. Presbyterian Church of Princeton, "Minutes of the Session," unpaginated.

12. Hageman, *History of Princeton*, 2:115–16.

13. P. Jones, *Life and Journals*, 326, 359.

14. Green, *Proceedings of Bible Society*, 5.

15. Birchenough, *Biographical Catalogue of Princeton Theological Seminary*, 14.

Christianity to the heathen, as it was then characterized, was simply not a sufficient reason for service.

Stockton's complex role in her previous life is outlined in Ashbel Green's extraordinary letter of recommendation to Jeremiah Evarts, the Corresponding Secretary of the Prudential Committee of the ABCFM, in Boston:

> A coloured woman by the name of Betsy [*sic*], was given as a slave by Robert Stockton, Esq. of this place [Princeton], to my first wife, his daughter. By me and by my wife she was never intended to be held as a slave—We deliberated seriously on the subject of dedicating her to God in baptism. But on the whole concluded not to do it.
>
> Betsey gave no evidence of piety, or any permanent serious-ness, till she was twenty years old. On the contrary she was, at least till the age of thirteen or fourteen, wild and thoughtless, if not vicious. She always, however, manifested a great degree of natural sensibility, and of attachment to me and to her first mis-tress; and a great aptitude for mental improvement. To save her from the snares and temptations of the city, which I feared threat-ened her ruin, I sent her to live in the country, with a minister of the gospel, Nathaniel Todd, who was married to my niece. With him she lived between four and five years.
>
> On Mr. Todd's change of place, and my coming from Phila-delphia to reside in Princeton, she returned to live with me. At the age of twenty, as near as I can judge, I gave her freedom; and have since paid her wages as a hired woman, except for a few months, when she chose to go to service in Philadelphia. This woman, as I hope and she believes, met with saving change of heart while she lived in my family, during the first summer after she returned to live with me, the summer of 1816. The exhortation of Mr. [Eliphalet] Gilbert (then a member of the Theological Seminary, and since settled as a minister of the gospel in Wilmington, Delaware) she attributes, under God, her first impressions of religion, which were abiding; and which, she trusts, eventuated her conversion. She was publicly baptized and joined the communion of the Presbyterian Church, in this place, in the winter of 1816–1817; and has remained in good standing in the church ever since. Betsey is now about 25 years of age, has never been married. Her health, till some time after she returned to live with me in 1816, was remarkably firm and vigorous. Since that, it has been several times interrupted and is habitually delicate; but I think is improving. I have paid her full wages [as] a hired girl, for two or three years past; her services

have been so valuable that I shall regret to lose them. But she had been, for a good while, exceedingly desirous to go on a mission and I am willing that she should. I think her, in many respects, well qualified for this. I hope she is fervently pious. There is no kind of work in a family for which she is not very expert. But I think her well qualified for higher employment in a mission than domestick drudgery. She reads extremely well; few of her age and sex have read more books on religion than she; or can give a better account of them. She has no small share of miscellaneous reading, and has a real taste for literature. She understands Geography and English grammar, pretty well. She composes her English [in] a manner that is very uncommon for one of her standing in society. She is tolerably skilled in arithmetic. She has made all of these attainments by improving her time and privileges in my family, without ever going to school at all. She calls herself Betsey Stockton.

Princeton, September 3rd, 1821 Ashbel Green[16]

This haunting and remarkably modern biographical sketch by Green recognizes Stockton as a socially and sexually complete adult who had chosen to remain celibate. It also reveals his intensely intimate relationship with the self-named fully adult woman Betsey Stockton.

It reminds that us that even a surrogate and loving parent like Green knew only approximate dates for the lives of former slaves. One cannot mistake the self-congratulatory tone of Green's spiritual reclamation of Stockton. He acknowledges and applauds her Calvinist work ethic and the self-motivated education of his surrogate daughter. The letter, really an essay, traces the subject's long personal evolution from the embryo naughty and bright child slave "Bet."

"She calls herself Betsey Stockton." The final line in Green's letter is Stockton's assertion of her free identity. No longer owned by Robert Stockton, Elizabeth Stockton Green, or Ashbel, she owned herself. Green's inclusion of it meant his full acceptance of her freedom from him, as her former owner.

Like Sojourner Truth, Harriet Tubman, Frederick Douglass, and John Brown Russwurm, self-aware freed slaves renamed themselves, adding a second name to a first one. They claimed their new identities, even as they forged new roles for themselves in a violently racist society.

Like Stockton, these former slaves wrested their humanity as fully individual beings from those who tried to deny it. And, like Stockton, these

16. Green, "Letter to Jeremiah Evarts."

courageous women and men rejected the names arbitrarily assigned to them by their slave masters. These names purposefully erased all ethnic or familial connections. Names assigned by others, almost always by owners, denied their personhood, as they were designed to do.

The acknowledged right of slave ownership—you name, you possess—was amid the owner's guttural utterance in the dismissive Sealy or Sukey or the ancient, generic Caesar. Each owner insured that slaves were called to unending work by appellations that never referenced Christianity; slaves' names were often less meaningful than ones for valued animals.

Stockton, instead of merely taking the familiar name of her former mistress—Elizabeth Stockton Green was called Betsy by her father in a manuscript letter—had assigned herself the surname of her mother's owner. Evolving from the child slave Bet, this twenty-five-year-old woman claimed her own full social persona.

By freeing Stockton when he did, Green followed his admitted objections to slavery. The 1804 law passed in New Jersey demanded that all slaves born after July 4, 1804, be freed after long apprenticeships to their mothers' masters, female slaves at twenty-one years of age, males at twenty-five.[17] Another part of this law bound children to original masters in a hired capacity. But this singular relationship between Ashbel Green and Betsey Stockton was complemented by the 1788 New Jersey law, which required slaveholders to teach their chattel slaves under the age of twenty-one years old to read and write.[18]

A closer reading of Green's published biography reveals a telling passage. Under the topic of missionary work, Green states that he, and not his wife, actually freed Betsey Stockton. In doing so, he was following his own and his father's convictions about slavery.

> When Mr. Stewart and his wife went to the Sandwich Islands, a coloured girl by the name of Betsey Stockton, (who had been given as a slave to my first wife, and with her concurrence was freed by myself) and who at the time was on wages in my family in Princeton, was invited to go in the character of a missionary, and as assistant to Mrs. Stewart in the concerns of the family. Betsey had become hopefully pious, and by the instructions received in my family, principally from my son James, had made laudable improvements in knowledge. She had saved wages, by which, with some small assistance from myself, she was able to prepare her outfit for the missions. Some of her letters to me

17. "History of Slavery in New Jersey."

18. Mitros, "Jacob Green and Slavery Debate," 33; New Jersey General Assembly, *Acts of Thirteenth General Assembly*, 488.

after her arrival at the island (where she became a teacher at a school) were so well written, that with very few corrections, I inserted them in the Christian Advocate, of which I was then the editor, and they were greatly admired.[19]

A search for Stockton's written document of manumission by Ashbel Green has, to date, turned up a cipher. But an interesting search in the historical record yielded another possible clue to her slave mother. As recorded in the Somerset County clerk's office, which published manumissions by Princeton, Montgomery, Bernards, Franklin and Bedminster from 1805 to 1862, a slave Celia, "slave of George S. Woodhull of Montgomery," was manumitted on August 31, 1825.[20] Was this Robert Stockton's former slave and/or Betsey Stockton's African American slave mother?

Green, as a major force within the Old School Presbyterian theology, writes historian Sean Wilentz, was quoted as observing that although slavery was a "gross violation of the most precious and sacred rights," the immediate emancipation of southern slaves would be "inconsistant alike with the safety and happiness of masters and slaves."[21] Thus Green once again followed in his father's ideological/theological footsteps, favoring gradual emancipation, a scheme whose intent was a tiered or timed manumission of freeing slaves by age and gender. Rev. Jacob Green's "Fast Day Sermon of 1779" foreshadowed Abraham Lincoln's view that war was God's punishment for the sin of slavery.[22]

The second recommendation for Betsey Stockton's mission work to the ABCFM came from a source who knew her, taught her, and, like Green, admired her. In September 1821, Michael Osborn, a student at Princeton Theological Seminary, also wrote to Jeremiah Evarts, the Corresponding Secretary of the ABCFM, recording Betsey Stockton's studies with him.

Osborn's letter highlights Betsey Stockton's household management, linguistic abilities, serious application to scholarship, her stated career goal of "taking charge of a day school for coloured children," and her friendship with Charles S. Stewart through Ashbel Green. Osborn also alludes to her friends' aversion to her stated plan to go to Africa, presumably under the American Colonization Society's banner, as reports of the deathrate there reached mainland America.[23]

19. J. Jones, *Life of Ashbel Green*, 326.
20. Van Doren Honeyman, *Somerset County Historical Quarterly*, 279.
21. Ashbel Green, as cited in Wilentz, "Princeton and the Controversies," 108.
22. Mitros, "Jacob Green and Slavery Debate," 21.
23. Osborn, as cited in Escher, "She Calls Herself Betsey Stockton," 79.

Theological Seminary, Princeton September 5, 1821

My dear Sir,

Leaning that the Rev.ᵈ Charles S. Stewart intended (in the event
of his being appointed by the ABCFM to the Sandwich Islands
mission) to ask permission of the Board to take out with him
in the capacity of domestic servant and assistant to the mission,
Betsey Stockton, a young mulatto woman of this place: I thought
I could give some necessary information respecting her, and
consequently offered to write to you with that view. I would say
in general, as the result of an intimate acquaintance with her, that
I think her pious, intelligent, industrious, skillful in the management of domestic affairs, apt to teach, and endowed with a large
portion of the active, preserving, self-sacrificing, spirit of a missionary. From my first acquaintance with her she has expressed
a decided wish to go to the heathen. Africa was the place of her
choice. The opposition of her friends has kept her until now.
For about a year and a half she has been a member of my class
in the Sabbath School at this place. Her recitations have been
chiefly from the *S[acred] Scriptures, the Larger Catechism, Jewish
Antiquities* and *Sacred Geography*. She has a larger acquaintance
with sacred history and the Mosaic Institutions than almost any
ordinary person, young or old, I have ever known. (By *ordinary
person* you will understand me to mean such as are not clergy-
men or candidates for the ministry). I recollected a multitude of
instances where, for my own information, I have questioned her
about some fact in Biblical history, or some minute point in Jewish Antiquities, and have immediately received a correct answer.
To a part of the questions proposed to her on Jewish Antiquities
she has given satisfactory answers *in writing*.

    She has enjoyed unrestrained access to the private library
of The Rev.ᵈ President of Nassau Hall (in whose family she was
raised, with the exception of three or four years, from her infancy) and I am persuaded has improved the privilege. I will
mention but one of the many instances of her love of study.
At the commencement of one of our six week vacations, I lent
her a copy of Bishop Horne on the Psalms, intending that she
should transcribe the table in which he classed the psalms
under their appropriate heads, and read his remarks on a few
of them, preparatory to committing them to memory. At the
end of the vacations, she had made time to study the whole
book, preface and all. That she had studied it thoroughly, I was
convinced by her frequent references to his remarks. She loves

to teach children, and has sometimes during vacation acted as teacher or superintendent of a sabbath school. During some months she has appropriated a part of every week to the instruction of a number of coloured children. For a considerable time, she has been studying with the view of taking charge of a day school for coloured children. Her knowledge of geography is respectable, she conquered the larger part of Murray's English Grammar, writes with a legible hand, and is now cyphering in the compound multiplication. On the studies specified, she had undergone an examination by myself and another student of the seminary. I am of the opinion that few pious young ladies of her age will be found to equal her knowledge of the Bible and general theology. Brother Wisner, if I mistake not, is acquainted with her, and will be able to communicate some facts which do not now occur to me.

Please give my best regards to Brother Wisner—

In haste I remain Truly Yours,

Michael Osborn[24]

What teaching methods did seminarian Michael Osborn use to teach Betsey Stockton? His goal was her mastery of advanced theological texts; it was a goal which teacher and student achieved.

Here are some answers. Stockton, then twenty-five, was a highly motived and unusually competent reader. She approached the texts of the books offered by Osborn with a singular tenacity. Her early reading with James and her catechisms by Ashbel Green showed the use of the Socratic method of student and teacher exchange.

In Stockton's case, for example, we know that she thoroughly understood the work on the Psalms, constructing a chart of her own, classifying them, and showing the finished chart to teacher Osborn. At twenty-five, she had already revealed the skills of a master teacher. She used *executive function*, an organizational scheme to create a mnemonic device for ready comprehension and retention of intricate material.

Osborn's letter reveals that Stockton possessed other intellectual gifts. The phrase "apt to teach" tells the reader that, while in her teens, she began to organize reading and writing materials (presumably) in English, for young children of color. She taught her young scholars on a regular basis. Stockton's repetitive classes for very young African American children may seem obvious today, but she was a teaching pioneer in 1822.

---

24. Osborn, "Letter to Jeremiah Evarts."

Did nature or nurture prevail in creating Stockton's brilliant mind? Did the uniquely academic household of the Greens nurture it? Had she inherited some traits from one or both parents? The ready answer is that *both* nature and nurture were present in varying degrees in one who today would be labeled intellectually gifted. Stockton's early and individual lessons, her very early literacy, proved a life-changing skill. That mastery catapulted her into becoming one of the most proficient practitioners of an international system of teaching, belying her gender, social position, or race.

As plans for Stockton and the Stewarts' missionary work solidified, Green, ever the privately paternalistic parent, mused in October 1822:

> I had in the evening a very solemn and affecting time in my study with Mr. Stewart and my coloured woman, Betsy Stockton, who were to set out the next day for Boston—being appointed as missionaries to the Sandwich Islands. I counseled and encouraged and prayed with them and charged them to remember me in their prayers—especially that I may never in the close of life dishonor my Christian and ministerial character. . . . The next day they went East and I West—probably to meet no more on earth.[25]

Green was consoling himself. At that juncture he was prepared, Christlike, to sacrifice his most precious being, "my coloured woman," to a lifetime commitment of missionary fieldwork. It was finished only by death on foreign soil. Fatherly pride and fatherly sorrow can be read in Green's farewell prayers and counsel with Betsey Stockton.

The board gave Stockton its endorsement to became an assistant missionary, accompanying the Stewarts to the Sandwich Islands. She remains the only unmarried freed slave whom the board sent to the foreign mission field. To guarantee Stockton's unique status and safety, the board wrote a contract with her, documenting the unique circumstances that demanded its creation.

Stockton's contract with the ABCFM did several things at once. It protected her physical safety from being impressed (kidnapped) by captains in passing ships. The written contract prevented her from being identified as a runaway slave on the watery leg of the Underground Railroad. It reiterated Stockton's legality to engage in mission work—just as a professional letter of hire would do today. Finally, the contract restated her status as a freed slave, an adult single woman who, in spite of being a person of color, was to do no more than anyone else's share of the drudgery of missionary work.

The contract is unique in the historical annals of freed slaves. A holograph copy is presented for readers, written by Jeremiah Evarts, Corresponding

25. Green, *Diaries*, 2206–7.

Secretary of the ABCFM, at New Haven, Connecticut, on November 18, 1822, prior to the sailing of the American whaler *Thames:*

> Betsey Stockton, a colored young woman brought up in the family Of Rev. Ashbel Green, having been received as a missionary to The Sandwich Islands by the American Board of Commissioners For Foreign Mission—it is thought that it may be useful, as there is something perculiar in her case, to specify in writing, the view of the undersigned in regard to her, and the part which she is to Act in the sacred work in which she is to be engaged.
>
> First. She is to be considered as, at all times, under the entire direction and control of the American Board of Commissioners For Foreign Missions.
>
> Second. With the approbation of the Board she is to be considered in the first instance as specially attached to the family of the Rev. Charles S. Stewart, and as constituting a member of this Family.
>
> Third. In this family, she is to be regarded & treated neither as an equal nor as a servant, but as an humble Christian friend, embarked in the great enterprise of endeavoring to ameliorate the condition of the heathen generally & especially to bring them to the saving knowledge of the truth as it is in Jesus.
>
> Fourth. She is to endeavor to lighten the burden of Mr. and Mrs. Stewart's family care as much as possible, consistently with her other engagements as a missionary and especially to relieve Mrs. Stewart in the more laborious parts of domestic concerns.
>
> Fifth. She is to see in Mr. and Mrs. Stewart her particular friends, patrons and protectors;—to look to them for counsel and aid, and to regard their opinions and wishes as the guide to her conduct, so far as these may consist with a Supreme regard to the glory and commands of God.
>
> Sixth. Out of the family of Mr. Stewart, she is to endeavor to render every service to the mission in her power, but not be called on, as of right, for any menial services, any more than any other member of the mission, as this might manifestly render her life servile, and prevent her being employed as a teacher of a School, for which it is hope that she will be found qualified.
>
> Seventh. It is understood that if Mr. Stewart should, at any time be disposed to separate Betsey from his family, or if she should be disposed to leave it, or if it should be mutually thought desirable that they should separate—all parties concerned will be at full liberty to do so—And in such event, Betsey will remain under the care and superintendence of the Board, like any other missionary.

The undersigned, having mutually and deliberately considered, and cordially approved the premises, have subscribed
the same at Princeton, New Jersey, this twenty-fourth day of
October, in the Year of our Lord, one thousand eight hundred
& twenty-two.

Ashbel Green

Chas. Saml Stewart

Betsey Stockton (holograph signatures)

New Haven, Nov. 18, 1822

Approved in behalf of the American Board of Commissioners
For Foreign Missions by Jerh. Evarts, Cor Sec. & Clerk of the
Prudential Committee

A true copy attest Levi Chamberlain[26]

Historians have raised many questions about this contract. What
exactly was Stockton's status? What was the meaning of the term assistant missionary? From their own actions and from the fact that no other
contract respecting the foreign missionaries existed, the ABCFM sending
institution wanted to ensure the uniqueness of its permission, granted to
a single woman of color who was sent as a teacher and not as a working
drudge. It was only later, in 1827, that the ABCFM sent four single White
women to the mission fields.[27]

We can also grasp the tone of the protective—even parental—concern
for Stockton's unique status as a woman of color. By putting their justified
concerns for misuse of Stockton's labor in writing, the gentlemen on the
board of the ABCFM insured Stockton's status as free. The contract might
have been carried on her person or included with the Stewarts' citizenship
papers, shown to harbormasters for passenger identity. Stockton could not
be claimed as anything other than what she was. Her job/role as a certified
missionary defined and protected her identity as a freed slave.

Touchingly, the Cooperstown friends of pregnant Harriet Bradford
Tiffany Stewart gathered their own recommendations for her welfare in the
Sandwich Islands in the form of a letter from Ann Pomeroy to Mrs. Harriet
Stewart on July 2, 1822. Pomeroy, who was treasurer of the Cooperstown
Female Missionary Society, included the following inventory of clothes and

26. Evarts, "Contract between Betsey Stockton." Used with permission of the
HMHS&A.

27. Ott, "'Peculiar Case' of Betsy Stockton," 18.

household items that would be packed in trunks for Harriet's use in her new life as a missionary, far from home: of "infant socks, 3"; "blankets," including "Small ones, 2"; and, prophetically, "Suits of Boys Cloths, 2."[28] These friends in Harriet Stewart's hometown had valued the articles in the box (or trunk) at $175.53 1/4 (cents), while their own work in gathering raw materials to be fashioned into clothes by hand and manufactured goods such as tin boxes, included as "the value of the work," was $46.71.[29]

As far as they could, those friends of Betsey Stockton, Harriet Bradford, and Rev. Charles Samuel Stewart tried to make and pack necessities to cushion the missionaries' daily life, which they knew from missionary letters already in the field would be one of physical hardship.[30] Letters from Hiram Bingham and other American missionaries, previously established at the Sandwich Island missions, had helped to inform those friends of the future missionaries. Conveyed to America by whaleships, those letters, sent between 1820 and 1822, revealed living conditions in the South Pacific Sea in the Sandwich Islands.

Goods packed in traveling trunks and letters of recommendation propelled the three Princetonians to the major adventure—and challenge—of their young lives.

28. Pomeroy, "Letter to Harriet Stewart."
29. Pomeroy, "Letter to Harriet Stewart."
30. Pomeroy, "Letter to Harriet Stewart."

Chapter 4: **Bidding the American Shores Adieu**

"HERE BEGINS THE HISTORY of things known only to those who bid the American shores a long adieu," wrote Betsey Stockton, then a brilliant twenty-two-year-old Mulatto woman, on November 20, 1822, from the ship *Thames*, about to depart from Thomlinson's Wharf, New Haven, Connecticut. So began her "Journal," written during her 158-day odyssey from Connecticut to Honolulu, Oahu, in the Sandwich Islands. Stockton and her Princeton friend Rev. Charles S. Stewart were instructed to keep journals by Ashbel Green. Structured as a Christian narrative of the voyage, Stockton's observations of whaling and the nautical world on the *Thames* anticipated Herman Melville's metaphorical masterpiece *Moby Dick*, published thirty years later.

Once again, Stockton's story began with a school. This time, it was the "heathen" or "Indian" school (Foreign Mission School) in Cornwall, Connecticut, where Native Americans, South Sea Islanders, and other young men were taught to read and write English. They were part of the American Board of Commissioners for Foreign Missions' global plan to send newly bilingual missionaries home to their indigenous peoples.

Betsey Stockton's calling to become a Presbyterian missionary stands a long-held historical theory about making Christians of the heathen on its head. In reality, the impetus for this cultural convergence in the Sandwich Islands did not begin with White Americans. Instead, it came through the person of a young Hawaiian native and recent Christian convert. He was 'Opukaha'ia; his Anglicized name was Henry Obookhiah (1790–1818). As a child, he had witnessed bloody wars in his native land. The legend surrounding his life includes the scene of this Sandwich Island youth found crying on the steps of Yale in 1809 "because nobody gives me learning."[1]

In 1818, his early death and apotheosis to Christian martyrdom at the heathen school in Cornwall, Connecticut, spurred New England Protestants to take action through the ABCFM. Over a thirty-year period, the

---

1. Demos, *Heathen School*, 16.

board sent a human armada of 155 missionaries in twelve groups to the Sandwich Islands.[2]

Paradoxically, from her humble fo'c's'le (forecastle) hammock in the *Thames*, Betsey Stockton carried with her the cultural tool so critical for preserving the indigenous culture she was entering: teaching English to Hawaiian natives at her "first school for commoners" there. Being sent to a foreign mission as a single woman of color, a freed slave who was uniquely well educated, Stockton's quest was unique. She came without the stance of White supremacy but as an ambassador for change within her missionary calling. To accomplish this goal, she conversed in the indigenous Hawaiian language on board the *Thames*, learning from native speakers William Kmoolla and Richard Kalauiula, both Hawaiian scholars educated at the heathen school in Cornwall. The pair had become the living legetees of the sainted Hawaiian Henry ʻOpukahaʻia.[3]

The original manuscript pages of Stockton's holograph "Journal" are lost. Stockton and Charles Stewart sent portions of their journals to Green in Philadelphia by passing whalers. By 1822, Green was editor of his new venture, a bi-monthly Philadelphia magazine, *The Christian Advocate*. While still an administrator for Princeton Theological Seminary, Green had been dismissed from the presidency of the College of New Jersey. He had moved to Philadelphia to oversee his new publishing venture. By serializing the publications of Stockton's "Journal" between Feb. 1823 and May 1826, Green featured the unfolding drama of the sea voyage and residence in the Sandwich Islands. He hoped to bolster readership and sales; some of Charles Dickens works were serialized in the same way.

In May 1824, Green emphasized Stockton's African descent and her early reading lessons in a private family. Actually, she had gained literacy while still a child slave of Green in Philadelphia and later in Princeton.

> The journal from which the following extracts are given, was begun immediately after the writer left the house of the Editor [Green] and been regularly continued ever since . . . . To us they appear interesting and instructive, especially when we consider that the writer is a young woman of African descent, who was never sent to school a day in her life, but acquired all her knowledge by a careful attention to the instruction which she received in a private family, and by her own efforts after she obtained her freedom at the age of twenty; her present age is about twenty-five.

2. Judd et al., *Missionary Album*, 3–12.
3. Demos, *Heathen School*, 16; Judd et al., *Missionary Album*, 4.

He closed with a tantalizing reminder to his readers: "A Missionary life at sea has not been so often and so particularly described as that on land."[4]

Green's publication of the "Journal" saved Stockton's work for posterity. With a wider reading of her journal, portions of which are included here, Betsey Stockton assumes her rightful place among early nineteenth-century authors, linguists, and educators. As an educated author, her writing is unique among freed slave narratives.

Stockton's literary voice is joined by two others. Reading the trio of whaleship journals enables armchair travelers to hear the voices of these early nineteenth-century writers. These eyewitnesses revealed details of the five-month voyage to the Sandwich Islands. While Stewart's whaleship journal were quickly published as two freestanding books, *A Private Journal of a Voyage to the Sandwich Islands* (1829) and *A Residence in the Sandwich Islands* (1830), Betsey Stockton's original salty "Journal" has remained a fragmentary work.

The third *Thames* journalist was Louise Everett Ely. Ely's manuscript diary added another distaff voice and vision of the voyage. Like Betsey Stockton, Ely had previous teaching experience, having been the "instructress" of the First District School of Cornwall, Connecticut. Forty years old at the departure of the *Thames*, Ely was joined by husband James, a former student at the Foreign Mission School at Cornwall. Her concern with neighborliness on the high seas, meal preparation, and packing goods in "barrels—not trunks" for sea voyages provides welcome details of New England domesticity by a school teacher in 1822.

This extraordinary account of Green's "mission family" sailing to the far side of the world—onto possible cannibal islands—was unique. Ashbel Green, ever the pragmatist, now sixty-one and in shaky health, needed to insure the commercial—as well as religious—success of his publishing venture.

The commercial mission of the voyage of the *Thames* was to catch whales and bring back barrels of spermaceti oil. But Betsey Stockton's voyage was famously recalled in 1960 in a stand-alone book, *The Missionary Whaleship*, researched and written by crew-descendant Thomas French. The *Thames* was to round the horn of South America, pass the dreaded Tierra del Fuego (Land of Fire), and continue into the Pacific Ocean. Its final destination for the missionary passengers: the Hawaiian archipelago.

The owners of the whaler were the New Haven Whalefishery Company.[5] The *Thames* was to cruise in the newly opened Pacific grounds for

---

4. Green, "Religious Intelligence," 232.
5. French, *Missionary Whaleship*, 61.

whaling, because the formerly abundant whaling grounds in the Atlantic had been depleted by 1822.

The *Thames* had been built at Saybrook, Connecticut, in 1818, four years before Stockton's voyage. She had been a packet ship, sailing between New York City and Europe, before its refitting as a whaler by 1822. She was 101 feet in length, with two decks and three masts. Her deck boasted between three and five long boats. Each carried a mate, a boatsteerer, the harpooner, and crew to row it. She was a square-sterned ship, and her investors hoped the "greasy luck" of bountiful casks of whale oil—and profits—would make the *Thames* the first in a series of such investments.[6] She was slightly smaller than the restored whaleship, *The Charles Morgan*, at the Mystic Seaport Museum in Connecticut, where the preserved wooden keel of the *Thames* currently remains.

Those profits, earned by whaling companies or ship owners, were transformed into stately neoclassical wooden or brick mansions, architectural testaments to the wealth garnered from the sea. These beauties, lining the main or front streets of New England towns, looked out on pastoral Sunday churchgoers and neighborly chats across white picket fences. But behind the white clapboard or brick facades lay the source of their beauty: the ugly physicality of harpooning leviathans, the sperm whales. The whaleship was essentially a factory ship. On its deck were the foul-smelling "try works," where the strips of the whale carcass were hoisted on deck, boiled into oil, then poured into waiting wooden casks stowed in the black maw of the ship's hold. This liquid wealth would light the lamps and grease the gears of early nineteenth-century America.

Waiting to give orders for the *Thames* to heave away was Master Reuben Clasby of Nantucket, the captain of a working crew of twenty-three souls. Here was an experienced sailing captain. Previously, Clasby had served as master of the ship *John and James* out of Nantucket in 1811 and made the treacherous voyage around the horn of South America five times before 1822.[7] Another crewmate would become known to Betsey Stockton and Charles Stewart: the nineteen-year-old boatsteerer from Nantucket. His infamous past would reveal itself to the Christian missionaries on the *Thames*, testing their Christlike acts of forgiveness.

After several frustrating inquiries on passage to the Pacific from Boston and New York City, the *Thames* out of New Haven was chosen for its capacity to provide comfortable accommodations for the departing missionaries. Betsey Stockton and seventeen fellows in her missionary family

6. French, *Missionary Whaleship*, 61.
7. Stackpole, *Sea-Hunters*, 388.

received free passage to the Sandwich Islands, a not uncommon practice at the time. Family members were almost all university- or common school-educated White American couples, newly married before their departure. Other passengers were four returning bilingual Hawaiian youths, former students at the Cornwall heathen school.[8]

In contrast, Betsey Stockton, a single woman of color, possessed a unique education from her studies at Nathaniel Todds's Woodbury school and tutorials at Princeton Theological Seminary. In her teens, Stockton was "apt to teach" African American children. Young as she was, her aptitude for teaching was already recognized. She came as a lone outsider within the mission family. Her bilingualism would conserve and protect the Sandwich Islanders' ancestral culture and heritage from the increasing presence of foreigners.

In November 1822, on the *Thames* deck, twenty-five-year-old Betsey Stockton wrote to Green in Philadelphia about Charles Stewart's inspection of the *Thames:*

> Sir—I have been waiting for some time to know something decisive respecting the mission, that I might write to you. Everything appeared so unfavorable to our getting off this fall, after we came to New York [City], that we all felt very much discouraged: But just as our fears had risen to their highest pitch, a merciful Providence interposed in our behalf. You know, the vessels which commonly go to the South Seas from our country are whaling ships, and that the accommodations are very seldom good. Dr. [Thomas] Holman, the missionary who lately returned from the Sandwich Island, told Mr. S[tewart] that the last mission family suffered very much from the size of the ship [the brig *Thaddeus*, out of Boston, with Captain Blanchard]. They were obliged to be stowed in their cabin [kept closely confined aboard ship] that they could admit no fresh air. Fearful that this would be our own case . . . Mr. Stewart left us to go to New Haven, intending to return and go to Boston in a short time. When we arrived at New Haven he was informed that a ship there was ready to put to sea, going to the South Seas and only waiting for a captain. He felt a strong inclination to see her, as he had heard much said of the vessels that sail in those waters. As soon as his wishes were made known, a boat was ordered from the ship to wait upon him [to transport him from the New Haven dock to the whaler], and he went aboard—to his surprise he found her a large handsome well-built ship, and learned that she was the *Thames*, built for a

8. Judd et al., *Missionary Album*, 73.

London trader. Her cabin is as large as your study, with twenty-three births [berths] in it and seven windows, the doors made of mahogany and every thing in her elegant. He told the officers that if he had known this vessel ten days sooner he would have engaged a passage for Mrs. S[tewart] and myself. They said it was entirely too late now—that they must go to sea immediately. He told me that he never felt so dejected in his life as he did at that time, when he thought of our situation, and the opportunity that was about to be lost. He spoke of it to many of his friends, who regretted very much that they had not known of this vessel sooner. At last the owners of the ship agreed to have a meeting, and take it into consideration. Mr. S went to a prayer meeting [in New Haven] in the evening—still quite dejected: but when he came from it, he found on the ground an agent just arrived from Boston, with orders to detain this ship, if possible and to engage a passage for the whole mission family. The owners met again and engaged to detain the ship ten days longer.[9]

Stockton confessed to Green her disappointment, her elation, and the fortuitous offer of free passage for the missionaries on the *Thames*.

Ever the academician, Charles Stewart began his whaleship "*Journal*," like Stockton, with a letter to Green to signal their progress:

On board ship "Thames" Long Island Sound, Nov. 20th, 1822

My respected and beloved friend—I sought in vain for an opportunity to write a few lines before our embarkation—I can still do it, however, and send [it] on shore by the pilot [boat]—we got under sail yesterday afternoon, and we are making our way out of the [New Haven] Sound, with every sail filled with a fair breeze.

We have been exceedingly blest in all respects. The [mission] family is truly a lovely one—perfectly satisfactory. The ship is of the first order of trading vessels—370 tons—packet built, with a fine cabin and every accommodation. The captain [Master Reuben Clasby] is not a pious man, but kind and affable, moral and polite. The crew also seem well disposed, interesting men. The inhabitants of New Haven were extremely kind and liberal, in providing stores, and we have every thing our health and comfort require. Our embarkation was solemn and affecting—every bosom, no doubt, was filled with inexpressible emotions; but, I presume among them were none of regret or fear. We might have wept, and from sorrow, but with it was mingled "the joy of grief."

9. B. Stockton, "Journal," *Christian Advocate* 1 (Feb. 1823), 88–89.

The captain's name is Clasby, the crew are 22 in number making 41 souls on board . . . . Mrs. S and Betsey are in good health and spirits and desire to be affectionately remembered to yourself and family—farewell.

STEWART[10]

Betsey Stockton's "Journal," Ship *Thames* at Sea[11]

Nov 20th, 1822—Here begins the history of things known only to those who have bid the American Shores a long adieu. We were employed in arranging our births [sic], clothes, &c. all day; and as the weather was calm, we were enabled to go on without much difficulty.

21. The weather became stormy, and the sea-sickness commenced.

22. It blew very hard in the day, and in the night increased to a gale; sea-sickness increased with it. I was myself very sick.

23. Saturday morning at daybreak shipped a sea. The water rushed into the cabin. I saw it with very little fear; and felt inclined to say, The Lord reigneth, let us all rejoice. I was so weak that I was almost unable to help myself. At ten o'clock I went on deck: the scene that presented itself was, to me, the most sublime I ever witnessed. How, thought I, can "those that go to the sea in ships" deny the existence of God. The day was spent in self-examination. This, if ever, is the time to try my motives in leaving my native land. I found myself at times unwilling to perish so near my friends; but soon became composed, and resigned to whatever should be the will of my Heavenly Father. I believed that my motives were pure; and a calm and heavenly peace soon took possession of my breast. Oh that it were always with me as it is this day!

24. Sabbath [Sunday]. The weather today still squally, and our family still in bad health. We had no publick service today. My soul longed for the courts of the Lord; but my heart was still rejoicing in the strength of my God.

25. The ocean has become much smoother than it has been for some time. Our family are recovering very fast; nothing particular had occurred to-day.

---

10. C. Samuel Stewart, as cited in Green, "Religious Intelligence," 89.

11. B. Stockton, "Journal," *Christian Advocate* 2 (May 1824), 232.

26. The weather is delightful, and we felt much better. The ladies wanted a pudding for dinner. Two or three volunteered their services and a pudding was made. I, for my part, felt no inclination either to make or eat it. I stayed with Mrs. S. In the midst of their business the man on the mast [in the crow's nest] called out, *A sail ho!* We were all in a state of elate for a few minutes. It we had seen a friend who had been absent for a long time we could not have hailed him with more delight. We bore for the ship, and soon discovered her to be the *[William] Penn of Philadelphia.* Preparations were made for speaking her [calling out to her in passing, at sea]. The sea was too rough to permit us to send letters. She came near enough to hail us, but we could only say, *All's well* after being at sea a week.[12]

December 1 [1822], Sabbath. My soul longed again for the house of the Lord; I endeavoured to find him present with me; and soon indeed found that he was near to all that call on him. I enjoyed the day although we were prevented from having worship until afternoon—owing to the roughness of the weather and the unsettled state of the ship.

2. Employed in making arrangements in the cabin; the day fair and the ship running at the rate of six miles an hour. The weather is much warmer than I have felt it since I left home. In the evening we had the monthly concert of prayer [assembled missionaries for a formal religious service].

3. We are almost settled and things are in good order. The [ship's] bell rings at daylight and we have prayers at sunrise. [Ships' bells ring at regular intervals to mark the time and the crew's watches, one to eight strokes for each four-hour period.] Mrs. Stewart is getting much better.

4. Nothing particular has occurred today; we are still on our course direct for Cape de Verd [the Cape de Verde Islands, fifty sea miles from the coast of Africa in the Atlantic Ocean].

5. The weather is good and all of us are in good health and spirits. The captain and officers attend our [prayer] meeting, and the sailors appear to treat the missionaries with respect.

Charles Stewart added on December 19 that the ship's crew were engaged "trying out the blubber." The missionary family's lamps needed it, he explained, as an "insufficent quantity of spermaceti" had been stowed on the *Thames* for the voyage.

12. Noted Charles Stewart, Nov. 30, 1822: "Our humble friend B[etsey Stockton] daily proves more and more kind, affectionate and faithful. She has been most thoughtful and assiduous, in her attentions to H[arriet, called Hattie], and we consider her an invaluable acquisition to our family," he wrote, less than ten days into the voyage.

Louisa Everest Ely's Description of a Whale Hunt on December 22[13]

Early this morning the man at Mast head [crow's nest lookout] announced the appearance of a whale—It was soon discovered to be the Fin Back [*Balaenoptera physalus*, a fast swimmer], a kind which they do not often attempt to take. Immediately after this was discovered a large shoal of black fish [*Globicephala macro-rhynchus*, pilot whales] perhaps 50 in number, but a little distant from the ship. They appeared like a company of swine as they rolled in the water. The whale boats were immediately let down after them. To this harpoon is fastened a rope so long that it will fill a half hogshead [coiled in a large cask]. After the harpoon was darted the fish run in various directions, towing the boat after him. You cannot conceive with what swiftness they will cause the little boat to ride upon the swelling waves [later known as the Nantucket Sleigh Ride]. In less than three hours they returned to the ship with two of the fish which may be truly said to be monsters of the deep. They were hoisted on to the ship by tackles. The longest was 21 feet long 5 feet in diameter. Both of them made 3 barrels and one half of oil. We considered our want providentially supplied as we had but a small quantity on board.

The next day, Dec. 23, 1822, Stockton wrote,[14]

The weather delightful; and the crew all engaged in making oil of the two black fish [pilot whales] killed yesterday. This is fine amusement for the missionaries. We have had corn parched in the oil; and doughnuts fried in it. Some of the company liked it very much. I could not prevail on myself to eat it. I tasted the flesh and liver of the fish, which were very good. The flesh is very much like beef, and the liver like a hog's.

Dec 24th, 1822. At 11 o'clock we had a heavy gale. It did not damage to the rigging [the shrouds, stays, braces, ropes securing the sails of the *Thames*]. I was very much amused during the gale by one of the landsmen, as they call them; who was ordered to *slack the weather bowling*, but did not understanding the phrase, *he let it go*. Such accidents in a squall cause not small noise, and make our captain lift up his voice like a trumpet. Some of our family like a gale very much. I have not got to that yet; however, I can view it with very little emotion in the daytime. In the night I sometimes feel unpleasantly. My [hammock] bed hangs so

13. Ely, *Diary of Missionary Voyage*, 7.
14. B. Stockton, "Journal," *Christian Advocate* 2 (May 1824), 232.

near the cabin windows [in the forecastle] so that I have full view of the water; and during a gale the waves appear as if they were coming directly into the cabin.

Dec 25th, 1822. Christmas. How unlike the last! But the day was pleasant, and I enjoyed myself very much; yet could not forebear thinking of my native land. We expected to have made St. Jago [St. Iago, a port in the Cape De Verde Islands]; but the wind was not favouring us, we were obliged to put about for Cape Horn, without landing [for supplies]. This was something of a trial, as it disappointed all our expectations of communication with our friends [sending letters home via passing ships].—Saw a large flock of flying fish. They rise from the water a little distance, when pursed by larger fish, and sometimes fly on board. They have a delicious flavor and are equal to any fresh water fish I ever tasted.

Betsey Stockton's "Journal," Ship *Thames*, N. at 24 2' W. Log. 20 43'[15]

Rev. and dear Sir [Ashbel Green].—Conscious of the deep interest you take in my welfare, I will endeavor to give you some faint idea of our situation—to describe all that we have seen and felt, would require an abler pen than mine. You no doubt anticipated many of the dangers to which we were to be exposed, but we were called to witness some, before you could have anticipated them. We embraced on the 19th ult. [ultimate]—The boat was sent to land, this pilot at 12 o'clock but having reached the extremity of the [New Haven] sound, the pilot discovered that we were drifting rapidly on the Race Rack, and returned as speedily as possible to save us from destruction. He remained with us till 4 o'clock, and was then landed at Block Island—by him I suppose you feel the motion of the water, of course the sea-sickness commenced. I cannot describe the scene which ensued—the most death-like sickness I ever felt in my life, was occasioned by the motion of the ship. Every person in the mission except Mr. Stewart and Kermoola [Hawaiian youth, returning to his native Hawaii] was sick at the same time. The weather became very boisterous on the following Friday—rainy and squally in the evening—and in the night it increased to a gale. I was up very early the next morning, and as [sic] I was looking toward the companion way [a ladderway through a hatch] when we shipped

15. B. Stockton, "Journal," in *Christian Advocate* 1 (Sept. 1823) 423–26.

a sea, and the water rushed into the cabin in a torrent. It was the first I had seen, and I felt alarmed for the moment but it was soon over. I am happy to tell you that since I left home, in all the storms and dangers I have been called to witness, I have never left my self-possession. This I consider as a fulfillment of the promise, that as my day is, so my strength shall be. But we have not yet come to the most trying part of the voyage. We are now near the coast of Africa, and I fear I shall not act the Christian, in the thunderstorms which are to be expected there.* [Added Green: "She has a natural timidity in regard to thunder."]. But I am glad to have in my power to say, that notwithstanding our difficulties, I have never looked toward home with a longing eye. I cannot say, indeed, sir, that I have not longed to see your family [i.e., Green's youngest son James, who helped to teach Stockton to read, and Jacob]. You are all so dear to me as life itself; and nothing but the consoling thought that we are destined to meet where parting will be no more, could support me.

My friends are all very kind to me. I have not been disappointed in Mr. and Mrs. Stuart [Stewart]. Their kindness lays me under renewed obligations to them. I share with them in all of our stores—If our water was good, we should be quite comfortable; but it was spoiled before we left port, and it has grown no better since. We have cider, porter, beer &c. but would gladly exchange them all for water. We hope the captain will take some in at St. Jago. The captain appears to be a well disposed man, and does every thing in his power to render the [mission] family happy. He attends prayers with us in the morning, in the cabin, and in the evening on the quarter-deck. We met the first Monday of the month, and observed the concert [service] of prayer; and the season was very precious to us. We frequently comfort ourselves by referring to our native country [America] and reflecting on the prayers which are there ascending in our behalf.

The mission family are, on the whole, as pleasant a company as I ever met with. The natives [Stephen Popohe, William Kamoola, Richard Kalaioulu, and Kupelii][16] are the kindest creatures I ever saw. They talk and sing for us in their own language, the sound of which is soft and pleasant.

I wish it was in my power to give the ladies of your family some account of our manner of living, but I cannot at present. Sometimes in imagination, I visit them in the night, and get a piece of bread; for there is nothing I have wanted so much since I left home, of the provision kind, as bread. Ours is pilot-bread

16. Judd et al., *Missionary Album*, 7.

and crackers, and by using them in our seasickness I took a dis-
like to them. But we have pudding, boiled rice, and mush once
a week, and beans, potatoes, boiled onions, fruit etc. The cook,
however is a dirty man, and we are obliged to eat without asking questions. While I was sick, they gave me a mug of chicken
soup—The grease, the pepper, and the feathers, floated together
on the surface. Being on deck, I was unable to get a spoon, so
I took out what I could with my fingers, and drank the rest. It
seemed as good as any I ever tasted; and it nourished me so that
I soon began to recover.

All the births [sic] in the cabin are occupied by the married
people; and it was thought best to make up one for by the dead-
lights [near the shutter fixed on the inside or outside a porthole
to keep water out in a storm]—for we are obliged to have them
all in. The captain [Reuben Clasby], who has doubled Cape
Horn five times, says that he had never seen the sea in such condition in his life. The bowsprit [large spar in front of the ship]
was at times buried in the sea, and again, almost perpendicular
in the air; so that every thing in the cabin which was not lashed,
was thrown from one side to the other. The vessel pitched and
rolled at the same time, in such manner that no one could stand
on their feet without holding. And as my birth [sic] was avast
the beam [fastened on the beam], whenever my head went to
leeward [turned in a direction away from the wind] and my feet
to windward [in a direction toward the wind], which was the
case every five minutes, it made me very sick—I found it would
not do for me to endeavor to sleep so. The captain therefore had
a hammock made and swung over the table [in the cabin] to be
let down at night and swung up in the morning. The first night I
tried it I rested very well—I was both sick and tired. The second
night the ship rolled without pitching and I was thrown back
and forth as fast as I could go [with it] until about 12 o'clock at
night; when a bed that been placed in one of the dead lights was
thrown down, and struck one corner of my hammock—This
threw me, first against the ceiling and then on the dining table.
As the same moment we shipped a sea and the water running
on the deck, and trunks falling in the cabin, allowed me to think
very little of myself. However I was soon accosted by Mr. Stuart,
who came to know if I was hurt. When I assured him that I was
not, I heard the rest of the [mission] family laughing heartily
behind their [cabin] curtains—It was fine sport for them and
the captain, for a few days. I did not venture into my hammock
again for the remainder of the night, but stayed with Mrs. S. But
I have learned to sleep very comfortably in it since. I go to bed

between between 9 and 10 o'clock, and get up at day-break—
ring the bell at day-light, and have prayers at sun-rise—then
have breakfast, and afterwards go about our business. Our study
hours are from 9 to 12 in the morning, and from 2 to 5 in the
afternoon.—Mrs. Stuart has suffered more than any of the family; but she now is recovering very fast.

We have had many remarkable interpositions of Providence already in our behalf. The first pleasant day after the
storm, we saw the *Prime* of Philadelphia and spoke her. It was
out of our power to write by her, yet it was very gratifying to
us to send word to our friends that all was well. We have seen
a number of vessels since, but have not been able to speak any
bound to America. We saw the *Winslow* of New Bedford and
sailed in her company for a some time. On Sabbath morning,
Mr. Stuart went on board and preached, and in the afternoon
the captain came on board our ship to church. Mr. Stuart observed when he returned, that he never expected to have gone
to preach in the midst of the Atlantic Ocean. The day will, I
think, be long remembered by us. The captain invited us all
on board his ship the next day that the weather should be fair.
But the wind, after blowing from several points of the compass,
died away in the night, so that the helm [the tiller] became
useless; and the two ships got so near together that immediate
destruction appeared inevitable. But the wind sprung up, after
a short time, and enable both ships to steer off. The *Winslow*
then left us, and we have had no company since—Company
that was very desirable, and yet we were glad to get rid of it, as
it was like to cost us too dear.

I have sir, already realized many things that you told me
when at home . . . But still, sir, I am as happy as I ever was in
my life.

It would do your heart good, to see with what firmness that
part of our family who has been accustomed to better things,
bear their trials. Here I do not insinuate that there are any who
have not borne them like Christians. But it was thought that Mr.
S would not bear them with as much fortitude as Mr. [Artimus]
B[ishop]; because one had been accustomed to a more delicate
manner of life than the other. If those who indulge that opinion
were with us, they would find that refinement in a missionary,
is no objection to him. I have seen your friend [Charles Stew-
art/Stuart] lie down on a pile of boards, or on top of the locker
[shipboard cabinet] when almost exhausted without a murmur.
He has already begun to "bear hardness like a good soldier." I
feel very much ashamed at times, when I look at him, and think

what he is, and what I am—If he bears hardships thus, how ought I to bear them?

Leaving home and becoming a missionary does not, I find, make peace with the great enemy—I find my heart still inclined to forget God, and to wander in the paths of sin. We have not a place in the ship to which we can retire, and spend a moment in secret with our God. This is one of my greatest privations: for the poor spark in my breast requires to be constantly fanned by prayer, to keep it from being extinguished—Sometimes I feel as though it were almost out . . . You will please to excuse my saying so much of myself.

Tell Mr. ___ [unnamed person, left blank; possibly James Green] that I have not forgotten him. I see many things to remind me of him constantly. This morning we saw and caught the *Portuguese man of war* [Mollusca] but could devise no plan to preserve one for him. The string of one of them hung from the ship to the water; it looks very much like a string of blue beads. One of the natives [Hawaiian youths] who was in the water bathing, says that one of these animals bit him. He brought a piece with him on his hand. Most of the missionaries this afternoon have been out in a small boat [one of the *Thames'* longboats] and found the sun very hot. The heat is not as yet very great in the ship.—No whales have been taken as yet, although we have seen a number—and the harpoons are all in readiness—You will please to excuse the defects of my letter. I find it hard, as yet, to think and write at sea. Remember me to ___ [unnamed person, left blank].

With feeling which neither time nor space can change, Yours humbly,

BETSEY STOCKTON

P. S.

After writing the above, we were driven off Cape Verde [the Cape de Verde Islands, off the coast of Spain] and were unable to stop there, and gave up all hopes of being able to send my letter—January 5th. A ship has just appeared in sight, and I have scarcely more time to tell you we are all well.

Jan. 4, 1823. We have crossed the line [the equator] yesterday and had the usual ceremonies. [Some ships' crews dressed up as Father Neptune and all the passengers had to bow before him and ask passage to cross the equator.] We have had a very interesting voyage thus far. We have caught a number of fish of different kinds, such as the black fish [pilot whales], sharks, dolphins, &c. The manner of harpooning them is very curious. I can say no more—We are taking in sail.

B S

Mr. and Mrs. Stuart desire to be remembered to you.

P. S. 2nd—We have been disappointed, the third time, in sending our letters. But this morning, at 4 o'clock, we discovered an Englishman, who has engaged to take them. Since I last wrote, we have had trying times, but no damage has been done to the ship. I have learned to be quite a sailor, and have not been frightened since I came on board—any more than to feel solemn. For this I desire to be very thankful.—The Lord has not forgotten me. We are now in S. Lat 44 degrees W. Long. 60 degrees—the family all well on February 2nd, 1823. We got some soundings yesterday for the first time after being out [of harbor] 75 days. I will write again by the first opportunity.

BETSEY STOCKTON

Dec. 30 [1822]. Sabbath. Had prayer meeting in the morning, and preaching in the afternoon at 4 o'clock. Mr. Stewart preached from I Cor. i.23. I enjoyed the Sabbath very much, and thought I felt something of the love of God in my heart. But still I felt as if I was declining in the spiritual life. I attend a little to the study of the Bible, and find it pleasant. Yet, I find a void within my breast that is painful. The scenes which constantly present themselves to my mind from Him who is, or ought to be my only joy. With the poor publican I will say, "God be merciful to me a sinner." At six in the evening, we caught two sharks, and saw a number of dolphins. The flesh of the shark is very good when young.

Dec. 31. I was much interested in witnessing the harpooning of a large shark. It was taken at the stern of the ship, about 6 yards from the cabin window, from which I had a clear view of it. It was struck by two harpoons at the same time. The fish, if we may call it one, for it has very little appearance of a fish, was so angry that he endeavoured to bite the men after he was on deck. His jaw bone was taken out and preserved by one of the missionaries. We see a great number of them, and take them frequently. I have not been able to preserve any curiosities for Mr. J[ames?]. If I were to return I could amuse him a long time, with telling the simple facts that I have witnessed, and the things I have seen; and at the close of the year I will mention a few. The colour of the water near land, is a greenish hue; and a little further out it is a bluish tint; and in the middle of the ocean it is of a dark blue, and very clear. I never saw a more beautiful green than the colour of the water off Cape Blanco [Africa] where we were nearly driven an an unfavorable wind. From this we steered S.W. by S. between the African Coast, and the Cape de Verde island and then directed our course S.S.W. to the coast of Brazil. If it were in my power I would like to describe the Phosphorescence of the sea. But to do this would require the pen of a Milton [author of *Paradise Lost*]; and he would fail, were he to attempt it. I never saw a display of Fireworks that equaled it for beauty. As far as we could see the ocean, in the wake of the ship, it appeared one sheet of fire, and exhibited figures of which you can form no idea. [Phosphorescent marine life comes closer to the surface at night.] We have bathed [in the sea] during this month frequently and find the water very refreshing. Yesterday, at 8 in the morning, the thermometer stood at 80 degrees. The missionaries all went in to bathe, with their pantaloons [long underwear]. Mr. B[ishop] wore his shirt also, and dived three times from the ship; the last time he staid too long in the water, so that the strength of his arms was exhausted, and he was not able to get into the ship alone. Mr. [Marcus] Lane, the second mate, dived from the bowsprit [long pole projecting from the bow], with a rope, and tied it round him. At the same time another [rope] was thrown from the side of the vessel. We felt alarmed for a few moments, but there was no real danger. Had he even fainted, the number of swimmers was so great that they could have kept him up until a [long] boat was lowered. I must finish the year by saying with the Psalmist, "When I consider the works of his hands, Lord what is man that thou art mindful of him."[17]

Betsey Stockton Meets Old Neptune and His Wife: The Earliest Nineteenth-Century American Description of the Crossing the Line Ceremony[18]

Jan. 4th, 1823. Crossed the line. In the evening old *Neptune* [Roman god of the sea] visited us, a little before we came to his *garden*, as he called it. His appearance was the most ludicrous thing I ever saw in my life. He announced his coming by blowing a large trumpet [shell]. The sailors were most of them new

17. Dec. 30 and 31 in B. Stockton, "Journal," *Christian Advocate* 2 (May 1824), 233.
18. B. Stockton, "Journal," *Christian Advocate* 2 (May 1824) 235.

hands [initiates, polliwogs], and the poor fellows were all put down in the forecastle, and afterwards brought up, one at a time, before his majesty, with their eyes covered, to answer a number of questions respecting their lives, business, &c. and why they had come to sea. He told the mission family, that as there were so many ladies on board, he had thought it expedient to bring his wife [*Amphitrite*, a sailor dressed as a woman] with him, and that she was as clever an old lady as ever was in the world. He introduced her to the family, but said he thought it not best for her to shake hands with them, as she had been handling so many of her dirty boys [unseen ceremonies below deck.] Nor did he think it proper to *shave* any one farther aft, among the ladies. But he would like *something else*. Accordingly they [the missionaries] sent him some Spirits [liquor] and Cakes, and he and his lady withdrew, telling us that we might cross his *garden* at all times. The manner in which they shave is very disgusting [e.g., shaving half of each crewman's face].

Jan. 5th, 1823. Sabbath. Pleasant and clear in the morning; a little squally in the afternoon. Had our usual worship. The day was solemn; Mr. Bishop preached for us: but "in vain I sought Him whom my soul loveth." I felt very much inclined to despair, and feared that I had indulged the hope of a hypocrite. Shall I after all become a castaway! Forbid it, O Lord! nor suffer me to injure the cause I have espoused.

Jan. 6th, 1823. Nothing new to-day. All going on in good order. I find my mind still dark; and do not feel quite happy. Yet for the sake of those around me I endeavor to appear cheerful. I am becoming more and more attached to Mr. and Mrs. S—and trust that God will make me a comfort to them.

Jan. 8th, 1823. Going very rapidly, at the rate of nine and a half miles an hour. The weather very pleasant. We have not suffered so much with the heat since we came near the line [equator] as we did some time ago. The air is much more like that on land than we felt it for four weeks past. Saw a large tortoise, but could not take it, without delaying the ship too long. We regretted the loss very much. Fresh meat would be very acceptable to us; we have had none since Christmas. Pork and beef [brought by the missionaries] are our standing dishes. Our table makes a curious appearance. It is spread over with *frames;* every plate, dish and cup is fastened; and even thus we cannot get a meal, at times, without holding with one hand, while helping ourselves to eat with the other. We have very little conversation at the table; all of us get through as soon as we can. There are eleven persons at each table; at the first, the captain and one of the mates, and nine of the missionaries. At the second, two mates, three of the missionaries, the four natives and myself. The provisions of both tables are alike. In the division of the missionary stores I always have my share, to that I have indeed a double portion of the good things of this life; for Mrs. and Mrs. S give me always a share with them. The last apple and orange were cut in three pieces, and divided between us. The impression that such little things make on my mind will not easily be erased. O that I were worthy of such favours, but I fear I am not.

Charles Stewart's *Journal* Records the Sighting of a Portuguese Slaver[19]

Thursday, Jan 9th, 1823: Early to-day, a sail was discovered, with signals for speaking; and we bore down to her. It was a Portuguese vessel of very indifferent appearance. Our captain put the *Thames* so close along side of her, that an apple could have been thrown on her deck. The commander could not speak English, and hailed through one of his crew: he merely wished to know our longitude; and informed us he was bound to the Western Coast of Africa. With the knowledge of her destination, the horrors of slave ship, at once, rose on the mind; and the probability of her errand, to that land of wretchedness, took entire possession of the imagination. The sighting of the captive, and the groaning of the oppressed, seemed already to be heard from her hatchways, and, as we dropped into her wake, gazing at her black hulk and bloody waist—colors well suited to her character—to the farewell wave of her hand, I could not add the customary ejaculation—*"God speed thee."*

Never before, was I so deeply impressed, with the enormity of this trade . . . . Oh! what perversion of feeling—what destitution of principle—must be in the heart, that can convert the ignorance and debasement of those, who, though sunk below the level of their race, are still "bone of our bone, and flesh of our flesh," into reasons for subjecting them to still greater degradation! Surely, if any thing on earth, calls loudly for the righteous judgment of God, it is the prosecution of the slave trade; and sooner or later, the retributions of a just avenger must fall on those who thus, make the heavens to echo the

19. C. Samuel Stewart, *Private Journal*, 48–54.

moanings of the bereaved, and the earth rich with the tears and blood of the enslaved.

Jan. 22nd, 1823: Sighting Flying fish [*Exocaetus volitans*]. We are all in fine health and spirits and truly happy. A very visible change has taken place in the general deportment of the crew . . . . Beneficial consequences are flowing from our Bible classes. Another exercise, connected with evening prayers,—the repetition, by each of the Missionaries, of a single text of Scripture, indiscriminately chosen from the Bible . . . . The officers and crew, like ourselves, are occupied with their Bibles, and other appropriate books . . . Evenings . . . It is a time in which I delight; and often, after most of our company are wrapt in sleep, I ascend the rigging . . . there to gaze on the heavens, "the work of the Almighty, and the moon and stars which He hath made"—and in view of their magnitude and sublimity, with the psalmist to exclaim—"What is man, that THOU are mindful of him, or the son of man that THOU visitest him?"

Jan. 23rd, 1823: Spoke the *Hebe* of Philadephia. The *Thames* was running, under a press of sail before a strong breeze, against which the *Hebe* stemmed her way, close hauled, with double-reefed topsails only . . . . Evening: The most tremendous squall we have yet encountered has just swept by. It came raging so suddenly, upon us, that the Captain had time only to exclaim—"All hands on deck! Hand the royals—and the top-gallant-sails too! clew up the mainsail!—mind your helm—quick! quick!"—while all became vociferation and confusion—before the wind struck us a full broadside, and, instantly, laid the ship almost on her beam-ends [on her side]. Everything cracked, in her struggle against the blast, and she shot forward like a racehorse, with her gunnels in the water, and the waves on her lee towering yard-arm high.

A shipwreck must, indeed, be horrible. I was not greatly agitated myself; the most unpleasant sensations I experienced arose from the terror of others; for there were many a pale face, and trembling lip, among both crew and passengers. Whatever the degree of danger may have been, the scene was of a character, deeply, to fix thoughts of that even by which sooner or later, we shall all be made to stand, before the bar of God.

Stewart Saves the Soul of a Murdering Cannibal on Board the *Thames*[20]

Jan. 25, 1823: My interviews with R[amsdell], since the gale off the Rio De la Plata, have been frequent. He continues, greatly interested for his own salvation. On two nights, recently, I have spent a part of his watch on deck, with him, and at both times, by the sight of the waning moon, have seen tears roll, in torrents, down his hardy cheeks, while he has spoken of the things, that relate to his eternal peace. To some of his ship-mates, he has become an object of ridicule, while others seem to be like-minded with himself.

But though the day has been one of gloom, it has been marked by a circumstance, which has given me more genu-ine satisfactions, than any thing since we left America. In the dusk of the evening, while leaning, alone, against the railing of the quarterdeck, feeling, in my own mind, something of the desolation of the scene around me, my arm was gently touched by some one, on the spars behind: it was R[amsdell], one of the hardiest of our crew. As my eye fell upon him, I at once anticipated his errand; and can scarce describe my emotion, when I ascertained it, indeed to be the sailor's query—*"What must I do to be saved?"* Perceiving me alone, he had stolen from his station forward, to say that his spirit, like the troubled sea, could find no rest .... His words were few, but his look, while he trembled under his guilt, as a sinner, and earnestly suppli-cated an interest in my prayers, spoke volumes. So unexpected, though greatly desired and prayed for, was this event, that I al-most doubted its reality. This state of feeling had been induced by a private conversation on the subject of religion, immedi-ately after the recitation of the Bible class, on the preceding Sabbath; and he had scarce eaten or slept, during the whole week. . . . Every thing, in his appearance manifested sincerity and contrition. I . . . yet cannot but hope that the Spirit of God has begun in his heart . . . and, should but one of this crew, be truly converted to the faith and practice of pure religion, through the example, the persuasion, and prayers of that indi-vidual, all his companions, were the voyage is completed, may be termed the Shepherd and the Bishop of Souls.

20. Jan. 1823 in C. Samuel Stewart, *Private Journal*, 57; Mar. 1823 in C. Samuel Stewart, *Private Journal*, 69.

March 6th A short time since, R[amsdell] was in great despondency . . . and said to me . . . "I feel that my soul will live forever; and without the grace of God, I know it must eternally perish! O, Mr. S—, I have found the right was to believe:—it was the righteousness of Jesus Christ I needed. Now the whole Bible is not *against me*, as it used to be, but every word is *for me;* because I see and feel, how God can be just and yet justify an ungodly sinner."

R[amsdell] is one of the happiest of creatures. All he says is worth twice its real value, from the manner in which it is communicated. [Another sailor had conversed with Stewart, and asked how *he* could be saved.] R told him, it was just so with himself once, "I did not know what faith was, or how to obtain it, but know now, what it is, and believe I possess it, but I did not know that that I can tell you what it is, or how to get it, I can tell you what is it not;—it is *not knocking off swearing, and drinking, and such like,* and it is not *reading the Bible—nor praying—nor being good*—it is none of these, for even if they would answer for the time to come, there is the old score still, and how are you to get clear of that? It is not any thing you have done or can do; it is only believing and trusting only what *Christ has done*—it is forsaking your sins, and looking for their pardon and the salvation of your soul, because He died and shed his blood for sin, and it is nothing else." A doctor of divinity might have given [his fellow sailor] a more technical and polished answer, but not one more simple, or probably satisfactory.

Charles Ramsdell, the nineteen-year-old Nantucket boatsteerer of the *Thames,* was one of four survivors of the earlier *Essex* tragedy. Seventy-three days after the shipwreck, Ramsdell survived in a longboat with his captain, George Pollard Jr. They drew lots, then shot and ate the murdered Owen Coffin, a Nantucket relative. Pollard and Ramsdell were rescued seventy days later, clinging to bones. Contrary to the scanty evidence of notes on the side margin of a holograph poem written decades after the event, "The Ship *Two Brothers*,"[21] Ramsdell never went on a second voyage with Pollard. The manifest of the *Thames*'s crew proves Ramsdell was instead on the *Thames.* Here, in Stewart's journal, we understand the power of saving souls, of Stewart's calling, acting as the representative of Jesus Christ on earth, offering the power of forgiveness to Charles Ramsdell, at the age of sixteen the murderer and cannibal of a shipmate.

21. Nickerson, "The Ship *Two Brothers.*"

In corroboration, on January 27, Louisa Everest Ely noted in her journal:

> One of the sailors has expressed anxiety for his soul as he affectionately took one of the brethren by the hand he said, "I am ignorant I wish to be instructed I want religion. I feel my time is short and I want religion before the missionaries leave the ship." May the lord grant his request and grant a listening ear to the requests made in behalf of these perishing immortals and get glory to his great name in their salvation.[22]

Betsey Stockton Narrates the Voyage of Rounding the Cape Horn—Twice[23]

Feb. 5th, 1823: All well and anxious to get round Cape Horn; a little blow in the afternoon. We are not without our fears; but the Lord reigneth, and we will rejoice. Lat. 490 40'—Long. 620 08'

Feb. 6th: The weather is beginning to be rather cold. I find my woolen clothes to be very comfortable; my health is very good again—a little homesick, but do not wish to return. O! thought I, if I could but spend one Sabbath evening in your study, how my healer [Christ] would rejoice. But I must look forward to that as through a glass [reference to 1 Cor 13]; and to meet you, with many others in my native land, pray for me. Were it not for that, I should almost despair. I find my heart more deeply corrupted than I had any idea of. I always knew that the human heart was [a] sink of sin, and that mine was filled with it; but I did not know until now, that the sink was without a bottom. I attribute much of my spiritual difficulty to the want of retirement and prayer. It is with the greatest anxiety that I mark the hours as they pass away, which once were devoted to God in secret, without having at present a place for retirement, or indeed at times a heart to retire. Ah! How soon may the people of God grieve away his Holy Spirit. But why should I thus complain and despond. He is still my Father and my God—and I still love him—Yes, my balm is still in Gilead, and my physician there. Lat. 560 41'—Long. 630.

Feb. 7. Still sailing all speed towards Cape Horn. Just as the sun was setting, we were called to witness one of the most sublime scenes that ever the eyes of mortals beheld.—no language

22. Ely, *Diary of Missionary Voyage*, 13.

23. B. Stockton, "Journal," *Christian Advocate* 2 (Dec. 1824), 563–66.

could paint it.—it was the setting of the sun. The scene kept changing from beautiful to more beautiful, until I could think of nothing but the bright worlds above, to which the saints are hastening. As soon as it was over, and the sun had disappeared, we were assembled on the quarter deck for prayers. Here my soul found free access to the throne of grace, and rose with delight in the contemplation of that God who is the author of all our joys and of all good.

Feb. 8. I was roused this morning by Mr. [Marcus] Lane [the second mate], who came into the cabin to inform the captain that there was land two points off the weather bow. The captain told him to brace and stand for it. I soon dressed myself, and went on deck to see it. Its first appearance was that of a dark cloud, but it became much darker as we approached it; until we came near enough to discover cragged rocks, with a whitish earth running between them. It was about 12 o'clock when we first saw the white streak, and at 1 we could see the greenish appearance of the mountains. Half an hour afterwards we saw a smoke rising from them, and at 2 a light blaze. It was, however, soon extinguished. What this fire was, no one on the ship could tell—perhaps a company of sealers [seal hunters] had stopped there, and seeing our ship, lighted it up to alarm [warn] us. Or it might be the signal of distress for some poor cast-away sailor— or possibly a volcanic eruption. Our captain had often passed *Staten land* [southern coast of Argentina]—before, but had seen nothing of the kind. But our situation was too critical to admit of a moment's delay to make observations; for we were now near enough to see the breakers dashing against this forbidden shore, and either a calm or squall might prove fatal to us. I thought of all the language of the poet, as I looked at these craggy cliffs—

"Alas! these rocks all human skill defy,

Who strikes them once, beyond relief, must die."[24]

We continued sailing near them until 4 o'clock, when a calm ensued. Our captain said nothing to us, but evidently appeared troubled. I then knew no danger, and talked to him as usual—asked him to send a boat ashore; and jestingly told him, that I would accompany him. I thought he looked solemn, and would give no reason for it. The truth was, that a strong current was drawing us towards these fatal rocks; and if the wind enough should not rise to render the ship manageable, we must inevitably be wrecked upon them, during the ensuing

---

24. Stockton is quoting from William Falconer's "The Shipwreck" (canto 3, lines 90–91), possibly from memory, and altering the punctuation.

night. Here you will indulge me with passing reflection. I have always remarked, that in the most dangerous situations, I have felt the easiest; and it was because I did not know my danger. And can there be any thing more like a sleeping Christian, or an unawakened sinner? Both in imminent danger, and both stupid. O that God may save me from the spiritual, as he has in mercy from the natural evil. A fresh breeze sprung up toward evening, and we were soon borne beyond the reach of the current; and in a few hours *Staten land* receded entirely from our view. But fresh dangers and anxieties awaited us.

Feb. 9th Here begins our tossing and rolling.—To-day we had the rain and hail in squalls. We cannot write or read with comfort; and if we attempt to eat, sitting on chairs that are not lashed, the chance is ten to one that we are thrown across the cabin, before the meal is over. I have had several pretty hard blows on my head, since we left the river Plate [the Rio de la Plata River, in Argentina]. Our latitude, as far as we can judge from reckoning and observation, is 55o 26'—Long. 350. Twenty-one days ensued after this, in which we were in snow, hail, rain, and one continued gale. Sometimes we could scud before the wind; but most of the time it was too strong to admit of that; we generally lay to under a close reefed top-sail [all mainsails were lashed to their masts, to avoid tearing or putting the ship on her beams, shipwrecked]. Oh! How cheerless every thing looked around us, in comparison with what it did some time ago. The sailors were all wet, day and night, the forecastle was half of the time filled with water; and the water that was shipped at the bow [front of the ship] ran as far as the companion-way [ladderway through a hatch to the next deck below]. All over the ship there was nothing but dirt and wet, so slippery we could not stand. One night at twelve o'clock, I went on deck, when the ship was laying [lying] to, under nothing but a close reefed top-sail. The wind was so strong, that I could not stand without holding by my hands to something fixed; it seemed as if the ship was going on her beam ends [falling sideways into the sea] every moment. The sailors were always pleased to see me on deck in a storm, and tried more than once to frighten me, but when they found that they did not succeed, they ended with saying, "well Betsey, you'll know how to pity poor sailors—we have not been dry since we left Staten land." My heart has often bled for these poor fellows. I slept whenever I could, night or day. Studying was out of the question; I found it impossible to put two ideas together, half the time. During this period, we caught several birds; one or two of which I tried to save for Mr. ___, but the rain continued so long that they were spoiled. The sailors call them *Mother Carey's chickens* [a species of petrol] and Mock Mollys. The most beautiful that I have seen is the Mock Molly. Of this species we took a number. They are a little larger than a goose. In viewing Cape Horn, I can truly say *the half was not told me.* It is indeed one of the most dreadful places ever seen; and if I double it again, I shall endeavor to do it by the way of Cape of Good Hope [tip of the continent of Africa]; this I know, is a blunder, but it conveys my meaning. In a gale we lost the waste-board of the ship [waist-board, protecting the deck from waves]; this left the deck three feet nearer to the water, and consequently we shipped [took on] more water than usual. I had always had the good fortune to be below when the deck got washed very badly; and as we were soon to be in the milder waters of the Pacifick, I wished very much to see our vessel ship one heavy sea, as the sailors call it [have one very strong wave wash across the deck, carrying sea water with it]. My wishes were answered in the following manner—One afternoon, when I had been suffering for some time with wet feet, I went to the caboose [the galley deckhouse, where the cook would have had a fire going] to warm them, just as I was coming out, I got both my eyes filled with ashes and embers, which put me in a very unfavourable situation for seeing what I wished to see; but at that moment I heard a sea strike the leeward side [from where the wind is blowing] of the ship, fore and aft; in an instant I sprang to the shrouds [the major side stays of the mast, huge wrapped ropes] and heard the water run in a torrent under me. My poor eyes were condemned to darkness; a liquid made of salt water and ashes did not improve them just then. However I felt no inconvenience from it afterwards, except that if afforded fine sport, for some time, to the captain, who often observed that Betsey had shipped a sea in her face. This occurrence however did not intimidate me; I went on deck very often to view the grandeur of the sea; and it is truly one of the most sublime objects in creation. I have spent hours since I left my native land in viewing this object. At times I have seen the waves rise mountains high before us; and it would appear as if we must inevitably be swallowed up; but in a moment our ship would rise upon the wave, and it would be seen receding at the stern [back end of the ship]. I stayed on deck one evening until 12 o'clock, looking at the waves break[ing] over the deck; while below it sounded like thunder or like rivers running over us. I could compare our sailing when going before the wind to nothing but flying. We were scudding [running] with the wind directly after, under a close reefed top and main sail [reduced area of sail] of course the ship rolled and pitched at the same time. Captain Clasby had told us, more than once, that if the wind was fair, we must take care of ourselves for he did not intend to spare us [steer the ship into calmer winds]. He was literally fulfilling his words; for he neither spared us nor the ship. I felt more afraid that the sides would meet the same fate that the waste-board did, than of any thing else. She labored very hard, and we shipped so much water, that the pumps [hand pumps used by the crew in the hold, below deck] were kept at work every four hours. I have thought at times, in the night, that we were on a rock, but on inquiry, the answer would be *nothing but Cape Horn.* However, we are almost done with it, and I am not sorry; nor am I sorry that I have been called to double it; for I have enjoyed more of the light of my heavenly Father's continence during the time we were off the Cape, than I ever did in the Atlantic. The only reason I can assign is, that here we have been called hourly to acknowledge his mercy in sparing our lives, and that while we here view his power upon this stormy ocean, we have felt helplessness and been made to adore and tremble. I am not writing to one who is unacquainted with the human heart; you know its dark deceitful nature; and that it is not always kept warm by tender treatment. For me at least it is necessary in order to keep me in my place, to have some doubts, some temptation, and some sickness to struggle with; and even then my garments are far from being kept white [without sin]. But hitherto has the Lord helped me, and I can raise upon this much dreaded landmark, a strong and lasting Ebenezer [a memorial stone or marker, reference to 1 Sam 7:12]. Long, I hope, shall I remember the mercy of God here. Here too the Spirit of the Lord has, I trust, been striving with some of the sailors, though many are yet, I fear, in the gall of bitterness; some, however, are rejoicing in the Lord. How would your heart rejoice with us, could you see these hearty sons of the ocean, who would scorn to complain of any earthly hardships, bowing with the spirit of children, at the cross of Christ. This fact we witness; and if I could do it as I wish, it would please me to give you an account of some of their conversations—their plain, abrupt, and sailor-like manner of expressing their thoughts and feelings, but I must leave this for an abler pen.

On the 16th of February, we saw Cape Noir [seventeen miles west of Tierra del Fuego] and were obliged to tack, to prevent being driven on it. [Twenty-seven days later:] The wind was against us; and the 3rd of March we were again near the same place, only a little to the west. On the Sabbath, Mr. [William]Richards

preached in the cabin, from these words: "Though you made
many prayers I will not hear"—warning those that refused to
hear the calls of God, of that day when God would refuse to hear
them. Oh! How appalling is the thought, that the day is coming
in which we must rise as witnesses against them or they against
us—if we have been unfaithful to them. We still retire for fifteen
minutes, every evening, directly after publick prayers, to pray for
them—I say retire, that is, we go to different parts of the ship;
some of us into the rigging [ropes fastened to sails], some out
in the [long] boats, and others on the spars [long wooden yards,
booms, gaffs]; yet in all these places we can find our God.

   We are now to bid farewell to high wind and dark blue water. I hope soon to be in that part of the Pacific, which deserves
the name; for this part Terrific would suit it best. Indeed it is so
terrible, that neither sun, moon, nor stars, condescend to visit it
often. Its constant companions are rain, hail and snow.

From Charles Stewart's *Journal* [25]

Thursday, Feb. 20th, 1823: Immediately after finished the preceding page, nearly a fortnight ago, we were assailed by the
fierce winds of the Cape. We had just fallen asleep, after an
uncommonly mild evening, when the rushing of an impetu-
ous storm, followed by the alarming cry, "all hands on deck!"
thundered with stentorian voice, down the maindeck, and
forecastle hatchways—roused us from our slumbers.—Some
apprehension excited at one time, of our being too much in the
neighborhood of the Diego Ramirez, a cluster of rocks thirty
miles south of Hermit's Island, on which Cape Horn is situated.
But, we shortly afterwards, ascertained ourselves to be well to
the westward of them; and on the morning of the 16th, at four
o'clock, made Cape Noir, an island near Cape Gloucester on
Terra (Tierra) del Fuego, twenty miles distant. We wore ship,
immediately, and had only time to clear the coast, before the
wind, blowing *"dead on shore"* increased to a perfect hurricane,
and for the last forty-eight hours, has driven us with irresistible
fury, far eastward again. H(attie) often says, *"with what terror
would our friends, witness our situation!"* at the very extremity
of the globe, surrounded by an immense waste of angry waters,
whose surface is unceasingly swept by wind, and hail, and rain,
and snow,—our only earthly hope, a few hundred feet of timber,

25. C. Samuel Stewart, *Private Journal*, 65–67.

which the ingenuity of man has formed to float upon the ocean; liable to many accidents, and hourly, exposed to a horrid death, . . . (might) make us fearful and unbelieving. But they do not. We have an unshaken confidence, that all will be well . . . . We often view our good ship, with a kind of sympathy: dismantled of much of her loftiness, and reefed and furled, almost to bare poles, she looks, in her conflict, desolate as a solitary oak, writhing in the contentions of a winter's storm.

Saturday, March 1st, 1823: After a tempestuous passage of twenty-one days, by the aid of a few hours of fair wind, we find ourselves completely around Cape Horn. The whole ship's company, passengers and crew, appear like captives on the eve of liberations, from a gloomy and uncomfortable prison . . . . We have scarce seen the sun for three weeks, and the moon but once . . . . Not one of the officers or crew, have had dry clothes, during the whole of the time; the deck has been constantly deluged, and the cabin dark and cold: for we have had no fire, though the mercury has stood as low as 34 degrees and 36 degrees [Fahrenheit] . . . . We could do nothing, but wrap ourselves in our cloaks, hold on to any thing within reach, and, whether sitting up or laying down, roll and pitch, with our labouring bark. Ships are often detained by them [winds and storms], three times the period we have been, and meet with weather far more dangerous and severe: so much so, that many vessels after striving, in vain, for weeks here, to make a passage into the Pacific, have been obliged to bear away for the Cape of Good Hope [the tip of Africa] and make their voyage across the Indian Ocean. Our crew has all been kept in life, where many a poor sailor has found a cold, unfathomed grave: and, our ship has rode in safety, where not a few have met an untold fate.

Betsey Stockton's "Journal," Continuing on March 4[26]

We have completely doubled Cape Horn; the sea is much smoother—I saw nothing remarkable during the day. My own health and that of the family is pretty good; it is a source of comfort to me that Mrs. and Mr. S enjoy their health so well: I have learned to love them, and they richly deserve it. My heart must be dead to every virtue, when it ceases to beat with gratitude to them. When I took the last look of those dear young gentlemen [Jacob and James Sproat Green], with whom I had spent my

26. B. Stockton, "Journal," *Christian Advocate* 3 (Jan. 1825), 36.

days of childhood and folly, and my more sober years of reflection, my soul sickened within me as I said—"Can I hope ever to find such friends like these? Can I ever find those who will take so deep an interest in my welfare, and with whom I shall spend such happy hours?" Yes, I have found such friends. When you think of me as a stranger in a strange land [reference to Exod 2:22], think of me still as one who has kind friends, to guide and protect her. 'Tis true the endearments of home cannot be forgotten. My mind often returns to your family altar. There I have often left my burden, and I cannot forget that consecrated spot. Nor can I forget the dear little boys, I have so often held in my arms—I comfort myself thinking that I shall hear from you all [the Green family] while in life, and with the hope that I shall meet you after the hour of death.

March 5th The weather much pleasanter than it has been. We are getting to the Pacific. Lat 460 22' Long. 820 30' W.

March 7th The weather not very pleasant, but much better than Cape Horn.

March 9th Sabbath. In the morning we had prayers in the cabin, and in the afternoon Mr. Stewart preached from Genesis vi. 3. "My spirit shall not always strive with man." I have seen nothing since I came on board that had appeared to produce so much effect. The Spirit of the Lord seemed striving with at least some of the sailors. They have been constrained since to say, *what shall we do?* And I hope some have fled to the only sure resting place for poor perishing souls. Lat. 460 22' Long. 800 35'.

March 10th Pleasant weather—all going on well. We are steering up the coast of Chili [Chile]. It is remarkable that off this coast it never rains; nor is it clear weather; it is always a little cloudy. The air is very refreshing at all times, but particularly so in the morning. Our deck presents a very odd appearance this morning. The fore-hole, or middle-hole, and the run [hatches on the deck of the *Thames*] are all open. The things that have been wet are airing in every direction; our medicine chests are unpacking and sailors are sending up the fore and mizzen, royal and top-gallant yards [ship's sails, to dry]. Picture to yourself our situation, when in the midst of all this, we hear the well known cry—"There she blows." This was repeated every minute or two for some time. The lines and water were hurried into the boats, and everything was soon in readiness. The sailors waited impatiently for the command to lower [the long boats]. Those in sight were sperm whales at four miles distance. The wished for orders were at length given, and in five minutes the [long] boats were seen gliding over the waves. How changed the scene, thought I—Four months ago, these boats would not have been lowered without having our ears assailed with oaths—Now not a profane word is heard. They pursued the whales some distance, but could not come up with them. The captain seeing this, hoisted the signal for return; the poor fellows were obliged to obey, and this ended the chase—and my day must end with it. The Lat. 390 16' Long. 800 40'.

March 13th—Steering N by W. Nothing occurred until 1 P.M. when we came up and spoke the English brig *Tiber* from Valparaiso [Chile's major port] bound to Valdivia. This is by the handsomest foreign vessel we have seen since we left America. The captain was very much of a gentleman. This conversation, as near as I can recollect it, was as follows:—Englishman— What ship is that? American—The *Thames* of New Haven. E[nglishman] How long have you been out? A[merican]—One hundred and ten days. E.—Are you bound to Valparaiso? A.— No, sire; I am bound to the Sandwich Islands. How long have you been out, and where are you bound? E.—I have been out eight days; I'm bound to Valdivia. Valparaiso is in a state of revolution. The Royalists have been defeated. The *Franklin 74* is there. What success have you had in fishing? A.—I have caught nothing [i.e., no oil-rich whales]. E.—I am sorry for that. I wish you success. Sir, what is your longitude? A.—810 10' A. [again]—I thank you sir. I wish you a prosperous voyage. All this passed in three or four minutes.

March 20th—There is a sameness in every thing that pass- es, which makes it almost impossible to write; unless I should give you a very minute account of every little incident that has occurred. This I will not attempt, for fear that I should aim at something out of my reach. Mr. Stewart will give you a full ac- count of every thing you wish to know. We are sailing slowly along the coast of Peru. The Lat is 200 38' Long. 910 52'.

March 24th—This morning was pleasant, but I could not enjoy it—I was wretched—I could not enjoy my friends, because I could not enjoy my God. The captain wishes to make a respect- able appearance when enters the port, and so he is painting the ship all over. Our Lat 150 29' Long. 960 47' W.

March 25th—Still dark in mind myself, but the family all in motion. Some packing clothes, some writing journals.—I just came to transcribe mine for you [for Green]. You would scarcely believe that so many different occupations could be carried on, on board a ship.—The painters, the carpenter and the black- smiths are all at work. This morning Stephen [a Tahitian youth] and Cooperree [nickname for William Kamoola, a returning

Hawaiian youth] caught a *Skip Jack* [a kind of fish] as they call it; I believe the proper name is *Bonetta*. Its flesh has a very pleasant taste, and fish, altogether, resembles a mackerel very much, only it is round, and when taken out of the water has some of the hues of the Dolphin.

March 26th—Nothing worth noticing occurred during the day. Painting and tarring, and writing, were carried on, as they had been for some time past. Towards evening, the dark cloud was removed from my mind, and I felt as peaceful as the ocean with which I was surrounded. There not a wave was seen rising abruptly, from any part of our ship; all rolled smoothly and gently along. The succeeding night was beautiful beyond description; and all was peace within. I thought of St. John's [from biblical book of Revelation] "sea of glass mingled with fire," when I beheld the ocean. Our tarring and painting had been completed; our studding-sails were spread; the full moon shone brightly on us, without one intervention cloud, while our vessel was wafted gently on the surface of the deep. It will be long before the impression of this evening will be erased from my mind.

March 29th—I still enjoy peace and comfort. The day has been much warmer than usual. I think I have not suffered more with the heat since I left America. The appearance of the crew has not been so favourable to-day as it was last Saturday. The strong man armed is keeping his palace [reference to Satan], but blessed be God there is a stronger power than he. Oh! That it would please him to come down and show his power amongst us.

March 30th—Sabbath. The first thing I heard in the morning, was that whales were seen spouting off the stern. The captain ordered the course altered, and for two hours all was confusion and noise. Alas! How unlike those Sabbath mornings I have spent beneath your roof [in Green's house], where all was quietness and peace. No spouting whales, no playing dolphins, no rattling ropes, nor hoarse commanding voices, were there heard.—Nothing there prevented our meditations, till the well known bell [at the First Presbyterian Church, Nassau Street] told us it was time to offer the morning sacrifice. But I am indulging myself too much in such recollections. I would not, I could not, I dare not, look with longing eyes toward my native land. No sir, my hand lies on the plough, and if my poor wretched heart does not deceive me, I would not take it off [the plough] for the wealth in America. It is not the "leeks and the onions" [reference to the Israelites' desired food in the desert after their exodus from Egypt] of your land that I long after, but for one such sermon as I have heard from Dr. A[shbel

Green]. It is the spiritual food I want. Excuse me, sir, when you remember that I have been spoiled at home [at Princeton]. After two hours detentions, we changed our course, and again pursed our way. At 10 we had our prayer meeting in the cabin, and in the afternoon Mr. [Joseph] Goodrich preached from Gen. xix 17.—"Escape for your lives." There was not many of the sailors present. Satan is very much out of humour, he is either losing, or securing some of his people on board. [Betsey Stockton is referring to the salvation of sailors.]

March 31st—The morning pleasant—the weather quite warm. Such a sudden transition from heat to cold and cold to heat, have a very remarkable effect on my health. They make me weak and dejected.

April 1st, 1823.—*All fools day;* but we I hope have laid aside our folly. The weather so warm that the tar is dropping from the rigging, and the water from my face; the ship almost in a calm, and we under a vertical sun—I am ready to think I have seen some new things under the sun [reference to biblical book of Ecclesiastes], if nobody else has. Lat. 30 25' Long. 1080 30.'

April 2nd—the weather very warm, and scarcely any air stirring. About 11 o'clock we had a shower, which is the first we have had since we left Cape Horn. In the afternoon our captain indulged with a view of the ship. He had promised me a *ride,* if you please to call it such, in one of his little boats [long boats] the first calm day so I reminded his of it to-day, and he ordered a boat lowered, and he, with four or five of the mission family and myself, went out in it. The women get into the boat before it touches the water, it is thrown up two or three yards by the swell, and it requires great dexterity to manage it so as to avoid the danger of being stove [hit] against the ship, while the men are getting in at the chains [to lower the longboat to the level of the sea water]. I enjoyed the excursion very much. We went around the ship twice; which having been painted lately makes a very beautiful appearance. Her bow, catheads [beams projecting on both bows of sailing ships, some with figureheads], and stern, have images on them, and all looked clean and cheerful. On the flying job-boom sat Stephen, the Tahitian youth; and on the bowsprit Coooperee [William Kamoola, Hawaiian youth], who is a diverting fellow, and in his quizzing way, hailed the captain as he passed. The quarter deck was filled with our family, whose eyes followed us as we passed bounding over the waves. When we returned to the ship I felt quite elated; it was the first time I had been *abroad* since we left New Haven, which is 132 days—a great while for me to stay at home, at one time.

April 4th Nothing but pleasant weather followed, until we came in sight of Owhyhee [Hawaii]. We then had frequent squalls of rain, and hard blows [winds], but not so as to make it uncomfortable.

Betsey Stockton's "Journal:" Betsey Stockton and Charles Stewart Deliver Harriet Stewart's Infant Son, Charles Seaforth, on the *Thames*, Mid-Pacific Ocean, in the First Mate's Cabin[27]

On the 11th Mrs. Stewart presented us with a fine boy, which I consider my charge. The little fellow beguiles many of my lonely hours; and you must excuse me if my journal is now *weekly* instead of *daily*. From the first moment that I saw the little innocent, I felt emotions that I was unacquainted with before. This, no doubt, arose from the peculiar situation in which I was placed, and from my attachment to his parents. It was one in the morning when I saw Mr. Stewart up in the cabin. Sleep forsook my eyes and with a heavy heart I asked—what is the matter? The answer was just what I had been fearing—Mrs. Stewart was unwell. I had hoped and prayed that the winds might waft us to our destined port, before her day of affliction should arrive. Although I knew that the sea would give up its dead at the command of God, yet the thought of entombing one that I loved so tenderly beneath its billows [burial at sea], was to me more than I knew how to bear. [Betsey Stockton contemplated the death of Harriet Stewart in childbirth.] I was soon, however, delivered from all my fears. Her hours of suffering were not many. At half past nine, we had our little stranger in our arms, and his mother in a comfortable situation. The wind blew so hard all the time, that it was impossible to set down a cup, or any thing else with safety. Her bed was at the windward side of the ship, and it required some exertion to keep her in it. Yet she felt no inconvenience from the circumstance, and suffered as little as if she had been provided with every convenience. Mr. Stewart and myself were her nurses. One of us sat up the fore part of the night, and the other the latter, for two weeks. The little boy had good health, and we got along very well. Most of my time was spent below, and I heard nothing that was passing on deck. I was happy to have it in my power to be of some assistance to my best friends. I found employment enough to engross all my

27. B. Stockton, "Journal," *Christian Advocate* 3 (Jan. 1825), 38.

attention, and nothing occurred worth mentioning. On the 24th we saw and made Hawaii. At the first sight of the snow-capped mountains, I felt a strange sensation of joy and grief. It soon wore away, and as we sailed slowly past its windward side, we had full view of all its grandeur. The tops of the mountains are hidden in the clouds and covered with perpetual snow. We could see with a glass [telescope] the white banks, which brought the strong wintry blasts of our native country to our minds most forcibly, as almost to make us shiver.

Harriet Bradford Tiffany Stewart herself, writing to her friend Olivia remembered the birth:

Most unexpectedly to me, about two weeks before we made the islands, my little boy was born; the bare possibility of such an occasion on board ship, where all was bustle and a crowd, had often filled me with dread, and I most sincerely hoped and believed, that it would not take place, but that we should be safely landed and settled before the coming of the anticipated hour; but the wisdom of Providence ordered otherwise, and subsequent events have unfolded most clearly, the goodness and tender mercy, that in disappointing our wishes, were only consulting our good, and providing for our superior comfort. Had our most sanguine hopes been realized with regard to reaching port, we should have found but once source of confusion, and as was the case, Mrs. [Lucy Goodale] Thurston on a sickbed with an infant three days old, who required all the time that our friends would spare from their own domestic concerns, and the general case of the family, which by the accession of our number, was increased to enormous size. No accommodations that the islands could have afforded would have equaled those I had on board ship, in the little stateroom, six feet square, which the mates were so kind as to vacate at midnight, and which was made uncomfortable by the very strong trades [winds] upon which we had entered, and which carried the vessel so much on her side, as to oblige me to exert myself, night and day, to keep from rolling on the floor—the infant we dare not trust anywhere but in his father's arms.[28]

28. H. Stewart, as cited in French, *Missionary Whaleship*, 110.

Charles Samuel Stewart, filled with joy and relief, wrote in his own journal:

> Another event has occurred to make me less anxious for the termination of our voyage . . . and is of deep interest—it is the safe and uncommonly favorable confinement of our beloved Harriet. She has constantly hoped to have reached the islands before this should have taken place; but the wise providence of God ordained otherwise, and we have great reason already to rejoin in it as a dispensation of visible and marked goodness and tenderness to us. At half-past nine o'clock on the morning of the eleventh instant, my wife became the joyful mother, and I the father of [a] fine, healthy son. You would scarce credit that a ship, at the close of [a] voyage of five months, could afford the comfort and convenience on such an occasion, that ours did and has since done She [Mrs. Stewart] occupied the state-room of the mates—has experienced no want that could not instantly be supplied, and has been sensible of no privations whatever. Both mother and son have been uninterruptedly in a better state, in point of health and ease, than thousands who, in like circumstances, are surrounded by every luxury that wealth can command, in a civilized and Christian country. Her faith and confidence in the providence of her covenant God, in leaving her home, as she did, against the affectionate solicita-tions of many of her dearest friends, have met a large reward; for He hath been faithful to his promises, and has not forsaken her in the time of trial. He has been with her, by the influence of His Holy Spirit, giving to her, great peace and quietness of soul, and imparting much of that Spiritual joy, "which none but they that feel it know."
>
> "The wind has literally been tempered to the shorn lamb" and no language can express the gratitude of my heart, for it is unutterable; in which I know my dear wife so cordially joins with me.
>
> The circumstance has given much joy to the captain, of-ficers and crew. Harriet is a great and universal favorite, and herself and the child are the chief objects of solicitude and attention. They were determined that the young stranger [the infant] should be an American: the captain immediately ordered the ensign hoisted, and Master Charles first saw the light under the proud waving of our national banner. I have seldom known the gleamings of its stars and stripes give more

animation and apparent joy; and I am sure that, in my eyes, they never looked so lovely.[29]

A relieved and proud father wrote of the birth of his son, Charles Clasby (later, renamed Seaforth) Stewart on the *Thames*.

On April 22, Louisa Everest Ely remembered,

> As we have nearly completed our voyage I have thought it might be a comfort to my friends should I relate to them the many favors we have enjoyed thus far. In the first place we have had a very indulgent Captain. I know not what a parent could have done more than he has done for this dear family. Our water for a few of the first weeks was very bad. Since then it has been excellent and we have a great supply. We have brewed a barrel of beer once in three days of the most of the time we have had new bread three times a week and an excellent cooking stove to bake it in. We have had a plenty of Beef, Pork, Hams, Butter, Cheese, Lard, etc. We have a number of barrels of Beef, Pork and Flour left for our comfort after we arrive and the brethern and sisters who are now at the Islands. Thus our wants have been supplied our lives preserved and we hope in a few days to behold the field of our future labors and trials . . . . Our preserves and dried fruits are as good as when we left America excepting the apple which were dried on strings. We have opened our trunks of linen within a few days past and find they are all well. We would advise any one calculating to take such a voyage to put the most of their things into casks, instead of trunks and boxes.
>
> 4 o'clock P.M. Now my dear friends we behold at the distance of 30 miles the eastern part of Owhyee [Oahu] where William [Kamoola, Hawaiian youth] says Obookiah was born. We can see smoke arising from different directions from their humble habitations . . . . When the sun has buried itself in the western ocean and the full moon bursting from a cloud threw its dim rays on the smooth surface of the deep we assembled on the side of the ship and fixing our eyes on the land for which Obookiah wept and prayed, sang the following hymn . . . "Wake, Islands of the South."[30]

29. C. Samuel Stewart, *Private Journal*, 76.
30. Ely, *Diary of Missionary Voyage*, 27–28.

Frederick Douglass. Daguerreotype portrait, studio of Augustus Moran (Brooklyn, NY), May 15, 1863. Used with permission of the Lynn Museum, Lynn, MA.

Charles Samuel Stewart. Daguerreotype portrait, studio of Augustus Moran (Brooklyn, NY), May or June 1863. Used with permission of Princeton Theological Seminary, Princeton, NJ.

Betsey Stockton. Daguerreotype portrait, studio of Augustus
Moran (Brooklyn, NY), May or June 1863. Original *carte de
visite*, N-0774, photograph collection of Hawaiian Children's
Mission Society Library. Used with permission of the
Mission Houses Historic Site and Archives, Honolulu.

Constitution Hill, Princeton, NJ. Birthplace of Betsey
Stockton in slavery; farmhouse of Richard Stockton, her
owner. Used with permission of the Historical Society of
Princeton, Princeton, NJ.

Departure of the Missionaries from New Haven, Connecticut for the Sandwich Islands, 1822. From a copy negative N-921, Hawaiian Children's Mission Society, Honolulu. Used with permission of the Mission Houses Historic Site and Archives, Honolulu.

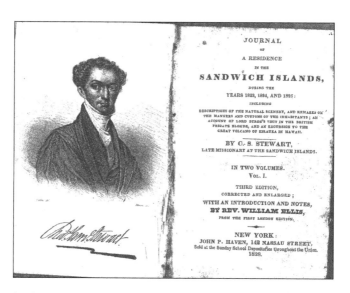

Charles Samuel Stewart. Frontispiece portrait, with title page. Used with permission of the Nantucket Historical Association Library, Nantucket, MA.

Cleopatra's Barge. Watercolor on paper 17 7/8 x 22 7/8" (45.403 x 58.103 cm), by George Ropes (American, 1788–1819), 1818. Gift of Mrs. Francis B. Crowninshield, 1953, M8255. Used with permission of Peabody Essex Museum, Salem, MA. Photograph by Mark Sexton.

Harriet Bradford Tiffany Stewart. Engraved portrait in oval frame, 1822. From *Mrs. Stewart*, an oil painting by Charles Ingrahm. From a copy negative N-840, Hawaiian Children's Mission Society, Honolulu. Used with permission of the Mission Houses Historic Site and Archives, Honolulu.

John Brown Russwurm. Oil on canvas, unidentified artist, c. 1850. Used with permission of the National Portrait Gallery, Smithsonian Institution, Washington, DC.

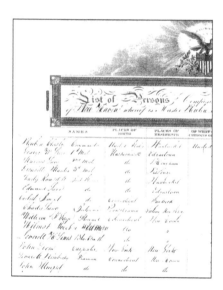

"List of Persons Comprising the Crew of the Ship *Thames* of New Haven whereof is Master Reuben Clasby Bound for the Pacific Ocean: Ship *Thames* Roll, October 8, 1822 [E 791, New Haven Crew List, Inward. 'Charley Ramsdell, Boatsteer, 19, of Nantucket, 5' 6.'"] Used with permission of the National Archives and Records Administration, Northeast Region, Waltham, MA.

A North-West Prospect of Nassau Hall with a Front View of the Presidents House in New Jersey. Copperplate engraving, drawn by W. Tennent, engraved by Henry Dawkins, 1764. In Savage, *Nassau Hall*, plate 2.

Ashbel Green. Engraved portrait by T. B. Welsh, from an original painting by Gilbert Stuart. Used with permission of Princeton University Archives, Princeton, NJ.

Situation of the Ship Thames *in a Squall off the Rio De La Plata.*
Engraving by Antony Imbert, in C. S. Stewart, *Private Journal,* 1828;
plate facing p. 27. Collection of Firestone Library, Princeton University.
United States public domain.

View of Maui from the Anchorage at Lahaina. Engraving by Antony
Imbert, in C. S. Stewart, *Private Journal,* 1828; plate facing p. 173. Image
shows an indigenous canoe and *Cleopatra's Barge* in foreground,
anchored in the deep-water harbor of Lahaina. Collection of Firestone
Library, Princeton University. United States public domain.

Thames keel on display at Mystic Seaport. Photograph by Russell A. Fowler, c. 2000. No. 71-11-173, Mystic Seaport, Mystic, CT.

First Infant School in Green Street New York. Engraving by Anthony Imbert, 1828. Edward W. C. Arnold Collection of New York Prints, Maps and Pictures; Metropolitan Museum of Art, New York.

Female Teachers.

Names	Residence	Entrance Date
M⁻ Caroline Thompson.	Jackson St.	1835 to 1848
M⁻ Ann Stryker	Green St	1848 - 49
" Jemima Squires	Witherspoon St.	1851 - 52
" Eveline Frasure	Green St	1848 - 49
" Charlotte Gordon (left ac 2639) Witherspoon "		1835 - 1845
" Laura Ford	" "	1849 - 51
Miss Betsy Stockton (Aunt Betsy)	Quarry St.	1835 - 1848
" Flora Vantyne	Green Street	" "
" Margaret Jennings (now Mrs Titus)	"	1848 - 49
" Susan Scudder	John's Alley	1849 - 51
" Catharine McCrag (up ac 1752)	Witherspoon St.	1852
M⁻ Flora Scudder — deceased		1835 - 48
Miss Cecilia Vantyne (Mrs. ... w th Rev. g. C. ...)		1835 - 48
M⁻ Anthony Simmons } Left before 1852 - 53.		1849 - 51
" Jane Scudder }		" "
Mrs Eliza Vanhorne)		1848 - 49

Miss Betsy Stockton	Treasurer — elected,	Sept 25th 1852.	
Miss Rachel Huston (now Mrs van orin)	Witherspoon St	1855 —	
" Amelia Craig	Green St	1841 -	
Mrs Charlotte Odom (renewed)	" "	1860 -	
Miss Mary Hackett.	Nassau "	1862 -	

"Female Teachers." Holograph list with names, residences, and entrance dates of teaching at the Sabbath School, 1835 ff. Photographic copy from First Presbyterian Church for the Colored, "Records of Morning Sabbath School," unpaginated. Used with permission of Special Collections, Princeton University Library, Princeton, NJ.

"Plan for Evening Prayer Concert, January 12, 1862." Photographic copy from First Presbyterian Church for the Colored, "Records of Morning Sabbath School," 274. Used with permission of Special Collections, Princeton University Library, Princeton, NJ.

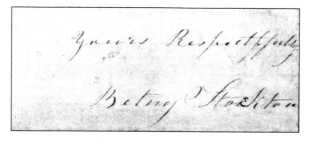

"Yours Respectfully, Betsey Stockton." Holographic signature. Gen Ms. (Misc) ALS of Betsey Stockton. Used with permission of Special Collections, Princeton University Library, Princeton, NJ.

> BETSEY STOCKTON,
> THROUGH HER DESIRE TO SERVE THE CAUSE OF CHRIST,
> ACCOMPANIED THE FIRST AMERICAN MISSIONARIES
> TO HAWAII AND OPENED A SCHOOL FOR THE COM-
> MONALTY AT LAHAINA, MAUI, IN 1823. AFTER HER
> RETURN TO THE UNITED STATES SHE WAS FOR
> MANY YEARS A VALUABLE MEMBER OF THIS
> CONGREGATION, A TEACHER OF ITS YOUTH AND A
> POWERFUL INFLUENCE FOR GOOD IN THE COMMUN-
> ITY. THIS MEMORIAL IS SET UP IN RECOGNITION OF
> HER FAITHFUL CHRISTIAN CHARACTER AND MOST
> USEFUL LIFE, BY FRIENDS WHO HONORED AND
> LOVED HER. SHE WAS BORN IN PRINCETON IN 1798,
> AND DIED THERE OCTOBER 24,1865. HER BODY
> LIES AT COOPERSTOWN, NEW YORK.

"Betsy Stockton." Commemorative bronze plaque on the interior of the Witherspoon Street Presbyterian Church, Witherspoon Street, Princeton, NJ.

> PRESENTED·BY THE·SCHOLARS·OF
> ELIZABETH· STOCKTON·

"Presented by the Scholars of Elizabeth Stockton." Stained glass window, interior of Witherspoon Presbyterian Church, Witherspoon Street, Princeton, NJ.

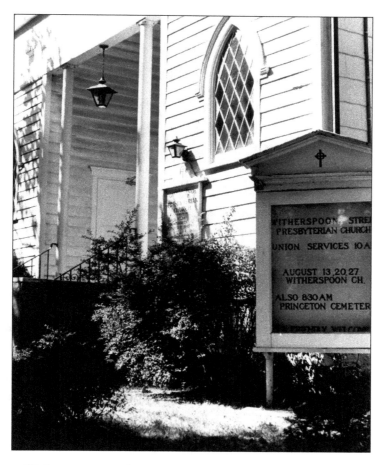

Witherspoon Presbyterian Church, front façade, exterior.
Photograph by Arthur M. Byers Jr., c. 1970.

Chapter 5: **"East of Eden"**

Betsey Stockton Names the
Lahaina, Maui, Mission[1]

BETSEY STOCKTON CONTINUED TO write sporadically in her journal during 1823 to 1825. These were her years as a teaching missionary at Lahaina, Maui, with the Stewarts. Once they had arrived on the *Thames*, Stockton and other missionaries fanned out among mission stations among the islands of Maui, Kauai, and Oahu, from a central base at the mission at Honolulu. There, from the Mission House of stone, on Missionary Row, the Reverend Hiram Bingham functioned as the spiritual and organizational head of American missions in the Sandwich Islands.

Glimpses of the primitive living conditions for these highly educated missionaries, primarily hailing from New England and the Mid-Atlantic states, seep through the words of their universally cheerful devotion. But the prospect of cooking for and serving "nineteen [individuals] at the communal dining table" was daunting and exhausting for the two women of the mission who did the work. Paradoxically, the bounty of local fresh fruit and fish was too costly for the missionaries because of tariffs by Hawaiian royalty on such items, meant to prevent native exploitation by international whalers and merchants.

In 1823, when Stockton landed there, Maui boasted a population of 25,000, while Lahaina itself had 5,000 residents. It was the fourth largest of the islands in the Sandwich Islands archipelago. The landform was dominated by two prominent volcanos, sweeping down to a shallow coast bordering the sea. Varieties of vegetation and of cultivated taro fields, close by tropical forests, were common.

Maui's principal port of Lahaina, on the northwestly (windward) coast, was already renowned for its excellent deepwater harbor. It remained a favorite mid-Pacific refueling port for foreign vessels under sail. The harbor also provided anchorage for interisland voyages for Hawaiian royals and Presbyterian missionaries, the sole means of interisland communication.

---

1. Bingham, *Residence of Twenty-One Years*, 191.

American, Russian, and English whalers and mercantile ships plied the Pacific waters, dropped anchor, and stepped ashore at Lahaina. Some of these whaleship captains, crews, and foreign merchants understood the change that the mission family would bring to the culture of this whaling port; others visitors resented their newly limited access to willing Hawaiian women or the strictures on the availability of alcohol. The American missionaries suggested these cultural changes to protect their indigenous benefactors from disease and denigration.

Stockton's startled first impression of the nearly naked Hawaiian men who paddled their canoes to greet the missionaries on the *Thames* was later changed. That culture shock was softened by the exchange of Western clothes for the Hawaiian men and the very welcome indigenous foods for the voyage-weary American missionaries.

Several recent developments favored Stockton's and the Stewart's work. The old king, Kamehamaha I, had died. All the islands had recently been united under one ruler, Kamehameha II. He had broken the *tabu* (taboo) of the native wooden idols, and the power of a chief goddess, the volcanic *Pele*, had also been broken. Previously, women were forbidden to eat in the presence of men. The cultural door was open for a different belief system and for religious conversions to Christianity.

Linguist Betsey Stockton had practiced oral Hawaiian on the five-month voyage from New Haven to Honolulu. Her conversations with William Kamoola, Richard Kalaioulu, and Kupelii, former heathen school students at Cornwall, Connecticut, fulfilled the ABCFM's plan for speading the gospel.[2] Besides Stockton and William Ellis, few other missionaries could speak the Hawaiian language. A critical catalyst for overcoming this difficulty between Hawaiian and English was printed bilingual material. At Honolulu, mission printer Elisha Loomis set up the "engine," the precious hand printing press, in a thatched house. It was the vehicle for churning out biblical tracts, primers, spellers, and hymnals, using both Hawaiian and English—a necessary breakthrough anticipating and facilitating the momentous cultural change in Hawaii from 1823 to 1826.[3]

Specifically, in January of 1822, Loomis set his type of the first page of the *Elementary Lessons*, afterwards called the *pi-a-pa*. Diplomatically, the printer turned to Hawaiian royalty in the person of King Keeumoku and asked the king to pull the lever and see the first impression made by this hand press.[4]

2. Judd et al., *Missionary Album*, 2.

3. Judd et al., *Missionary Album*, 140.

4. A. Loomis, *Grapes of Canaan*, 148.

Beginning in August 1823, Loomis was assisted by Levi Chamber-lain, the mission's agent for accounts. They began to build a new perma-nent building to house the printing press. By December 1823, a new grey coral building was constructed to replace the temporary thatched one, finished with a temporary timber roof. Next, two workers sent to Canton for ceramic roofing tiles. After the materials arrived and the building was finished, Loomis began one of the American missionaries' most ambitious and successful projects for cultural convergence: the first hymnal in both English and Hawaiian.[5] Charles Samuel Stewart soon organized a choir at Lahaina, using this book of hymns.

After resting in the single frame house at the American missions' headquarters in Honolulu for several weeks, Stockton, the Stewarts, and the Richards family were requested by Queen Kaahumanu, King Kamehameha II's favorite consort, to establish a new mission station on Lahaina, Maui. The six adults and baby Charles Seaforth Stewart were assigned to their labors there. As one of the most powerful people in all of the islands, the queen and the missionaries sailed from Honolulu to Lahaina on the beautiful sloop with the improbable name of *Cleopatra's Barge*. Two years before, in 1820, the seagoing yacht had dazzled King Kamehameha II, who promptly purchased and renamed her *Haaheo o Hawaii (Pride of Hawaii)*.[6]

Paradoxically, a steady food supply and adequate housing were scarce in this otherwise tropical paradise. Some crops from the field, such as the starchy taro plant, could be harvested without cultivation. The missionaries were occasionally given fish fresh from the sea. But Western food tastes and stringent funds from the ABCFM were two stumbling blocks to the mission family's steady diet. Thatched houses with reed mat floors and walls proved to be flimsy shelters compared to brick or woodframed houses, their former homes in the States. And the missionary food budget was always in compe-tition with successful whaling captains who could afford to pay high prices for goods sold by *haole* (White residents, non-Hawaiian) merchants in La-haina and elsewhere in the islands.[7] Missionaries could use the mission's credit account at local stores, but only with an added 20-percent interest on sales there. The ABCFM's solution was to ship casks of food around the horn to feed its missionaries in the Pacific. In the meantime, cash purchases of such items as large fish and pineapples were essential.

5. A. Loomis, *Grapes of Canaan*, 186.

6. Johnston, "Million Pounds," 6.

7. A. Loomis, *Grapes of Canaan*, 123.

The natives are very pleasant people, wrote Stockton, at first sight, "but much dirtier than I expected to find them. They eat baked dogs, raw fish . . . [and] the houses are so small that they have to creep in at the door."[8]

As daily life at the mission station at Lahaina became more settled, Stockton wrote that Harriet and Charles Stewart had been assigned a largish thatched house with an adjoining room that Stockton and infant Charles, the baby whom she had delivered on the *Thames*, shared.

Nearing the end of the five-month voyage, Stockton had written of her first sight of the island archipelago:

> On the 24th [of April, 1823]. We saw and made Hawaii (Ow-hyee); At first sign of the snow-capped mountains, I felt a strange sensation of joy and grief. It soon wore away and as we sailed slowly past its windward side, we had full view of all its grandeur. The tops of the mountains were hidden in the clouds, and covered with perpetual snow. We could see with a glass [telescope] the white banks, which brought the strong wintry blasts of our native country to our minds so forcibly, as almost to make me shiver. But it was not long before objects that were calculated to have a chilling effect of another kind, were brought to our sight. Two or three canoes, loaded with natives, came to the ship; their appearance was that of half man and half beast—naked—except for a narrow strip of *tapa* [woven fiber] round their loins. When they first came on board, the sight chilled our hearts. The ladies retired to the cabin, and burst into tears; and some of the gentlemen turned pale: my own soul sickened within me, and every nerve trembled. Are these, thought I, the beings with whom I must spend the remainder of my life! They are men and have souls—was the reply which conscience made. We asked them where the king was—at Hawaii [the Big Island] or Oahu? They said at Oahu. We informed them that we were missionaries, come to live with them and do them good. At which an old man exclaimed, in his native dialect, what may be thus translated—"That is very good, by and by, know God." This beginning of missionary labours seemed very encouraging; and in a short time our unpleasant feelings were much dissipated and we conversed with them freely, through the [former heathen school Hawaiian] boys, who were our interpreters. We gave them old clothes; and in return, they gave us all the fish they had caught, except one large one, which we bought. They remained with us until our boat went on shore, and brought us some potatoes, taro and cocoanuts, which were very refreshing

8. B. Stockton, "Journal," *Christian Advocate* 3 (Jan. 1825), 39.

to us after our voyage of five months; part of which time we had
no other diet than meat and [ship's] bread. I brought my little
boy on deck [Master Charles Seaforth Stewart], who was two
weeks old; some of them took him in their arms and in ecstasy
exclaimed, *araha matitai—very great love to you;* and kissed
him. The last expression of affection we could have dispensed
with very well; but we have to become all things to all men, that
we may gain some. They then bid us many *arohas*, [alohas] and
took their departure.[9]

At Lahaina, twenty-five-year-old Betsey Stockton would deepen her
friendship with missionary brother Charles Samuel Stewart. His medical
education at the College of Physicians and Surgeons in NYC was crucial to
the survival of all at the Lahaina station, which lacked a trained physcian.
His law studies allowed Betsey Stockton and others to negotiate international issues, such as presentation of papers of citizenship. In turn, Stockton was to became his growing family's lifeline as bilingual interpreter,
teacher, medical nurse, baby nurse, and housekeeper in their primitive,
isolated, and tiny cabin. No tropical paradise, the 1823 missionary station at Lahaina consisted of a cluster of thatched-roof huts hugging the
shoreline of the deep harbor.

Hailing from an aristocratic family, Stewart formally described Betsey Stockton as "a coloured female, a domestic and assistant missionary in
my own family," in his 1828 version of the mission published in *A Private
Journal of a Voyage to the Pacific Ocean and Residence at the Sandwich Islands.*[10] Stockton's and Stewart's years of 1822 to 1826 were to become one of
the most critical periods in the history of the Sandwich Islands—a cultural
turning point for Hawaiians, who were ruled at the outset by a dynasty of
indigenous royal queens and kings who eventually made fast friends of the
Presbyterian missionaries from America.

Stewart wrote the final entry of his sea journal, documenting the mission family's arrival at Honolulu, Oahu:

In the *Thames*, at anchor off the Harbour of Honoruru [Hono-
lulu], Monday, April 28th 1823: At twelve o'clock on Saturday
night, by the light of a full moon, we made the south-east end of
Oahu, five miles distant.

At sunrise, we were close under Diamond Hill [Head], a
principal point, on the south side of the Island. It is the crater of
an extinguished burst on the eye in beautiful panoramic view:

9. B. Stockton, "Journal," *Christian Advocate* 3 (Jan. 1825), 38.
10. C. Samuel Stewart, *Private Journal*, 69.

presenting first the Bay of Waititi [Waikiki], encircled by heavy groves of the cocoanut, and other luxuriant trees . . . . At the farther end of the plain, three or four miles distant, lay the town of Honoruru: to which a fort with its floating banner, the American Consulate, the Mission House, and a cluster of masts in the harbour, give something of an aspect of civilization.

At nine o'clock, Mr. Bishop, Mr. Richards, and myself, with the natives William Kamhoula, and Richard Karaioula [Heathen School graduates], accompanied the captain [Reuben Clasby] on shore. We rowed half a mile along the coral reef,—by which the coast here is bound, and on which the surf breaks, some hundred rods from the beach,—before coming to the narrow opening, forming the channel into the harbour. The entrance is short; and we were soon in the midst of ten or fifteen ships, principally American and English whalemen, and some five or six of the native vessels—brigs and schooners— all anchored near to the beach, and some, at moorings on the short. The bay is small, not more than half a mile long and a quarter broad, but deep and perfectly safe.

Perceiving a low, stone quay on a point under the fort, we were about to land on it, when a party of Islanders exclaimed, *"tabu!—tabu!"* and informed our interpreters, William and Richard, that the largest of the houses was the residence of the king; and he had prohibited any one from landing at that place. William replied, *"new Missionaries have arrived"*: when they ran to the place, and a fine looking young female in a European dress of pink satin with a wreath of yellow feathers on her head, made her appearance. It was *Tameha-maru* [Kaahumanu], the favorite queen of *Riho-Riho* [Kamehameha II, the young king].

On landing, we were introduced to her Hawaiian majesty by Mr. Jones, the American Consul. She received us very cordially, and after biding us welcome to the Islands, consigned us to the care of Mr. Jones. The appearance of the queen appeared about twenty or twenty-two years of age, and though well formed, is tall and masculine, in figure. Her countenance is open and intelligent, with fine black eyes and hair; but her features are too broad and flat for beauty; and her complexion that of a dark mulatto—the general colour of the Islanders.

The news of our arrival, soon reached our Missionary friends . . . . We had the happiness of receiving the warm salutations of Mr. [Elisha] Loomis [the mission printer], and the Rev. Mr. [William] Ellis, an English Missionary, under the patronage of the London Missionary Society. Mr. Ellis has been many years at the Society Islands, and is but recently established at this group. His experience in Missionary labour, and his acquaintance with dialects of the South Seas, make him a most valuable accession to the Mission here.

Thronged by a crowd of chattering and noisy natives, who expressed their pleasure at our arrival, by hooting, and dancing, and running along our path, we proceeded immediately with these gentlemen to the Mission Houses, . . . where we were introduced to the rest of the [mission] family, consisting of the Rev. [Asa] Thurston, and Mrs. Thurston, Mrs. [Sybil] Bingham, Mrs. [Mary] Ellis, and Mrs. [Elisha] Loomis. Mr. [Hiram] Bingham was absent, at Waititi, three miles distant.

We had completed a long voyage, and were permitted to tread the shores of our destination under circumstances of peculiar mercy;—and now had the privilege of paying our vows of gratitude to God from one of his peaceful temples though in the humblest form. I can never forget the excitement with which I entered its lowly roof, trod the matted ground—its only floor—and looked at its unbarked posts and rafters, and coarse thatch of grass;—primitive as every thing appeared, I felt, that it was a House of God and one of the happy Gates of Heaven.

On returning to the mission house, we had the pleasure of meeting the Rev. Mr. (Hiram) Bingham . . . and one of the queens of Riho-Rhio had been sent with him as a messenger from the chiefs there to request a visit from us.[11]

At the Missionary Row of thatched houses in Honolulu, Stewart wrote of his family's accommodations there:

Our house might be . . . only fourteen feet long, and twelve broad—three feet high at the eaves, and nine feet at the peak of the roof. It is composed of pole and a thatch of grass, having no floor, but the ground spread with mats: for window, three holes cut through the thatch, without sash or glass . . . . In this little cabin, H[arriet] and myself, C[harles] and B[etsey], with all our personal luggage are stowed: . . . with the exception of a bedstead and cot, they [our trunks] constitute the whole of our furniture.[12]

11. C. Samuel Stewart, *Private Journal*, 86–88.
12. C. Samuel Stewart, *Private Journal*, 105.

In describing the populace and governance of indigenous Hawaiians, Stewart listed the ranks of the royalty and added,

> Such is the civil condition of the masses of the nation. Their only birthright is slavery; and its highest immunities cannot secure to them, a right to life, much less an inferior possession. Surely to such, the message of salvation must prove, indeed, *"glad tidings of great joy."* May they receive them with thanksgiving and adoration; and through them, become free in the spirit of the gospel, and rich in the inheritance of eternal life.[13]

From another quarter also, Stockton and the Stewarts were officially welcomed. On May 3, 1823, Captain Reuben Clasby received the following letter from King Riho Riho [Liholiho, or Kamehameha II] Iolani in translation from newly written Hawaiian, forgiving the Nantucket captain of the *Thames* the usual harbor fees:

> To Capt. Clasby,
>
> Love to you.
>
> This is my communication to you. You have done well in bringing hither the new Teachers. You shall pay nothing on account of the harbour—no nothing at all.
>
> Grateful affection to you.
>
> Riho-Riho Iolani[14]

Stockton wrote of the new dwelling:

> On Saturday, the 10th of May, we left the ship, and went to the mission enclosure at Honoruru [Honolulu]. There had been assigned to us a little thatched house in one corner of the [mission] yard, consisting of one small room, with a door, and two windows—the door too small to admit a person walking in without stooping, and the windows only large enough for one person to look out at a time. Near us was another of the same kind, occupied by Mr. [Thomas] H[olman], and opposite one much larger where Mr. H[olman] and E[ly] resided. Next to them stood another small one, in which Mr. [Rev. William] Ellis of the London Mission Society resided; and in the mission house (which at home would be called small) there were Messr. [Hiram] Bingham, [Rev. Asa] Thurston, [Elisha]

13. C. Samuel Stewart, *Private Journal*, 105.
14. C. Samuel Stewart, *Private Journal*, 102.

Loomis, [Joseph] Goodrich, [Rev. Abraham] Blatchely and [Daniel] Chamberlain.

The family all eat at the same table, and the ladies attend to the work by turns. Mrs. Stewart and myself took each of us a day separately. I found my time fully occupied during our stay at Oahu, which I was not sorry for. Had I been idle, I should not in all probability have been so happy in my situation as I was. I was obliged to stay within the enclosure all the time, except on the Sabbath when I went to church, which was a few rods [yards] off; and in the morning early I went three or four times, with Mr. [Charles] Stewart to Mr. Anthony Allen's [an African American resident of Lahaina] about a mile and a half from home for [goat's or cow's] milk. Mr. Allen was very kind to me, and seemed happy to see one of his own country people. I think he told me that he had resided on the island twenty years, and had never before seen a coloured female [i.e., Betsey Stockton]. His wife is a native woman [Hawaiian], but very pleasant, and to all appearances innocent. The first time I visited her she presented me with a very handsome [woven tapas] mat, and appeared happy to see me. They are in good circumstances, and friendly to the mission. I regretted leaving them very much.[15]

The Missionaries Board *Cleopatra's Barge*

Stockton wrote:

On the 26th of May, we heard that the barge was about to sail for Lahaina with the old queen [Keopuolani] and princes and that the queen was desirous to have missionaries to accompany her; and that if missionaries would consent to go, the barge should wait two days for them. A meeting [of the missionaries] was called to consult whether it was expedient to establish a mission [station] at Lahaina. The mission was determined on, and Mr. S[tewart] was appointed to go; he chose Mr. [William] R[ichards] for his companion, who was also appointed the next day. On the 26th we embarked on the mighty ocean again, which we had left so lately.[16]

15. B. Stockton, "Journal," *Christian Advocate* 3 (Jan. 1825), 39.

16. B. Stockton, "Journal," *Christian Advocate* 3 (Jan. 1825), 40; see also A. Loomis, *Grapes of Canaan*, 330, for an overview of Hawaiian royal names.

From the Pacific Ocean to interisland travel: enter a legendary vessel, recently purchased by King Kamehameha II, who was "second in line of America's only authentic royalty."[17] Originally named *Cleopatra's Barge* by the Crowninshield family, its American owners, this magnificent ship was a seagoing yacht crafted in Salem, Massachusetts. Built by Retire Becket for George Crowninshield Sr., head of the very rich and peculiar Crowninshield family, this unique seagoing yacht was to undergo a singular future.

She had been sailed to the Sandwich Islands in 183 days, arriving in Lahaina on November 6, 1820. Dazzled by the beauty of the yacht, King Kamehameha II partially paid for it in kind through the barter of a parcel of precious sandalwood, then worth about $80,000. Kamehameha II promptly renamed his proud vessel *Haaheo o Hawaii (Pride of Hawaii)*.[18]

Hawaiian royalty allowed the American missionaries free passage among island missions aboard the beautiful sloop as continued gestures of kindness and generosity toward these newcomers from another culture.

Stewart recalled:

> On board the *Cleopatra's Barge*, at sea, May 30. 1823, on Wednesday, the 28th .... H[arriet] and myself, B[etsey] and C[harles] with William Kamihoula, and Loomis—who makes the voyage to see us established at our station—embarked with the [old] queen Keopoulani, for Maui.[19]

The party sailed on May 28 and reached Lahaina on the 31st, after a rough passage of a little less than one hundred miles.

Stockton's wrote while aboard *Cleopatra's Barge* about her first sight of Lahaina:

> The morning of the 31st, we all came on deck, and were in sight of land. In the middle of the day we came to anchor; the gentlemen left the vessel to see if they could obtain a house, or any accommodations for us. They returned in a few hours with Mr. Butler, an American resident, who had kindly offered us a house. In the afternoon our things were landed, and we took our residence in Lahaina. We had not seen a tree that looked green and beautiful since we left home until we came here. The water, too, is very good, and the house one of the best that I have seen on the island—. It is the same that Dr. [Thomas] Holman

17. Johnston, "Million Pounds," 4.

18. Johnston, "Million Pounds," 6–7.

19. C. Samuel Stewart, *Private Journal*, 169; see also Johnston, "Million Pounds of Sandalwood," 6–7, for use of *Cleopatra's Barge* in conveying the missionaries from island to island.

had while he was in this country. Mr. [Abraham] B[latechly] was very kind to us, and did ever thing in his power to make us comfortable. His wife is half-breed, and one of the prettiest I have seen on the island. The next day, being the Sabbath, the gentlemen went down to the village in the morning, and preached by an interpreter. The people were very attentive, and requested that their instruction might begin the next day; and accordingly the following day it did begin.[20]

Stockton continued,

Near the last of June I had another attack of the pain in my breast, with a little spitting of blood. At the time I was seized, we were without a lancet, or any means of obtaining one, except from a that ship that had just come into the harbour. [The heroic system of medicine demanded bleeding to balance the four humors] .... [Found] one from a ship and Mr. [William] R[ichards] bled me. In a few minutes I was relieved, but was not able to leave this place until the 24th, when a brig came in sight.—Supposing it to have a deputation on board, I walked to the beach and arrived just in time to see his royal highness land, amidst hundreds. He appeared very well at the time, but we found out soon after that he was in a frolic [a drinking party], and had left Oahu without its being known where he was going. The day previous to his arrival a schooner came in quest of him; and the day after, his own barge came [*Cleopatra's Barge*] with two of his queens—he has four. In his manners he is quite a gentleman. He reads and writes [English] well. We regret very much that he is given to drink. He says he is afraid of the [hell] fire, and has made several attempts to refrain, but he is unsuccessful. On the 29th [of June, 1823] was the Sabbath. I went in the morning with the family to worship; the scene that presented itself was one that would have done an American's heart good to have witnessed. Our place of worship was nothing but an open space on the beach, with a large tree to shelter us; on the ground a large mat was laid, on which the chief persons sat. To the right there was a sofa, and a number of chairs; on these the missionaries, the king and principal person sat. The *kanahas*, or lower class of persons, sat on the ground in rows; leaving a passage open to the sea, from which the breeze was blowing. Mr. R[ichards] addressed them from these words, "It is appointed unto all men once to die, and after death the judgment." Honoru [one of the heathen school

20. B. Stockton, "Journal," *Christian Advocate* 3 (Jan. 1825), 39.

graduates] acted as an interpreter; the audience all appeared very solemn.[21]

In an unforgettable scene, the powerful Queen Kaahumanu requested that Betsey Stockton join her on the royal Chinese silk sofa.

> After service the favourite queen called me and requested that I should take a seat with her on the sofa, which I did, although I could say but few words which she would understand. Soon after, bidding them *aroha*, I returned with the family. In the afternoon we had an English sermon at our house: about fifty were present and behaved well.[22]

In this instance Stockton used her conversational facility with the Hawaiian language to great advantage. She was able to address one of the Hawaiian royalty in her native tongue, even though, as Stockton modestly adds, she spoke briefly; but she was understood by Queen Kaahumanu. Barely a month after her arrival in the Sandwich Islands, Stockton bridged the cultural gap through a friendly spoken exchange. That linguistic skill was soon to be put into even greater use for the mission, as Stockton began to shoulder her designated duty of teaching, this time in a bilingual setting.

Stockton's first school began on June, 29, 1823, barely a month after Stockton's mission family had arrived in the Sandwich Islands. She recounted its founding:

> In the morning one of the king's boys came to the house, desiring to be instructed in English. Mr. S[tewart] thought it would be well for me to engage in the work at once. Accordingly I collected a proper number and commenced. I had four English, and six Hawaiian scholars. This, with the care of the family, I find as much as I can manage.[23]

To Ashbel Green she reported: "I have now a fine school of the *maka ainina*, or lower class of people, the first I believe that was ever been established."[24] Stockton's characteristic modesty was coupled with her understated pride in this bilingual school.

But Stockton's "domestick" duties occupied her as well. On July 3, 1823, she wrote:

---

21. B. Stockton, "Journal," *Christian Advocate* 3 (Jan. 1825), 40.
22. B. Stockton, "Journal," *Christian Advocate* 3 (Jan. 1825), 40.
23. B. Stockton, "Journal," *Christian Advocate* 3 (Jan. 1825), 40.
24. B. Stockton, "Journal," *Christian Advocate* 3 (Jan. 1825), 39.

In the afternoon I went, with a number of natives, to purchase pine apples. After walking through Taro [indigenous starch plant] patches and water, we came to the pine apples, which appeared very handsome. They grow on the edge of a pond of water; and fruit generally hangs in the water—one or two on a bunch—sometimes only one—which grows straight up on the bush. I obtained two apples and several plants, and returned home before night.

In the morning [of the next day] Mr. S[tewart] returned from prayers with Mr. Ellis, the London missionary, who had just arrived from Oahu, on his way to [the island of] Hawaii. I was very much disappointed to see him without receiving letters from America. When we left Honolulu [in May], two vessels were expected; one from New York and the other from Boston. I often visited the beach to watch for sails; the vessel at last arrived, but brought me no letters. Oh may I be taught, to be submissive at all times.[25]

In this journal entry, Stockton allows us, her readers, a window into her watery world and ends with the introspective musing of a young woman. She projected an image of a lonely captain's wife on her elevated walk in Nantucket, calico sunbonnet flapping in the breeze, looking seaward for news and solace from distant loved ones across the ocean—in her case, a letter from Ashbel Green.

At that time and place Betsey Stockton rose to her challenge: to teach her young scholars in two languages. This was Stockton's avowed vocation. She was labeled "apt to teach" as early as her years as a teen in Princeton. Early literacy at the household of Green and his sons, and Michael Osborn's Sunday tutoring at Princeton Theological Seminary, were now to bear fruits.

In their report of September 17, 1823 at the Fourteenth Annual meeting in Boston, the ABCFM listed "Betsey Stockton, a coloured woman," with the notation as to why she had been sent in the Reinforcement Company "qualified to be a teacher."[26] Stockton became an unlikely poster woman for literacy in the Pacific.

Stockton's school was supported by regular efforts from many of the American missionaries—ordained or married women with small children, Harriet Stewart and Sybil Moseley Bingham among them. A great desire for universal literacy swept through the Sandwich Islanders on every

25. B. Stockton, "Journal," in *Christian Advocate* 3 (Jan. 1825) 40.

26. American Board of Commissioners for Foreign Missions, *Report*, 115.

island. It became a new cultural fashion. Called the *palapala*, it meant "the writing" and "the new learning."[27]

How did Betsey Stockton and the other American missionaries create such a phenomenon of cultural change? Again, the written records of the ABCFM in September 1825 report exactly how this explosion of literacy occurred:

> At the commencement of the current year . . . . Hiram Bishop [is] preparing a hymn book for their [the people's] edification. Twenty five hundred copies of the Owhyean Spelling Book had been distributed; and the [only] thing which prevented a new edition [was] but the want of paper.[28]

Stewart noted Stockton's and his progress in creating a school for adults, mostly farmers at Lahaina, as he wrote:

> Application was made to us by them [the farmers] for books and slates and an instructor and the first school—consisting of about thirty individuals ever formed—has been established in our [mission] enclosure, under the superintendence of B[etsey], who is quite familiar with the native tongue.[29]

Assisting Stockton in this larger school were Harriet Stewart, still a nursing mother with an infant son, and Classica Lyman Richards. The women of the Lahaina mission labored on a daily basis as teachers in a bilingual setting.

The cornucopia of printed materials from the mission press in Honolulu supported this growing fervor by Hawaiians for the *palapala*. Printers Elisa Loomis and Daniel Chamberlain worked "the engine" to its limit, but the missionaries also needed the permission of the Hawaiian royalty. From Lahaina came their cry:

> Our books are gone. There are two schools where the number of books equals half the number of scholars. If we had the books, we could establish many schools.[30]

The rulers had spoken and given their blessing: the *palapala* was good. From the island of Kauai, Queen Kaahumanu, traveling with a great company, inquired how the people

---

27. Bingham, *Residence of Twenty-One Years*, 195, 215–16.
28. A. Loomis, *Grapes of Canaan*, 200.
29. C. Samuel Stewart, *Private Journal*, 259.
30. A. Loomis, *Grapes of Canaan*, 200.

were making out with the *palapala* . . . tell the Longnecks [American missionaries] to send more books down here. Many are the people—few are the books. I want . . . 800 Hawaiian books to be sent hither . . . . By and by perhaps, we shall be wise.[31]

By January and February of 1824, Stewart wrote about the changing pastimes of Hawaiian royalty. The queens and princes, he noted, had changed from surfing "with boards" to "writing at their desks." They increased their demand for books in the native language (Hawaiian). Previously claiming the right to be taught by the missionaries as the exclusive right of royalty, now their intention was to "have all of their subjects enlightened by the *palapala*."[32]

On February 2, Stewart wrote of establishing an important school:

Today we have been permitted to establish a large and regular school using their domestics and dependents. We have always had several scholars at the establishments of different chiefs, amounting in the whole to fifty individuals, under regular tuition; and Mrs. [Clarissa Lyman] Richards, H[arriet] and B[etsey], besides instructing the boys in our families in their own language, have daily taught a few persons in our houses. But we have never till today, had a regular, systematic school, except with the chiefs, and the special favourites of their respective trains. The school formed, entirely from the household of the young prince, and was held in a neat and spacious house prepared by him for the purpose. The names of twenty-five boys and young men were entered as scholars. The young chief himself presided as head of the school, under our superintendence.[33]

One week later, he wrote:

In addition to the school of the young prince, each of the chiefs now has one similar under his special superintendence. The number of schools thus formed is ten, including in the whole, one hundred and fifty scholars . . . and [we] soon expect to have five hundred persons under regular tuition in this district.[34]

Because of this explosion of the number of schools, Betsey Stockton has been credited with the founding of learning at Lahaina and, in a larger

---

31. C. Samuel Stewart, *Private Journal*, 263.
32. C. Samuel Stewart, *Private Journal*, 259.
33. C. Samuel Stewart, *Private Journal*, 259.
34. C. Samuel Stewart, *Private Journal*, 262.

measure, with successfully establishing schools for non-royal learners in the Sandwich Islands.

In retrospect, schools might have seemed the inevitable outcome of the printing and language acquisition by missionaries. In contrast, Stewart's journal reminds us of the great physical cost to missionary life:

> A violent storm on March 13. Rain and storm comes through the chinks of our doors and windows .... The water, to the depth of a foot, is running in a rapid current through B[etsey's] room—forming a small wing to ours—and Mr. Richard's house is entirely overflowed. We are now seeking partial refuge from the rain under our umbrellas;—and H[arriet] has been sitting for hours with C[harles, their eleven-month-old baby], in her arm, watching the motion of the rafters in the contentions of the wind—ready to make an escape with him from the ruins of our cabin.[35]

By the spring of 1824, five hundred scholars took part in the quarterly examinations and Queen Kaahumanu was among those who agreed to reveal her accomplishments of reading and writing.

> "This is my word and my hand," she said, followed by "I am making myself strong," with her signature, KAAHUMANU. As the first in her class, she herself orally spelled twenty Hawaiian words. One group at a time, the scholars chanted in unison the passages which they had committed to memory.[36]

Before her celebrated death on September 16, 1823, as a converted and baptized Christian, the Regent Queen Mother Keopuolani, too, had counseled her people:

> Protect the teachers who have come to this land of dark hearts; give heed to their instructions; reject not the commands of God .... Give heed to the *palapala*.[37]

Charles Stewart's February 1824 entry at Lahaina recorded additional growth of the schools, as ever greater number of printed books were requested for distribution.

> In consequence of this spirit [of increased learning], we have today been permitted [by royalty] to establish a large and regular school among [the royal Hawaiians'] domestic and dependents.

35. C. Samuel Stewart, *Private Journal*, 272.

36. C. Samuel Stewart, *Private Journal*, 299.

37. Bingham, *Residence of Twenty-One Years*, 216.

Later in that same week in February, 1824, Stewart added, as information came to him,

> We have the happiness of stating, that in addition to the school
> of the young prince, each of the chiefs now has one similar,
> under his special superintendence. The number of schools thus
> formed is ten, including in the whole, nearly one hundred and
> fifty scholars. Applications have been made for the institution of
> several more, and we soon expect to have at least five hundred
> persons under regular tuition in this [mission] district.[38]

These were the networks of schools for royal Hawaiians, perhaps the foundation for the modern school at Lahaina, Lahainaluna.

In May 1824, Betsey Stockton and Harriet and Charles Stewart landed at the Mission House at Honolulu. Stewart listed his principal duties there as preaching in the native language at Waititi, as well as "the instruction of twenty or thirty native teachers, in reading, writing and singing, three afternoons in the week."[39]

"Yesterday at daybreak, B[etsey] tapped at our door, to announce the arrival of the Tamahmaah of New York . . . with letters," Stewart wrote on August 9, 1824.[40]

This beautiful brig was the answer to so many prayers by Stockton and Stewart for their news-hungry souls. Two weeks later, Stewart wrote:

> For some time past the chiefs have expressed their determina
> tion to have reading and writing extended to the whole popula
> tion . . . only waiting for books, and an increase in the suitably
> qualified native teachers . . . to put [it] into effect. A knowledge of
> this reading, the maka ainama or farmers of Lahaia, application
> was made by them to us for books and slates and an instructor;
> and the first school—consisting of about thirty individuals—
> ever formed among that class of people has, within a few days,
> been established in our enclosure, under the superintendence of
> B[etsey] who is quite familiar with the native tongue.[41]

Stockton's school at Lahaina, held in the yard of her thatched-roof house, had grown from the four England and Hawaiian scholars of June 1823 to a school of thirty adult Hawaiians in August of 1824. Betsey Stockton, "who is quite familiar with the native tongue," had realized her pledge

38. C. Samuel Stewart, *Private Journal*, 297.
39. C. Samuel Stewart, *Private Journal*, 283.
40. C. Samuel Stewart, *Private Journal*, 310.
41. C. Samuel Stewart, *Private Journal*, 318.

to the ABCFM as a teaching missionary. Here were the fruits borne of her advanced education at Princeton. Here was the specific example of teaching the *papapala* to indigenous Hawaiians. It was the tool they were to use to preserve their culture during a period of great cultural change. Coming to their culture as an outsider, Betsey Stockton's invaluable skill as a linguist became her legacy for her young scholars and the adult *maka aniama* (common, non-royal Hawaiians) of the Sandwich Islands.

During their Honolulu residence, from April to August 1824, Stockton was among a party of nine who visited the salt lake four miles from the Mission House. Harriet and Charles Stewart left with Levi Chamberlain. Robert Haia, an islander educated at the Cornwall Connecticut school, acted as their translator.

The following extraordinary entry in Stockton's journal, dated September 15, 1824, was prompted by Green's requests for frequent letters from her, as well as for specimens of the natural world. Stockton, the student of anthropology, regretted her inability to purchase a wooden idol, as well as prized shells, salt crystals, and flora and fauna at the Sandwich Islands. Her introspective musing on the burdens of her daily life are minimized in comparison to her "want of spiritual food and Christian converse." So, in spite of the success of her schools and the rigors of child-drearing and housekeeping in a primitive setting, Stockton recognized unfulfilled needs of her interior life.[42]

From Lahaina, Maui, Stockton addressed her entry to "Rev. and dear Sir [Green] by the [brig] *Tamahamaha*":

> I received your kind letter, and found it truly refreshing. At the time I received it, I was at Oahu with Mrs. and Mrs. Stewart. We went there in April and did not return until August.
>
> What I shall say to you respecting my journal I know not. Perhaps I am guilty of neglect—and perhaps not. During the first six months after we came here, I was pretty much engaged with the domestick [sic] cares of our family; and had but little time to write and but little matter to write about. I however wrote when I could, although I knew but little personally of the general state of the mission; and was fully aware that Mr. Stewart would send you constant and full accounts of it, which would be much more of interest that any thing I could say. With this in view, I have disobeyed one of your parting commands; but let me entreat you not to attribute it to ingratitude or to the want of any proper feelings. [Green had reminded Stockton to keep her journal entries for him.]

42. B. Stockton, "Journal," in Christian Advocate 3 (April 1825), 188.

In your last letter you tell me "to keep up my spirits," I wish it was in my power to say that I have always done so; but here I fear I must plead guilty. My spirts often sink very low; and that this is criminal I do not pretend to deny. I know that the work in which I was to be engaged was great and glorious, and that it demanded all my faculties of body and wind in its performance. Still I am of the opinion that Christians at home, surrounded by all of the ordinances of the gospel, and by their Christian friends at all times accessible to them, cannot judge what are the heaviest trials a missionary is called to bear. I have found them to consist, not in the relinquishment of those outward comforts which I once enjoyed, so much as the want of spiritual good and Christian converse. This want I feel very keenly. When in my native land, my Christian privileges constituted much of my happiness; and now, the privilege of mourning their loss will surely not be denied me. But though sorrowful, yet I rejoice. The missionaries' sorrows and the missionaries' joys are mine.—The missionary's grave, and perhaps the missionary's heaven, will also be mine.

Mr. [William] Ellis [English missionary and linguist] has always been kind to me, and I regret his loss [from the mission] very much. But it is the Lord's doing, and we will be still. I hope he will visit Philadelphia, that you may have an opportunity of seeing him. You will, I think, find in him both the Christian and the gentlemen. Mr. Stewart intends giving him letters [of introduction] to you.

I have been looking over my journal and find but little that is fit to send you, and that little I shall probably not be able to send at this time; ad I expect to embark for Oahu tomorrow, or the day after, with Mr. [William] Richards, who is going to take one of Mr.[William] Ellis' children home, that has been living with us. My business there is to render Mrs. [Mary Mercy Moor] Ellis what assistance I can, previous to her embarkation; and then to sail to Lahaina as soon as possible. The vessel in which we expect to sail has not yet arrived; and if in my power I will yet collect my scattered papers and send them to you.—But if not by the present, but the next opportunity, which I expect will be soon.

Please to give me love to all the family . . . . The health of the family is but *so, so* [italics in original]. Mr. Stewart has not been well since we returned from Oahu. The most of the time he does not enjoy good health. Little Charles grows finely, and is a pleasant boy. Mr. [Artemis] Bishop and Mr. [Joseph] Goodrich have each buried a child on these heathen shores. . . .

Please excuse all my blunders, and consider me still your humble servant. BETSEY STOCKTON.

Dear Sir,—I should think myself highly criminal, if I did not embrace the first opportunity to tender you my warmest gratitude for your kindness. I know you want no fine speeches nor apologies. You are fully aware that, however widely separated from you, still the home and friends of my youth hold their place in my heart, and that time and distance only tend to endear them the more to me. The reflection that if I am faithful, we shall soon meet where sin and sorrow are no more [reference to eternal life], is a support to me under every trial. I do not say that this reflection had due influence at all times on my mind for I am often defected in this land of darkness. If I walk abroad, there is little but sin and misery presented to my view; or if I look within, there is a still more appalling sight; and when I miss the *alanui palole.* [(Editorial note from Ashbel Green:) We cannot translate these words—they seem to denote an *unerring guide.*] I have not so many friends to direct me right as I once had.

You wish to hear of *shells, lizards,* and *stones,* etc. etc.; and I regret that it is not in my power to send you more of them. I have seen many things which I should have liked to send you, but have been unable to purchase them. Not long since, a boy brought one of his former [wooden] gods to sell, which was about a yard and a half long, carved with much ingenuity, and painted black. The value of the article he wanted was about thirty cents, which I was unable to give [pay], as Mrs. Stewart was not at home at the time. All that I have collected I sent some time by a Nantucket whaleman—the third mate of which was a coloured man, who promised to present them to you himself if nothing prevented; and if prevented to see them safely shipped for Philadelphia. Perhaps the most curious thing among them is some lava, taken form the volcano on Hawaii. In many respects it is said to exceed any in the known world.

A very able work will soon appear [in publication] by Mr. [William] Ellis, who was one of the deputation sent lately to explore these islands; in which a description of the volcano, accompanied with a drawing will be seen. At the same time you will probably have the *Hawaiian Conversion, of the Life of Keopuolani,* the late queen, who was our best and most lamented friend. She was perhaps the first true convert to the Christian faith, and at the same time the greatest chief on these islands—the mother of the present king, prince and princess. But to the point—Handsome shells are not very abundant here. Coral we have in great quantities, and some of the specimens are very beautiful—I hope to get you some before long. Lizards we have by the thousand, and of almost every colour—some with long tails, and some with short ones. They often fall on our table, and run over our beds. The natives are in general afraid of them, for during the *tabu* system, they were worshipped as gods. I am one of their avowed enemies, and murder them whenever I can. Snakes and toads we have none—lice and fleas of a superior quality and quantity; cockroaches and ants without number—and all of these belong to our household. While I was at Oahu, I visited the Salt Lake, which is about a mile and half in circumference, and nearly surrounded with fresh water. The orifice from which the salt water issues is not more than an inch in diameter. As we approached it, it had the appearance of a lake frozen over, and then covered with snow. The salt crystallizes at the bottom I went in some distance, and broke off some specimens, with the stone on which it had crystallized to send you. Mr. [William] E[llis] is of the opinion they cannot be sent; but I think I shall try by the first good opportunity.

Give my love to cousin Flora [Stryker, a woman of color, a friend from Princeton], and thank her for the information she gave me. Tell her to write and let me know how all my relations are, and how many of them have turned their feet into the narrow path of life and peace. I have now a fine school of the *Maka ainana*, or lower class of people, the first I believe that has ever been established.[43]

Stockton's anthropological efforts were successful, despite William Ellis's doubts about the viability of shipping specimens by whaleship. In the May 1825 issue of his bi-monthly *Christian Advocate*, Green published the results of Betsey Stockton's specimen collection from the Sandwich Islands:

She had forwarded [them] to us in a trunk, containing articles of the product of the Sandwich Islands. The trunk has arrived in safety, and the articles have received no injury. They consist of shells, lava, coral, and a rick, apparently make of the tooth of an animal, presented by the wife of the chief *Boki* to Betsey Stockton, and various other manufactures of the native. The manufactures are truly curious—several pieces of Tapa, or native cloth, variously and very handsomely coloured, and a large parcel of coloured mat, such as those which the floors of the chiefs are covered, and on which they sit.[44]

43. B. Stockton, *Journal*, in *Christian Advocate* 3 (Apr. 1825) 187–89.

44. Green, "Sandwich Islands," 234.

Stockton's letter to Levi Chamberlain, on December 25, 1824, from Lahaina, reveals another side of her character. To the agent for secular affairs of the ABCFM, she wrote:

> I have a fine school, nine persons came from Ranai [Kauai?] who have joined it. One of them is a chief. . . . I trust the Lord wills it [the learning] to their souls.

And in a moment of levity, she compared her upset stomach to a recent sea voyage from island to island:

> but this is nothing compared with my last voyage in the *wash tub* [originally underlined] of deliverance . . . . My poor little Charles has been sick for four weeks past, he is something better but very thin. I remain your humble and affectionate friend, Betsey Stockton.[45]

The reference to a ship as a wash tub reveals the same sense of humor that supported her on the *Thames*, where she was affectionately teased by members of its crew. She closed her letter with her ever mindful vigilance as her Charles's nurse, coupled with her role as school founder and teacher.

In January 1825, Stewart mentioned the location of this same school at Lahaina: "In these walks I am often accompanied by H[arriet] and C[harles] while B[etsey] is engaged in a fine school kept by her every afternoon, in the chapel adjoining our yard."[46]

Despite Stockton's help with household chores and child-minding at Lahaina, Harriet Stewart's health continued to deteriorate. Husband Charles wrote of the birth of their daughter on March 7, 1825, named Harriet, after her mother. Although the baby seemed healthy, the birth nearly killed the mother, noted her husband. He decided to take action to save his twenty-seven-year-old wife's life. A sad solution came by sea. Through an unanticipated source, Stockton and the Stewart family became players on an international stage.

The Stewart's plan for saving Harriet's life came with the arrival of naval commander Lord Anson Byron. *HMS Blonde's* arrival at Lahaina's harbor on May 6, 1825, presented the Stewarts with a chance for rest and renewal. Departing from Spithead, London, eight months previously, the ship carried the bodies of missionary friends Queen Kahamaulu and King Kamehameha II, victims of measles in London. Their bodies, in triple coffins of mahogany, oak, and lead, were returned to the Sandwich Islands for Christian burial, a diplomatic gesture.

45. B. Stockton, "Letter to Levi Chamberlain."
46. C. Samuel Stewart, *Private Journal*, 263.

The *HMS Blonde* carried the artist Robert Dampier, Episcopal ministers, an English crew, and a ship's physician. A formal funeral for their Hawaiian majesties was conducted on May 11, attended by Stewart and other American missionaries. "At this extremity of the globe," Stewart noted, the ship would takes months to refit and restock. A fifty-six-gun ship, Stewart described it as "a fine model, and perfectly new, this being her first voyage."[47]

During meetings with Stewart, Lord Byron grasped the dire situation of Harriet Stewart's health and graciously extended an invitation to the young American couple to join him for several months aboard the *Blonde*. Accordingly, on July 5, 1825,

> Harriet was carried down [to the ship] in an arm-chair and his Lordship's gig [horse-drawn carriage] waiting, we were immediately rowed off to the vessel, a distance of two miles in the open [ocean] roads: the possibility that Harriet might not live to return to Oahu, made the separation of her children a severe trial. We left them [Charles, two years old, and three-month-old Harriet] however, with the persuasion, that they will receive every kind and affectionate attention from our faithful friend B[etsey], and from the ladies of the [mission] station.[48]

Unencumbered by the physical demands of two close pregnancies and the dangers of childbirth, Betsey Stockton would assume the duties for which she had been trained at Princeton, a place which must have seemed ages before and worlds away.

Harriet Stewart was first placed on a sofa in Lord Byron's cabin, but before the company on board the *Blonde* sat down to dinner, she was moved to her own cabin, adjoining the dining room. Oil portraits of His British Majesty King George IV and Lady Byron looked down on the suffering young mother. Months of restful ocean breezes, coupled with the luxury of regular hot meals of foods suited to Western tastes, partially restored Harriet's—and Charles Stewart's—declining health.

Understandably, Stockton had shouldered the major burden of the lives of the Stewart children. Perhaps the availability of cow's milk, greater quantity of fresh food, better shelter, and Stockton's support by mission women at Honolulu somewhat alleviated the daily tasks of childcare without electricity or running water. She knew that death was no stranger to the children of missionary parents at the Sandwich Islands; Sybil and Hiram Bingham had already buried two children. One son, Jeremiah Evarts Bingham, remembered

47. C. Samuel Stewart, *Private Journal*, 328.
48. Bingham, *Residence of Twenty-One Years*, 350.

as "an engaging child of sixteen months," had died of croup.[49] Mother Sybil's debilitating depression after his death was to last for months.

Unfortunately, the three-month cruise on the *Blonde* did not restore Harriet Stewart's strength. A decision was made for the four Stewarts and Betsey Stockton to return to America in an effort to save her life. According to Hiram Bingham, the head of the American missionary deputation in the Sandwich Islands:

> Mrs. Stewart's health in the estimation of the mission to justify her removal to the United States . . . and the offer of a gratuitous passed to England made by Captain [Charles] Dale of the *Fawn*, availing themselves of the medical advice of Dr. Short, the surgeon of the homebound ship.[50]

The *Fawn* sailed into the harbor at Oahu for refitting in the early part of October. She was bound directly to London, and her accommodations for the mission family were "superior to those of most ships navigating the Pacific," wrote Bingham. Rev. Charles Stewart was officially released from his mission "with the hope of receiving him again in due time." Harriet Stewart was so feeble that she was "carried in the arms to take her leave of Mrs. [Sybil] Bingham, who was equally feeble," noted Bingham about the sad parting women, both suffering from post-partum debility.[51]

The price of human health had been high, but the Regent Queen Mother Keopuolani's wishes were to come true for her people. In September 1826, a month before Stockton and the Stewarts' departure, Bingham himself turned in the spreadsheet on the progress of schools at Sandwich Islands. The number of schools were multiplying as rapidly as books and teachers could be furnished and already contained fifteen thousand pupils—ten thousand of whom were supposed to be capable of reading intelligibly in their own language.[52] Bingham knew that the foundation of the schools (now three in Lahaina) was based on the hard work of the missionary press: "Some 16,000 spelling books or elementary lessons, were printed and put to use from March to October [1825]."[53]

No doubt Betsey Stockton had used those spellers and books of elementary lessons in her two schools at Lahaina.

On October 17, 1825, the *Fawn* carried its precious passengers and entered the open ocean roads at the harbor of Honolulu, passing Tahiti in

49. Bingham, *Residence of Twenty-One Years*, 274.

50. Bingham, *Residence of Twenty-One Years*, 273.

51. Bingham, *Residence of Twenty-One Years*, 273–74.

52. C. Samuel Stewart, *Private Journal*, 393.

53. Bingham, *Residence of Twenty-One Years*, 272.

November. She continued her voyage around the Cape of Good Hope, the southernmost tip of Africa. The *Fawn* arrived in London on April 9, 1826, at the new London Docks. Before continuing their voyage to America, Stockton and Stewarts were to rest for three months at the residence of the Adams family in Homerton College, a northeastern suburb of London. English missionary William Ellis had provided a reference for his friends, made at the Sandwich Islands.

Due to circumstances beyond her control, Betsey Stockton, in 1826, became the first woman of color to circumnavigate the globe. In contrast to their six-month voyage, Honolulu had seemed to the first missionaries there "like the delights of an Eden," wrote Hiram Bingham. Stockton's prophetic statement, in contract, reveals a Christian pragmatist: "On further acquaintance with Lahaina, B[etsey] Stockton remarked, that though it had been compared to Eden, she thought it more like the land, 'East of Eden.'"[54]

From her studies of the Scriptures at Princeton Theological Seminary, Stockton was referring to the land to which the biblical murderer Cain was exiled. Living east of Eden at Lahaina and Honolulu meant hardship and illness for members of the second company of American missionaries. Friends from America sent a wooden frame house by ship for the Stewarts and Stockton, but it arrived after their departure from their Sandwich Islands mission.

In the final analysis, Betsey Stockton became the unassuming poster woman for the revolution of bilingual literacy in the Sandwich Islands. Coming as a woman of color, her legacy of early schools stabilized Hawaiian culture. Teachers often ask the question "Have I made a difference in my students' lives?" Stockton's knowledge of the Hawaiian language gained on board the *Thames* led directly to the establishment of bilingual schools. Her work was supported by others in the mission at Lahaina and by the fruits of Elisha Loomis's productive printing press at Honolulu, Oahu.

However, Stockton alone was the catalyst, the agent of change, between young American missionaries and the acquisition of a written indigenous language by a top-down Hawaiian hierarchy. Realizing the usefulness of literacy—especially bilingualism—the rulers had turned to the missionaries to teach the *palapala* to all of their subjects.

54. Bingham, *Residence of Twenty-One Years*, 191.

Chapter 6: **Departures and Accusations, 1824–1826**

BETSEY STOCKTON WAS TO become a player in an international drama during the years 1824 to 1826. An international incident had been caused by published allegations of missionary wrongdoings at Lahaina, Maui. The flash point was the denial by the missionaries of an evening's entertainment of "a magic lantern show" to Hawaiian royalty. These false charges, stemming from the British fear of the increasing presence of American missionaries in the Hawaiian Islands, demanded public refutation. The moral stance of Stockton's sending agency, the American Board of Commissioners for Foreign Missions (ABCFM), seemed to hang in the balance.

Having successfully established schools, erected churches, and distributed thousands of printed items, the American missionaries heard, with rising skepticism, of a plan for the then reigning King Kamehameha II and his Queen Kamamalu to sail to London, to meet George IV, King of Great Britain.

The royal Hawaiians had shown willingness to befriend the missionaries at this critical time, when the number of mission stations in Hawaii increased. Americans Hiram Bingham, Charles Stewart, and others were quick to understand the difficulties of language, a hazardous voyage, and the trusting nature of the two Hawaiian monarchs. To ensure the safe return of their royal friends, they suggested English missionary Rev. William Ellis as traveling guide to the Hawaiians. Ellis was well known and greatly loved by them, a twenty-year veteran of the Pacific Islands culture. He also wanted to return to England in 1824. It seemed a foolproof plan to all interested parties.

But the outcome of the royal Hawaiians' proposed voyage to London proved tragic to the Hawaiian nation, beyond the American missionaries' worst imaginings. According to Hiram Bingham, Hawaiian mission head:

> Having been assured of the friendly regards of George the Fourth and the President of the United States [James Monroe], [they] cherished a desire to visit their countries, and having a propensity to roving, hastily resolved on making a voyage to England and America.

Capt. [Valentine] Starbuck, a Nantucket master of the English whaleship, *L'Aigle*, who had shown kindness, in touching at the islands this season, homeward bound, offered the king and his suite a free passage to England, which he [the king] readily accepted.

The more sagacious chiefs were not without their apprehensions that evil would befall him or them, if he should pursue his plan without a competent and trustworthy interpreter and instructor . . . therefore in concurrence with the king and Kamamalu, they interested themselves to secure the services of Mr. Ellis. The Hawaiian rulers offered to pay Capt. S[tarbuck] for [Ellis's] passage, but he [Starbuck] refused first, because he had not the room . . . . The captain then affirming that he was not allowed to carry passengers to England for money, and that to overcrowd his ship might affect his insurance, [he] persevered in declining.

The party embarked from Honolulu on the 27th of November, 1823. . . . The king [Kamehameha II], as he had done before, again recommended attention to the instruction of the missionaries; and [Queen] Kamamalu distinguished herself as she was wont to do. This Amazonian lady, about twenty-six years of age, tall and portly, of queen-like air, yet affectionate, filial, courteous, patriotic, and friendly to the missionary cause, breaking away from mother, sister, home, and native land, appeared exceedingly interested in taking leave of the nation.[1]

The royal suite, or party, sailed from Honolulu on November 27, 1823. On board the *L'Aigle* were King Kamehameha II and Queen Kamamalu; Governor Boki of O'ahu; Boki's wife, Lilihia; and John Young's son, James Young. The Frenchman John Rives took a secret passage, although he was the king's trusted French secretary. The suite carried $25,000 in gold coin to pay for expenses during the voyage and after landing in London. Having passed around Cape Horn, the party arrived in Portsmouth, England, on May 22, 1824.[2]

At Portsmouth, the royal Hawaiians were abandoned by Capt. Starbuck.

The whole of the king's baggage including the money had been left on board the *L'Aigle* in Portsmouth, to go round the river in the ship and when the ladies were first seen in London they

---

1. Bingham, *Residence of Twenty-One Years*, 202–3.
2. Bingham, *Residence of Twenty-One Years*, 204.

were dressed in very strange habiliments [clothing]. The queen wore trousers and a long bed gown of coloured velveteen, and her friend, Liliah, wife of Boki, had something of the same kind . . . complaining bitterly of the cold.[3]

Because the king and queen had been robbed of almost all their gold, the royal party stayed at Osborne's Hotel in the Adelphi as guests of Mr. and Mrs. Chaplin, owners of the hotel. Learning of their plight, King George offered protection.

His majesty's government immediately deputed a gentleman to . . . perform the office of a guardian to them . . . The Honorable Frederick Byng.[4]

Saved from further embarrassment, the king and queen were now the personification of high fashion at London social events.

The [Hawaiian] chiefs were much delighted with the politeness of the Duke and Duchess of Gloucester, who were of the party. The queen particularly felt gratified with that kind of urbanity of manner which distinguishes her royal highness . . . . It might perhaps cause a smile . . . [with the] remembered description of [Captain James] Cook, who found the king Taraipu and his queen with nothing but their waist clothes, to their grandchildren wearing coats made by a London tailor, and [with] stays and gowns by a Parisian modiste; but that the dresses were fit and becoming we all remember, and, moreover, that more than one [London] lady [was] begging to have the pattern of Kahamalu's turban.[5]

The next day [Monday, May 31], the king permitted his box at Convent Garden to be decorated for them [to see the play *Pizarro*], and they were received with ceremony, though not with state, by the managers. Their behavior was greatly admired; no awkwardness, not inattention on their part. Their bows in return for the congratulations they received on entering, were quite European. This was one of their greatest gratifications: they knew they were in the royal box, and that it had been prepared and appointed for them.[6]

3. Byron, *Voyage of H.M.S. Blonde*, 59.
4. Byron, *Voyage of H.M.S. Blonde*, 59.
5. Byron, *Voyage of H.M.S. Blonde*, 62.
6. Byron, *Voyage of H.M.S. Blonde*, 63.

Indeed, a formal portrait of the king, queen, and their attendants at Drury Lane was quickly made and showed happy faces attending the theater production.

Charles Stewart had often remarked on the natural dignity of the royal Hawaiians, now seen by Londoners:

> The chiefs, male or female, are at once known, not only by their size but by their walk, general air and manners. A consciousness of natural superiority . . . give them an ease of action, and an unaffected dignity of department, that would distinguish them as persons of rank, in whatever company they might appear.[7]

Reigning King Kamehameha II was coached in protocol and wanted to present his entourage at court, outfitted in fashionable clothing. When the bill was presented, the king found that half of his money was missing. But plans went forward for an audience with King George IV and a state reception to honor the Hawaiians.

Sadly, without immunity to Western disease, between June 12 and June 19 "the whole of the Sandwich Islands chiefs and their attendants were taken ill."[8] They had been stricken with a virulent strain of measles. Attended by physicians of King George IV, all quickly recovered except for King Kamehameha II and Queen Kamamalu. The queen died on July 8, followed by her husband a week later on July 14, in London.[9]

The bodies of Kamehameha II and Kamamalu were placed in triple coffins of mahogany, oak, and lead, having been laid to rest previously in the vaulted cellar crypt of St. Martin-in-the-Fields, a central London church.[10] King George had the unenviable task of sailing the dead queen and king to their home, the Sandwich Islands.

Captain George Byron, the Right Honourable Lord Byron, seventh Baron Byron, cousin of the poet, was deputed by the English crown to carry the bodies of King Kamehameha II and Queen Kamamalu to the Sandwich Islands for a state funeral. On board the *HMS Blonde* were its master, Commander Lord Anson Byron; James Macrea, the Scottish botanist from the Royal Horticultural Society; naturalist Andrew Bloxam; and the naturalists's brother, Richard Rowland Bloxom, the ship's chaplain. The ship's artist, Robert Dampier, painted the ship's portrait and several other paintings during the voyage from London to Honolulu.

---

7. C. Samuel Stewart, *Private Journal*, 130.

8. Byron, *Voyage of H.M.S. Blonde*, 65.

9. Byron, *Voyage of H.M.S. Blonde*, 59.

10. C. Samuel Stewart, *Private Journal*, 333.

The *HMS Blonde* sailed from Woolwich, England, on September 8, 1824, with the dead king and queen encased in their triple coffins.

The first intelligence of the King and Queen's untimely deaths in London was recalled by Charles Stewart:

> March 10th [1825] from ships the *Persus* and *Almira* came into port [Lahaina] with much needed supplies of food and materials, and news for the mission. But every other feeling is lost in the melancholy intelligence [information] of the death of our friends Kamehamaru and Liholiho [Kamehameha II]. The truth is a shock to us—so much so, that we frankly confessed, our tears are mingled with those of the chiefs and people who are almost overwhelmed by the bereavement.

Remembering that the American missionaries had urged the royals to include the Rev. William Ellis to accompany them—and that they had refused—Stewart added with a sigh, "there were circumstances in their embarkation . . . against the wish of the Mission and of the nation, the privilege of having a pious teacher, interpreter and guardian with them."[11]

After eight months, the *HMS Blonde* itself was sighted off the Sandwich Islands in early May, 1825. It landed at the deepwater harbor of Lahaina on May 4, 1825, where the Hawaiians who survived the London visit then disembarked.[12] Two days later, on May 6, 1825, smaller boats carrying the British dignitaries landed at Honolulu with Lord Byron and his company. There the state funeral for King Kamehameha II and Queen Kamamalu took place amid great international honors.

Lord Byron Extends Hospitality to the Stewarts aboard the *HMS Blonde*

Increasingly concerned about his wife Harriet's ill health, Charles Stewart sought advice and help from the newly arrived British doctors.

> Thursday, May 26, 1825; The physicians . . . [from] the *Blonde*, having recommended a change of air, as most likely to benefit H's health, Lord Byron has most kindly assigned us accommodation in the *Blonde* for a trip to the harbor of Waiakea—at Hilo on Hawaii—where he is going for a month to refit and explore the

---

11. C. Samuel Stewart, *Private Journal*, 333.

12. Bingham, *Residence of Twenty-One Years*, 262.

windward side of the Island, with the intention of returning to this port again.[13]

On Board *HMS Blonde,* June 5, 1825

> We left them [our children], however, with the persuasion, that they will receive every kind and affectionate attention from our faithful friend B[etsey], and from the ladies of the station.[14]

While mother Harriet was afforded care aboard *HMS Blonde* during the month of July 1825, her husband Charles Stewart accompanied a group to investigate the volcano of Kiraura on the island of Hawaii, listing all of the natural and geological specimens in his journal. When he returned, he found his wife "more ill than when I left her."[15]

The necessity of the leaving the islands now became a matter of life or death for Harriet Stewart. Husband Charles wrote that "three requisites were essential . . . in the same ship—a physician . . . accommodations sufficiently large for a family—and a ship homeward bound."[16]

In early October 1825, all of his requisites for a safe voyage home were met in the circumstance of the ship *Fawn*, when Captain Charles Dale of London "touched at Oahu for refreshments." From Dale, Stewart learned "that the *Fawn* was bound directly to London, had large accommodations and that a 'Dr. Short,' a surgeon was attached to her." Captain Dale immediately offered a passage for the whole family, "provided it was accepted gratuitously, as an expression of his friendship and good will."[17]

Stewart was overcome with gratitude at the generosity of the captain and his ship's physician and immediately met with members of the American mission at the Sandwich Islands to ask about his release from the mission, as well as their opinion about whether the offer of a passage for the Stewart family and Betsey Stockton should be accepted.

Stewart put two propositions to the mission heads:

> 1st—Whether it was my duty, under the existing circumstances of my family, to return, at least for a time, to the United States? And 2nd—If so, whether the kind offer of Captain Dale, of a gratuitous passage to London, should be accepted? Both of

---

13. C. Samuel Stewart, *Private Journal,* 350.
14. C. Samuel Stewart, *Private Journal,* 352.
15. C. Samuel Stewart, *Private Journal,* 362.
16. C. Samuel Stewart, *Private Journal,* 389.
17. C. Samuel Stewart, *Private Journal,* 395.

which were fully and unanimously decided in the affirmative; and we began to [prepare to] embark at the end of eight days.[18]

Before their departure for London on the *Fawn*, Stewart paused and allowed himself a brief reflection of the work of Betsey Stockton, Harriet Stewart, and his missionary labors during the past two and a half years. Of them, Stewart wrote:

> The highly encouraging state of the people, thousands of them delighting in our instruction, . . . in a [mission] field ripe for the sickle—all caused us to bid farewell to the Sandwich Islands, with feeling of the most painful depressions. . . . Tears of affection and the beautiful and classic ground on which our eyes rested, as we waved a last adieu to the American shores-than any we experienced on the *19th of November 1822*.[19]

Many years later, in his published account, mission head Hiram Bingham offered these explanations for the American missionaries' departure to their former homes from what was meant to be a lifelong commitment to the ABCFM. Bingham painted a portrait of the sacrifices of personal health of women missionaries:

> We were called to a reluctant parting with Mr. and Mrs. Stewart on the 17th of October, 1825, after their residence of two years and a half on the islands. Several of the [American] females of our mission suffered materially from debility, which was attributable in part to the climate of a perpetual summer, whose temperature in the shade by day averages 75° throughout the year, and in part to their solicitude for the success of our enterprise, and in part to the privation and unaccustomed modes of living and hardships to which, in straitened circumstances, they were subjected. Mrs. Stewart was so feeble that she was carried in the arms to take her last leave of Mrs. [Sybil] Bingham, who was equally feeble, and whose course [life], it was apprehended, would be sooner finished than that of Mrs. S[tewart—i.e., Sybil Bingham would die sooner than Harriet Stewart]. After the early death of our little J[eremiah] Evarts [Bingham], an engaging child of sixteen months, who after a variety of suffering, was seized with croup, Mrs. B[ingham] was brought low, at a period when the demands for the strength of all the labourers was so great as to render [her] inability to labor a peculiar trial. She was for weeks confined to her couch with alarming symptoms of a

18. C. Samuel Stewart, *Private Journal*, 395.
19. C. Samuel Stewart, *Private Journal*, 396.

broken constitution; but the kind arm that has been so often stretched out in mercy to our mission, raised her up again.[20]

Bingham failed to mention the missionary wives' frequent pregnancies, the dangers of childbirth without medical help, or previous illnesses, as reasons for their debility.

Betsey Stockton and the Stewart family arrived at the new London Docks on April 9, 1826, after six months aboard the *Fawn*. Outward bound from Honolulu, their ship passed Tahiti in November 1825, sailing on to round the Cape of Good Hope, the tip of the African continent. It completed the circumnavigation of the globe of the missionary family, marking Stockton as the first woman of color to do so.

In London, the family recuperated for three months at

> Marshgate House, the residence of the Adam[s] family of Homerton, a northern suburb of the city [now Hackney]. . . . This is one of the households into which myself and the [missionary] family were received with all Christian hospitality on our arrival in London from the Sandwich Islands, 1826.[21]

With the family safely resting among Christian friends, Charles Stewart faced a firestorm of newly published criticism questioning the behavior of the American missionaries at the Sandwich Islands. In reality, as timely documents came to light, the false accusations by the British were seen for what they were: British suspicion of the growing sphere of influence by the presence of so many American missionaries.

Purportedly written by Richard Bloxam, the chaplain of the *HMS Blonde*, the account accused the resident American missionaries, referencing Charles Stewart by name, of disallowing a Saturday entertainment of the "magic show lantern by candlelight" to the assembled Hawaiian chiefs, because it would be a sacrilege of the Sabbath. For Presbyterians, the Sabbath began on sundown on Saturday. The account, published as the *Voyage of the H.M.S. Ship Blonde* in London in 1826 was a chance to curtail the increasing cultural—and future political—influence on the hereditary royals, the government of Hawaii, by the American missionaries. The goal of the British, of course, was to maintain the Sandwich Islands as a valuable area of political and commercial interest to the British Crown.

The author of the scurrilous attack? Further research points to one Maria Graham, the book's editor, later known as Lady Maria Callcott, as the real author of the accusation. Not surprisingly, Richard Bloxam had fled

---

20. Bingham, *Residence of Twenty-One Years*, 274.
21. C. Samuel Stewart, *Sketches of Society*, 1:129.

from England via Portsmouth before Charles Stewart and Betsey Stockton's April 1826 arrival in London.

Luckily, Charles Stewart had been an eyewitness to the misunderstanding of the previous events in Hawaii. As Mrs. Graham's pseudo account unraveled, he was residing in London. He could and did offer a personal refutation of the magic lantern incident. Stewart went on to voice the positive contributions to the Hawaiian people by the American missionaries. On the world stage, he mounted a rebuttal to the unfounded charge of missionary control of the Hawaiian chiefs by his sister and brother American missionaries.

Adding to Lord Byron's verbal rebuttal of the false charges, Charles Stewart addressed the London meeting of the British and Foreign Bible Society, publicly refuting the charges.[22] As the controversy followed him "across the pond" of the Atlantic, Stewart continued to write and to publish his eyewitness interpretation of this trumped-up international crisis. In doing so, Stewart defended the ABCFM, whose objective was to save souls for Jesus Christ through the path of teaching literacy.

Championed by the Rev. William Ellis, Charles Stewart's English colleague in Hawaii, the war of words continued. *An Examination of the Charges against the American Missionaries at the Sandwich Islands as Alleged in the Voyage of the Ship* Blonde *and in the London Quarterly Review* was published in Cambridge, England, in 1827. In this work, Ellis noted:

> It is true that Mr. Stewart was told by Lord Byron himself, that the magic lantern was to be exhibited to the natives, at the solicitation of [Queen] Kaahumanu; and that he [Lord Byron] replied he thought the natives would be pleased.[23]

Lord Byron met Charles Stewart in London under cordial circumstances.

> When he [Lord Byron] became acquainted with all the facts . . . he declared himself, in a note now in the possession of Mr.

22. C. Samuel Stewart, *Sketches of Society*, 88–89.
"But not until Lord Byron had given a satisfactory proof of the sincerity of his assurance to me on parting at the islands, by a public speech, before a highly respected and numerous audience—the late Mr. Butterworth, M.P. in the chair—in which he mentioned the American missionaries with commendation, and gave a highly favorable account of their success.
"Such are some of the reasons which lead me wholly to disbelieve that his lordship has been an accessory to the detraction of the reviewer. Yours, &c. C. S. Stewart" (C. Samuel Stewart, *Residence in Sandwich Islands*, 338).
23. Ellis, *Examination of the Charges*, 41.

Stewart, to be perfectly satisfied . . . [and the incident] left no impression unfavorable to the mission.[24]

Byron spoke from personal knowledge of Stewart's Christian character and loyalty to the mission. Lord Byron was reminded of their friendship during the month-long cruise when Harriet and Charles Stewart had been his guests aboard the *HMS Blonde* in Hawaiian waters in the summer of 1825.

In 1827, to William Ellis's published rebuttal was added William Orme's *A Defense of the Missions in the South Sea and Sandwich Islands against the Misrepresentations Contained in a Late Number of the Quarterly Review, in a Letter to the Editor of that Journal published in London*. Orme, a clergyman himself, published his defense from the Mission House, Austin Friars, London. In one of the most poetic descriptions ever of the work of Stockton and the Stewarts, he wrote:

The [Hawaiian] club is changed into the plough share and the spear into a pruning hook. . . . The howl of superstitious fear had given place to the language of prayer.[25]

The American missionaries, Orme asserted,

have added fresh languages to the vocabulary of the earth, and have presented in written forms, alphabets and tongues unknown in the literature of the world.[26]

Mrs. Graham's attempted propaganda became a chance for review and assessment of the work of the American missionaries in the Sandwich Islands. In addition, it opened a window of reason for reexamination of any other negative charges that might disallow contributions to the mission—in either goods and cash—to be questioned. All told, it proved counterproductive to its intended damage to the Americans' mission in Hawaii.

No higher praise for the school founding and bilingual work of Betsey Stockton, Charles Stewart, Hiram Bingham, and Elisha Loomis was ever offered on the international stage at the time. However, within less than three years, a public vindication was to come to light from the Hawaiian people themselves, a clear-eyed assessment of the value of the American missionaries' work in the Sandwich Islands.

With his usual mixture of perception and eloquence, Stewart published two letters to Jeremiah Evarts, the corresponding secretary of the ABCFM,

24. Ellis, *Examination of the Charges*, 40.
25. Orme, *Defense of the Missions*, 77.
26. Orme, *Defense of the Missions*, 77.

the institution that had sent Stockton and the Stewarts as missionaries to Hawaii. Those two Stewart letters were published "from Boston" on July 9 and July 10, 1827. But Stewart actually wrote them and handed them to Orme while he was still living in London in the summer of 1826. They were the postscripts included in Orme's London publication *Defense of the Missions* and were entitled "Letters from the Rev. C. S. Stewart, in Defense of Himself and his Brethren, against Charges of the *Quarterly Review*."

Taking up the verbal gauntlet, Stewart wrote,

> The review of a "Voyage of His Majesty's Ship *Blonde*," in the years 1824–25 is made the occasion of presenting to the public the characters, instructions, and influence of the American Missionaries residing in the Sandwich Islands, in a most erroneous and unjust light, and of conveying impressions of the design and result of their establishment here, as unfavorable as they are unfounded. [The *London Quarterly Review*] . . . is chargeable with *gross error, misrepresentation and falsehood* . . . . For some object—and no other is discoverable, than that of wresting from the American Missionaries, the credit of having introduced the religion of the cross at the Sandwich Islands—the writer, supported, as it appears, by Mrs. Graham (a lady employed by the publisher of the voyage, to prepare a work for the press, from notes of the Rev. Mr. [Richard] Bloxam, chaplain of the frigate, says that Christianity "was planted at the Sandwich Islands by the *spontaneous will of the natives*, before any mission ever of persuasion had reached them."[27]

In his published letter to Jeremiah Evarts, dated July 10, Stewart took the editor of the *London Quarterly* to task, referring to the facts published by his friend William Ellis in *Journal of a Tour through Hawaii*:

> that in the course of three or four years, that thousands are capable of reading and writing [a language] and tens of thousands are, by it, making advances in the elements of knowledge.[28]

Stewart saved his final blast against the criticisms of the American missionaries' work in the Sandwich Islands, especially against the idea that

> the Preachers at the Islands, "from the nature of their education are unfit to instruct the natives in the doctrines and duties of religion." . . . The ministers of the gospel who first landed at the Sandwich Islands, and those with whom I was more specially associated, in leaving this country, three years afterwards, were

27. C. Samuel Stewart, in Orme, *Defense of Missions*, 110.
28. C. Samuel Stewart, in Orme, *Defense of Missions*, 110.

all men of liberal education. For nine years at least, before their embarkation from America [in 1819], they had been pursuing a regular course at of classical, collegiate, and theological study, at the first institutions of our country.[29]

Specifically, those institutions included Charles Stewart's own education as an 1815 graduate of the College of New Jersey and his graduate work at Princeton Theological Seminary. Sandwich Island missionaries were early Ivy Leagues graduates—before there was an Ivy League. They graduated from Harvard, Yale, Middlebury, and Andover Theological Seminary. In short, they were a clique of America's finest Protestant minds.

Nor was Betsey Stockton's advanced education at Princeton Theological Seminary Sunday classes unique among women missionaries. Lucy Goodale Thurston was a graduate of the Bradford Academy in Haverhill, Massachusetts, and was a teacher. Stockton's *Thames* whaleship journalist companion Louisa Everett Ely was a certified teacher at District School #1, Cornwall, Connecticut. These three women pulled their educational weight at their missions at the Sandwich Islands. Other women had been privately educated, such as Sybil Moseley Bingham and Harriet Bradford Tiffany Stewart, Stockton's sister missionaries and teachers.

Stewart also defended Betsey Stockton and the returning Hawaiian students of the Heathen School who sailed with the mission family on board the *Thames*, as Ely wrote,

> They bore with them, to their distant destination, the respect of their tutors and professors, for good native talent, and for attainments in literature and science, equal to those of their fellow-students; and as a body they are as well fitted for the stations they occupy as the clergy of England and America are for their duties at home.[30]

Without mentioning Betsey Stockton by name, Stewart's letter to Jeremiah Evarts, the ABCFM's agent, was his justification for the work that Stockton accomplished by beginning schools for young non-royal Hawaiians, the *maka ainama*, and for adult farmers in Lahaina. Stockton's accomplishments must be weighed against charges that the American missionaries were "unfit to teach."

Later, in America, Stewart's two letters were republished in summary of the controversy in an anonymous review entitled "American Missionaries at the Sandwich Islands" in *The North American Review.*

29. C. Samuel Stewart, in Orme, *Defense of Missions*, 110.
30. C. Samuel Stewart, in Orme, *Defense of Missions*, 110.

Arriving at the New York City dockyards in August 1826, Rev. Stewart and his missionary family parted ways after having traveled together from Honolulu for eleven months. Stewart traveled to the American South. Betsey Stockton traveled north. In the passenger list of the steamship, Betsey Stockton was labeled as "Nurse, 31"; ailing Harriet Stewart as "Lady, 26"; toddler as "Charlie, 3"; and his infant sister as "Hattie."[31] The family group journeyed up the Hudson River to Cooperstown, New York, Harriet's ancestral home. A new chapter in all of their lives had begun.

Rev. Charles S. Stewart came to love life at sea. Perhaps he found solace for the illness and impending death of his beloved Harriet. After a preaching tour of the Presbyterian churches in the South with the ABCFM, Stewart enlisted as a naval chaplain aboard the US ship *Guerriere* in November 1828. Ever the reporter during his watery travels, Chaplain Stewart was warmly welcomed at Lahaina, Maui, as his ship docked there. Of this reunion after three years away from his Hawaiian friends, he wrote:

> My reception by the chiefs, the governor and his wife, the princess . . . former parishioners and special friends was warm-hearted and affecting, many of them bathing my hands with tears as they pressed them to their hearts and lips . . . . As the news of my arrival spread rapidly through the district, . . . [they called,] "Aroha Mita Twata . . . Aroha Mita Twata-Vahine, aroha [lowercase in original] Kali, Aroha Harieta a me Behe!" . . . "Love to Mrs. Stewart, love to Charles, together with Betsey" . . . . Betsey Stockton is held in grateful recollections, both by the chiefs and the common people. It was under her immediate auspices and instruction, as you know, that the first school among the farmers and their families in Lahaina was established, at the close of the year 1824. Schools of the kind are almost as extensive as the population . . . . Several of her scholars have become pious; several are among the best qualified and efficient of the native instructors.[32]

Published by Charles Stewart in New York in 1831, *A Visit to the South Seas* was followed in London in 1832 in a two-volume set, edited and abridged by Rev. William Ellis. It was a written ledger of Betsey Stockton's missionary work in Lahaina from the mouths of her former students, open for international readers to peruse.

31. "New York Passenger Lists."

32. C. Samuel Stewart, *Visit to the South Seas*, 1:322.

Chapter 7: **Tragedy and Transitions**

BETSEY STOCKTON'S NOVEMBER 1822 contract with the American Board of Commissioners for Foreign Missions documented her as a free woman sent as an assistant missionary to the Sandwich Islands for life. Three years later, she was officially released from her contract by the board: Stockton and the Stewarts were directed to return to America in an attempt to save Harriet Stewart's life. The ghost of a "protracted and dangerous illness" of the summer of 1819 (never diagnosed) had reappeared.[1]

While Stockton and the Stewart children headed north for Harriet's childhood home in Cooperstown, New York, Rev. Charles Stewart traveled south, joining Jeremiah Evarts of the ABCFM. The board engaged Stewart for a domestic mission, a fundraising tour of the prominent Presbyterian churches in the southern United States. Given his wife's continuing frail health, Stewart must have felt honor bound to accompany Evarts in an effort to raise funds for the mission and the friends at the Sandwich Islands, whom he loved and to whom he hoped to return with a healthier Harriet.

Stockton, too, experienced competing interests for her time and skills. By accompanying Harriet Stewart and the children, Stockton would continue her role of the past four years as companion and nurse. Poor health had plagued them all: Rev. Charles, Harriet, son Charlie—and to a lesser degree—Betsey, during their years at the Lahaina, Maui, mission.

On March 21, 1827, in Cooperstown, a soulful Harriet Stewart wrote to her very close friend of Betsey's nursing help:

> Betsey is still with me, and quite well at present—her health during the winter has been poor—she is out this evening, but I presume would desire to be remembered to you—my dear little ones are quietly sleeping near me—they are remarkably well at present, and much grown since you saw them.[2]

She wrote to unnamed recipients, presumably to Olivia Murray. She also gave news of her husband's travels:

---

1. "Harriet Bradford Tiffany Stewart."
2. H. Stewart, "Letter to My Very Dear Friend."

114

I received a long letter from Mr. Stewart on Monday [March 19], dated at Washington—he was well and very busy as usual in his missionary pursuits; he is accompanied by Mr. [Jeremiah] Evarts, and both are strenuously endeavoring to rouse our southern brethren to action in the great cause [i.e., Christianity] which [they] themselves have so warmly espoused—. They are going to Norfolk in Va. and from there commence their return north, through the principal places, stopping only long enough to form associations, & this route will take my husband 200 miles farther south than he expected [causing a further delay in Stewart's return].[3]

Nearly two years later, on December 19, 1828, Harriet Stewart wrote to an unnamed friend—presumably Olivia again—about her growing son.

Charles goes regularly to school and is learning pretty fast— these little creatures are a great solace to me in the absence of their father, and afford me constant employment for mind & body—.[4]

These "little creatures" now included infant daughter Martha, born in 1828, the third and last child born to Harriet and Rev. Charles Stewart.[5]

Betsey Stockton's continued childcare and nursing skills for her beloved mission family was critical at this time, as Rev. Charles Stewart had become an international advocate of the mission cause through his prolific published writings.

Following his monthslong tour through prominent Presbyterian churches in the south, Rev. Charles Stewart decided to serve as a minister of God in a different capacity. In 1829, he enlisted as a naval chaplain on the US ship *Guerriere*, out of Hampton Roads, Virginia. On February 10, 1829, he wrote to Harriet:

Letters from Washington will have appraised you, dear H_____, of my departure from that city on the 25th ult [January]. I arrived in Norfolk by the way of Baltimore on the 29th, and joined this ship on the 30th . . . . *The Guerriere* is a frigate of the first class, and having yourself been a passenger on board a man of war of the same force, a particular description of her is unnecessary. Her size, model, and whole external appearance, as she sits proudly on the water, are so much those of H.B.M. ship *Blonde*, that were you rowing alongside, her dark hull and

3. H. Stewart, "Letter to My Very Dear Friend."
4. H. Stewart, "Letter to Unnamed Recipient."
5. H. Stewart, "Letter to Unnamed Recipient."

heavy batteries below, and lofty masts with light spars tapering graceful to the sky above, would appear the same.[6]

Stewart was a man in love with God, his wife, and children, but also a man in love with ships, the sea, and sailors, whom he fondly thought of as "rough sons of the sea."[7]

To inform both his wife and future readers of his carefully edited and published travelogues, Stewart noted:

> The after cabin, handsomely fitted as a library and cabinet . . . [and near] to others, one appropriated to Andrew Armstrong, Esq., U.S. naval agent at Peru—a passenger—and the other to myself . . . . It is long since I learned to love the character of the sailor: not the vulgarity and low vice too often found under the name, but the nobler traits which belong more distinctively to him than to any other order of men. I mean the warm heart and generous soul, the clan-like tie which leads him to hail every round jacket and tarpaulin hat, as it they were the features of a brother . . . . . [In the age of sail,] there are none to whom the world stands more indebted—none to whom every class of society are under stronger obligations of good will [an avowal of Christian humanism]. . . . I have already ascertained that two or three of our crew are professedly and decidedly religious.[8]

His published letter closed with the wish "Let your prayers, dear H____, be with me in this behalf, and let all who love me pray not only for my own safety and prosperity, but for the rich gift of the spirit of grace upon our ship, and the crew with which I sail."[9]

For Betsey Stockton as well as Harriet Stewart, Rev. Charles Stewart's decision to enlist as a chaplain must have come as personal blow, as they surely missed the steadiness of his care, his companionship, and his sustaining Christian spirit during their voyages around the known world.

The four years of 1826 to 1830 were years of transitions for them all. Stockton left Harriet Stewart's bedside in 1828 to realize—very briefly, perhaps very reluctantly—the next two chapters of her own teaching in Philadelphia and Canada.

She was to fulfill her stated ambition to become the principal and teacher in a Philadelphia "infant school for colored children," wrote her adopted

6. C. Samuel Stewart, *Visit*, 16, 17.

7. C. Samuel Stewart, *Private Journal*, 68.

8. C. Samuel Stewart, *Visit*, 15, 16, 19.

9. C. Samuel Stewart, *Visit*, 20.

son, Charles Seaforth Stewart, in 1899.[10] Unidentified sources erroneosly wrote of this school as an infant African American school for boys only. But it was not just for boys. For it was the innovative institution the School for Coloured Infants at No. 60 Gaskill Street, Philadelphia. There Stockton was to become the principal and teacher, filling a position recommended by her faithful advocate and surrogate father, Ashbel Green.

Harriet Stewart died on September 6, 1830, in Cooperstown, a young mother of three, at thirty-two years old.[11] With their mother in the grave and their father somewhere on the high seas, Betsey became both surrogate mother and father to Charlie, Hattie, and Martha Stewart in Princeton. In 1833, she enrolled Charlie in the Edgehill School for Boys. Prophetically, the role of single motherhood—and of a working professional—was one that Stockton embraced throughout her lifetime.

Decades later, in 1870, Rev. Charles Stewart's obituary revealed the secretive abduction of his missionary bride.

> So dreaded was the anticipated trial of the farewell on leaving her sister and aged mother for a lifetime among the savages, that Mr. Stewart arranged to spare them the parting agony by taking [Harriet] her out, apparently for a [carriage] drive, from which she never returned, until after some two years of missionary life, she was brought home on a sick bed, to die.[12]

These published words bared the soul of Rev. Charles S. Stewart, minister, College of New Jersey graduate, and internationally acclaimed travelogue writer. The obituary author thus allowed readers a window into the complexity of the marriage of this handsome and vital scholar-missionary of the Romantic Age and his gentle patrician wife, Harriet Bradford Tiffany Stewart.

10. C. Seaforth Stewart, "Letter to Martha A. Chamberlain."
11. Judd, et al. *Missionary Album*, 185.
12. Judd et al., *Missionary Album*, 185.

Chapter 8: "When We Set Forward Wilderspin, We Set Back Fagin"

"When we set forward Wilderspin, we set back Fagin."
—Betsey Stockton's school at No. 60 Gaskill Street, Philadelphia[1]

"COLOURED INFANT SCHOOL": "It is with much pleasure that the infant school for Coloured Children has been opened in Philadelphia under the patronage of the Infant School Society of that City."[2]

BETSEY STOCKTON AND THE Stewarts arrived in the United States in August 1826 from London. They had departed from Honolulu, Hawaii, almost eleven months earlier. Once in the United States, Stockton's energies and abilities were torn between nurturing invalid Harriet Stewart in Cooperstown, New York, and accepting Rev. Ashbel Green's recommendation for Stockton's professional life. A principalship and teaching position at a new school in Philadelphia was in the offing.

Upon arrival, the brilliant and tireless Rev. Charles Stewart immediately accepted a missionary call from the American Board of Commissioners for Foreign Missions, now internationally recognized, to participate in a tour of influential Presbyterian churches in the American South. Some of these churches were deeply connected with the institution of slavery.

In November 1829, Stewart returned to the sea as naval chaplain on the United States war sloop *Guerriere*, then was reassigned from July 1829 to July 1830 to the *Vincennes*. Stewart's American tour of churches and his work for the US Navy placed Stockton squarely in the roles of nurse for his wife Harriet and surrogate mother of the Stewarts' two very young—soon to be three—children.

By 1827, and a world away from the exotic customs of the Sandwich Islands, the Industrial Revolution had created dire socioeconomic problems on both sides of the Atlantic. Children of the urban poor—both Black and white—were the hardest-hit victims of these changes. Through the newly

---

1. McCann and Young, *Samuel Wilderspin*, n.p.
2. Russwurm, ed, *Freedom's Journal*, May 9, 1828.

instituted factory system, both parents spent long hours as wage earners outside the household. By necessity, they daily abandoned their offspring to perilous neighborhood streets during working hours. Urban children faced a triple threat: serious physical injury, kidnapping, and illiteracy. These conditions alarmed conscientious citizens because they threatened the structure of one of the most cherished social institutions: the family.

In addition to these socioeconomic changes, slavery continued to limit freedom and opportunities, even in the northern states, for newly free African Americans. Slave laws were a veritable briar patch of inconsistencies across the United States. The peculiar institution however, was undeniably strengthened by decades of withholding basic literacy from African Americans. "Education and Slavery are Incompatible with each other," trumpeted Frederick Douglass.[3]

In 1799, New York State had adapted a gradual abolition law; after that date, children born to slave mothers were free but were required to work for the mother's master into their late twenties. Existing slaves kept their status. Also according to this law, all chattel slavery was to end on July 4, 1827.[4]

That same year found the first solely owned and edited African American newspaper. *Freedom's Journal* could be found on newsstands and by subscription in New York City. "Devoted to the Improvement of the Coloured Population" read its masthead. One of its editors, John Brown Russwurm, a man of color, was to become an important link in the network of individuals supporting Betsey Stockton's school in Philadelphia.

In Pennsylvania, an 1808 emancipation law meant that children born to a woman held in slavery after that year were born free.[5] By the 1820s, the city of Philadelphia, lying north of the Mason-Dixon Line, was a magnet for growing communities of self-supporting—and self-protecting—free African Americans and fugitive slaves. Manumission societies, stations on the Underground Railroad, and Quaker ideals made the City of Brotherly Love a node of qualified safety, where free African Americans could work and plan for a more prosperous life.

Some women, men, or children in Philadelphia had been freed by their masters through written or spoken—voluntary—manumission. Other former slaves had been freed through their own petitions to courts, and some had fled the more restrictive 1804 New Jersey emancipation law. As a case in point, Betsey Stockton had been freed by verbal manumission in 1816. Elizabeth Stockton Green, long deceased, and husband Rev. Ashbel Green

---

3. Douglass, cited in Blight, *Frederick Douglass*, 35.
4. Wikipedia, "Slavery in New York."
5. Diemer, *Encyclopedia of Greater Philadelphia*.

had been her original owners. Now, by their previous agreement, Betsey Stockton was freed from slavery, baptized, and joined the First Presbyterian Church of Princeton, as documented by Green himself.[6]

Leaders in American cities responded to the need for child safety by creating new institutions of education. In the early decades of the nineteenth century, infant schools were established to educate the youngest and poorest urban children, both Black and White. This system seemed to be a solution to the immediate social crisis of urban children's physical safety. Initially, these schools were held in rooms or houses outside of the child's home; the earliest schools could not afford an entire school building.

In Philadelphia, wealthy men such as Swedenborgian minister Rev. Maskill Carll, Quaker Robert Vaux, and Irish Catholic Mathew Carey were strong supporters of the plan.[7]

However, the real force for educational change came from prominent women, single and married, in several northern cities. In the 1820s and 1830s, dedicated women flexed their public muscle, formed Infant School Societies, and quickly opened local charity schools in Boston, New York City, and Philadelphia. All told, these societies started sixty schools across America.

These bluestockings created and ran charity schools, stepping out of confining arenas of hearth and home. Their actions were augmented by the Dorcas Association (formerly the Fragment Association of African American women) who posted their constitution in Russwurm's newspaper, *Freedom's Journal*, in 1828. These sisters clothed and shod needy African American children, readying the children for school attendance. Like author Mary Wollstonecraft in England, these women, Black and White, exhibited the quality known as agency, a self-conscious empowerment that leads to community betterment.[8]

In the case of Betsey Stockton's future school, by January 1828, the Infant School Society of Philadelphia was the force behind the planning, execution, and sustenance of "The Infant School for the Coloured." From the start, it was to be a separate, segregated school under an umbrella that included several similar schools for White children. The business of the colored school was to be entirely entrusted to a committee of eight: Mrs. Susanna Latimer, Mrs. Acron, Miss Kittera, Miss Sparhawk, Miss Eagles, Miss Amelia Davidson, Mrs. Robert Vaux, and Mrs. Pearsall.

This committee of eight had done their homework. The women's letters of request for information about this new teaching method—used at

---

6. J. Jones, *Life of Ashbel Green*, 326.

7. Beatty, *Preschool Education*, 26.

8. "Agency," in Brown, *New Oxford Shorter*, 1:40.

the Infant School—were aided by Philadelphia philanthropist Rev. Maskill Carll. A year earlier, in 1827, having recently visited such institutions in England, Carll reported in person about his London observations to the women members of the Philadelphia Infant School Society:

> The practical utility and importance of Infant Schools, as es-
> tablished in England are suited to the circumstances of this
> community [incomplete sentence] .... Whereas no public insti-
> tution exists in Philadelphia for instruction of the poor children
> . . . and whereas the constant labor required of poor parents
> for the maintenance of their families . . . the greatest benefits
> have been found to arise in London and other places for the
> establishment of schools for the care and instruction of infant
> children .... Encouraged by the knowledge and successful la-
> bour of many benevolent persons abroad [who] have associated
> for the purpose of establishing an institution to be called, "The
> Infant School Society of Philadelphia [incomplete sentence]."[9]

What school had Carll visited in London? Almost certainly he had vis-ited the prototype infant school at Quaker Street, Spitalfields. It was situated in East London's most squalid neighborhood, between Commercial High Street and Brick Lane.

By July 1820, Samuel Wilderspin, a self-described London Cockney, was the founder and first teacher of the Quaker Street Infant School. Its mis-sion was to shelter and to teach children from eighteen-months to six years old, just as reported by Carll. The school was purposely founded among the most savage conditions of squalor, crime, and illiteracy in Spitalfields, East London. This ghetto-like pocket was the habitat of French Huguenot im-migrants employed in the silk weaving industry. Several families crammed into each steamy tenement house, where attic looms operated day and night. As the progeny of two working parents, children faced the hazards exposed by Charles Dickens in *The Adventures of Oliver Twist*, Dickens's most sav-age indictment of England's social system. By introducing the memorable characters of Fagin, the Artful Dodger, and the gang of kidnappers, Dickens portrayed the daily realities of urban childhood in neighborhoods of urban squalor such as Spitalfields's notoriously lethal lanes.

To combat such conditions, Wilderspin became the principal interna-tional proselytizer for the infant school method. Many critics were not per-suaded that infants as young as eighteen months old could really learn any useful knowledge. Others wrote that Wilderspin confused instruction with education. Still others poked fun at his efforts, such as the 1843 caricature

---

9. Carll, as cited in Beatty, *Preschool Education*, 26.

drawing "Baby-Lonian University" by English artist George Cruikshank. This
pen and ink lampoon depicts a baby professor seated on a dais, capped and
gowned, who lectures to many tiny scholars. Quotations from Thucydides to
Newton spout from the mouths of gibbering infants.[10]

What the blueprint for Wilderspin's educational philosophy *did*
emphasize was oral recitation, group singing, planned lessons, and daily
outdoor exercise in his newly imagined necessity: the school's playground,
contiguous to the building itself. In 1820, in East London and other center-
city locations, the radical idea of the daily use of dedicated space for urban
children to play, protected from predatory adults and other children, was
precisely the drawing card that Wilderspin's new school demanded. To
make sure his readers understood the importance of a playground for
each school, he included engravings of a school playground in many of
his published works.

Infant schools' interactive lessons also drew on the entertainment
value for very young children. Under Wilderspin's plan, school rooms
were to be fitted with specific educational equipment, including a "gallery"
where the youngest eighteen-month-old "scholars" could sit and observe
their three- to five-year-old compatriots, answering fact questions in unison, while marching around the spacious classroom, grouped in twos and
fours. In addition to this, number grids and animal picture cards were
used to stimulate math facts as well as vocabulary for primary reading.
Large color lithographed plates of animals were set on easels, educating
and entertaining many children at once. Teacher-posed questions about
the visual materials were then answered through oral recitation by selected groups of students.[11]

Ashbel Green writes a letter of recommendation

The committee of eight of the Philadelphia Infant School for Coloured Children needed a teacher who could use these imported methods of instruction. Could London's experimental mode of instruction successfully cross
the Atlantic?

Ever vigilant for the continued success of surrogate daughter Betsey
Stockton, Ashbel Green emerged to shape another of the pivotal events
of her life. Between 1825 and 1828, Green had evolved from being the
publisher of her writing—her whaleship "Journal"—to becoming her primary advocate for a paid teaching position. He gave his nod to Stockton's

10. McCann and Young, *Samuel Wilderspin*, 146.

11. McCann and Young, *Samuel Wilderspin*, 20–24.

potential employers in Philadelphia, possibly through correspondence, now lost, between them.

Correspondence came from that employer to Betsey Stockton on February 18, 1828, from Philadelphia's Coloured School's Committee of Eight. It must have been a red-letter day for her, marking the acknowledgment of her teaching prowess.

Their two holograph letters to Stockton urged her to join them as the school's first principal and teacher at the infant school. Amelia Davidson, the Corresponding Secretary, wrote:

> The committee for the establishment of a coloured school in this city, were gratified to learn through Dr. Green that you are willing to accept the situation of principal of that institution . . . . They wish you to consider yourself engaged to be their teacher.[12]

The women's enthusiasm for the school permeates the handwritten page in their second letter to Stockton on April 1, 1828: "The Committee . . . [has] great pleasure to announce . . . that funds sufficient to enable them to commence the school have been collected."[13] In Philadelphia, the free African American community supported the idea of this school, even before it opened its doors. The school's Record Book noted that in March 1828, "coloured persons" subscribed to half of the 234 dollars, "monies received for the coloured school."[14]

With difficulty, the school's committee had located and rented a "large and airy" school room,[15] to open on the first of May 1828 at No. 60 Gaskill Street, between 3rd and 4th Streets. Safety was among the committee's concerns, and other neighborhoods, such as Vine Street, were considered simply too dangerous for young children.

Stockton Observes Joanna Bethune in NYC

With the school's location set, the committee wrote to Betsey Stockton:

> It is important that you should be here [in Philadelphia] a week or ten days before that time, in order to attend at our present school, and obtain a complete knowledge of the mode of instruction, and also desire that you spend a day or two in N[ew] York, to visit

---

12. Davidson, "Letter to Betsey Stockton."
13. Infant School Society of Philadelphia, "Letterbook," unpaginated.
14. Infant School Society of Philadelphia, "Record Book," 40.
15. Davidson, "Letter to Betsey Stockton."

the schools there, and ascertain whether any improvements have been made upon the system generally adopted.[16]

Wilderspin's infant school system had crossed the Atlantic. In Philadelphia, the committee wanted their own African American scholars to adhere to the methods and materials suggested by Wilderspin in London.

With apologies, they reconsidered their initial offer of $300 annually to Betsey Stockton. Instead, they offered Stockton $200 per year, "with the proviso that [her] salary could be increased as the school grew . . . in favor with the public." In a postscript, Amelia Davidson noted that the two letters to Stockton had been "directed to Cooperstown [NY] where Betsey Stockton was then living with Mrs. Stewart. She arrived in Philadelphia April 21."[17]

Through earlier correspondence, the Philadelphia committee knew just where to send their newly hired teacher to spend a day or two observing New York City's infant schools. Traveling to New York City, Betsey Stockton met the brilliant powerhouse Joanna Bethune, a mature fifty-year-old Scottish woman and a social activist, known for previously having founded an orphans' asylum (with Mrs. Alexander Hamilton), Sunday schools, and a Society for the Promotion of Industry among the Poor in New York City.

The master teacher whom thirty-three-year-old Betsey Stockton met and observed was an extremely religious fifty-seven-year-old visionary whose "greatest delight was in edcation of the young."[18] Bethune had been taught by a Scottish teacher of rhetoric "in the knowledge of the art of speech and gesture, which made herself the best teacher of elocution," wrote Rev. George Bethune, her son and biographer.[19] His mother's handwriting was "of a peculiarly bold, free" style, he added.

With an eye toward the future and the young, infant schools soon became Bethune's chief concern. Her first infant school had opened the previous year in 1827, probably in the basement of the Canal Street Presbyterian Church. As she had noted: "July 15, 1827 . . . . Tomorrow I begin the first infant school."[20]

Both Philadelphia's school committee and Bethune wanted the authentic teaching materials from London; they sent abroad for the books written by Wilderspin. They sought the teaching plan and understanding of it for themselves. Bethune was one of the first successful American practitioners

16. Second letter of committee to Betsey Stockton, Apr. 2, 1828, in Infant School Society of Philadelphia, "Letterbook," unpaginated.

17. Davidson, "Letter to Betsey Stockton."

18. Bethune, *Memoirs*, 122.

19. Bethune, *Memoirs*, 183.

20. Bethune, *Memoirs*, 168.

of Wilderspin's infant school system. "It is not surprising . . . that the infant-school system as organized by Wilderspin on the basis of Swiss educational philosopher Johann Pestalozzi's plan of development should have deeply interested her," wrote George Bethune in his memoirs of his famous mother.[21]

About two months after Bethune had opened the first free infant school, the society had at least nine such schools in New York, with over 180 scholars, all of which she superintended and one of which, at the Five Points location, she taught herself. Five Points was the Manhattan equivalent of the savage conditions of poverty, squalor, and crime of London's Spitalfields. A true Christian woman, Bethune wrote in February 1831:

> Blessed by God that He has put it into the hearts of some of His servants to make the attempt to reclaim the moral waste at the FIVE POINTS . . . . [Hear] the prayers put up by Thy servants for the wretched inhabitants . . . . Publicans and harlots go into the kingdom, when God has purposed of mercy toward them, before many proud professors and formal hypocrites.[22]

Did Betsey Stockton chance a personal visit to the crime-infested Five Points in Manhattan? Given Stockton's extraordinary common sense and her narrow escapes from personal danger and death in her recent past—probably not. As a young, presumably unaccompanied mulatta woman, she probably deemed it too dangerous to visit Bethune's school there. More likely she chose to visit another school, the First Infant School in Green Street, New York, as documented by two interior views of its school room. This location for Bethune's first school would have been far safer for Stockton to fulfill her recommended visit to observe Bethune.[23]

During that visit to New York City, Stockton learned the refinements of speech, gesture, and handwriting from a master teacher, adding to Stockton's own unique teaching expertise at Lahaina. Afterwards, the Committee for the Coloured School also wanted to possess a set of Bethune's specific teaching *tools*—colored lithographs—sent from England for that purpose and known to be in New York City.

On June 11, 1827, a year before Stockton's visit to Bethune, the society's Record Book noted:

> Resolved: That a letter be immediately addressed to Mrs. Divie Bethune of New York, for such information as she can offer respecting articles used in teaching and if satisfactory information

21. Bethune, *Memoirs*, 122.
22. Bethune, *Memoirs*, 183.
23. Smylie, *American Presbyterians*, 61; Jackson, *Encyclopedia of New York City*, 106.

is not obtained, a correspondence on this subject shall be opened with Mr. Wilderspin in England. It is understood [that she], has imported a complete set [of plates] from England, from which it is probable copies could be procured for the Philadelphia School, in a short time and at a small cost.[24]

It is unclear whether or not Joanna Bethune responded to their plea for copies of her lithographs—ones which Betsey Stockton surely saw in use in Bethune's New York City school. But another way to receive their lithographic prints for their school presented itself.

Enter John Brown Russwurm

Scanning any news of the whereabouts of the desired set of imported lithographs, the Philadelphia committee responded to a March 28, 1828, advertisement in *Freedom's Journal*.[25]

John Brown Russwurm, the newspaper's editor, was born in Jamaica in 1799, the son of a White plantation owner, Russwurm, and an unnamed Black slave. As a young child, he was almost hidden in a boarding school in Quebec in 1807 by his father. He was later sent to Hebron Academy in Maine, graduating in 1819 as John Brown. His stepmother urged the elder Russwurm to acknowledge his son and grant him the surname of Russwurm. After graduation from Hebron, John Brown Russwurm moved to Boston, where he taught at Primus Hall, a school for African American children. He became Bowdoin College's first graduate of color in 1826, where he joined a literary society whose president was Nathaniel Hawthorne. As an editor and activist in New York City, he was in a position to help the embryo Philadelphia Infant School, a place where members of his race would be taught in a safe setting.

On April 1, 1828, within a few days of seeing the ad and barely one month before the Philadelphia school was to open, corresponding secretary of the society Amelia Davidson wrote to Russwurm:

> Mr. Russwurm: Sir: In consequence of a communication in your paper of the 28th ultimo, respecting some Lithographic engravings, sent from England for the use of a coloured Infants' School, I have been directed to make an application to you for

---

24. Infant School Society of Philadelphia, "Record Book," 13, 14.

25. Russwurm, ed., *Freedom's Journal*, Mar. 28, 1828.

the same, and to state the circumstances of the Society here [in Philadelphia].[26]

Davidson reviewed the current status of Philadelphia's Coloured School with Russwurm, giving a brief account of its progress to date. Next, she requested the set of lithographs known to be at his newspaper office in New York City, possibly sent through Londoner slave trade activist William Wilberforce, with whom Russwurm corresponded and who was a known supporter of the infant school movement.[27] Davidson continued: "A suitable room [for the school] has been procured and a pious and well-informed female, with whom they have every reason to believe qualified for the undertaking is engaged as a teacher."[28]

Betsey Stockton was the "pious and well-informed female" now known to John Brown Russwurm by reference. She had arrived in Philadelphia on April 21, directly after her mandatory visit to Joanna Bethune in New York City, having personally observed in action the highly touted infant system of education of Wilderspin.

The committee of eight women did not have long to wait for Russwurm's reply. By April 28, Amelia Davidson responded to Russwurm: "Your letter was duly received, and I must present to you the thanks of the Committee on the very pretty Lithographs, which arrived safely and were handed to me on Friday morning last." She concluded her letter with a warm invitation for Russwurm to visit the school, grateful for his previous help. "Should your expectation of visiting this city be realized, we hope you will do us the favor to call at the school, No. 60 Gaskill St. and have no doubt you will be much gratified."[29]

A few days later, on May 1, the set of lithographs in hand, Stockton opened her Philadelphia school at No. 60 Gaskill Street, with forty-five scholars attending.

> The School room has been fitted up, at very small expense, almost all of the required expenses, except lumber, having been obtained as donation, and all the work having been done gratuitously by coloured persons. Betsey Stockton arrived in the city on the 21st of April after having visited the Infant School at New York as requested by the Committee. The salary is $200—per annum to commence at the time of her leaving the service of Mrs. Stewart, on or at the 1st of May. If the latter, the Committee

26. Davidson, "Letter to John Brown Russwurm," Apr. 1, 1828.
27. Bacon, *Freedom's Journal*, 233.
28. Davidson, "Letter to John Brown Russworm," Apr. 24–28, 1828.
29. Davidson, "Letter to John Brown Russworm," Apr. 24–28, 1828.

5

[will] defray expenses of her journey from Cooperstown. Rebecca Call, a coloured girl, nineteen years of age and having been recommended by the teacher of the Public Female Coloured School has been engaged as Assistant for three months at the rate $100 per annum. The Lithographic pictures for which application was made to the Editor of the *Freedom's Journal* were received on 25th April—they consist of 10 engravings of animals, and are accompanied by explanatory sheets.[30]

As the school's first principal and head teacher, Betsey Stockton's progress was swift and sure.

The committee for the Coloured School, report that since the opening of the school on the 1st of May twenty-nine children have been admitted into the school. It was not be expected that in the short space of one month any material change could be affected in the manners and habits of children, ignorant and uneducated . . . . Your committee however have the satisfaction of being able to state that the improvement of the children, in every respect, equals the most sanguine expectations. They have become now more cleanly in their persons, more regular in their attendance, and more attentive in their exercises. Many can already repeat hymns and the other lessons, and interesting accounts have been received of the attachment of some to the school. A Sabbath School has been opened and is regularly taught—about two hours previous to the public worship—morning and afternoon. It is attended by many of the Infant School scholars, their brothers and sisters and others. The principal Betsey Stockton has not disappointed the expectations of the committee. Active, energetic, and intelligent, she appears well calculated for all the situations in which she is placed. Considering her capability and the trying nature of her duties, your committee have thought proper to increase her salary to $250 per annum, commencing from the 1st of June. Therefore your committee have every reason to rejoice in the blessings of these efforts, and should this perseverance and zeal equal the importance of the undertaking, cannot doubt that a blessing attend it, and that the aide necessary for a continuance of the work will not be withheld.[31]

Stockton had triumphed, her teaching practices were acknowledged, and her salary was raised.

30. Davidson, "Letter to John Brown Russworm," Apr. 24–28, 1828.
31. Infant School Society of Philadelphia, "Record Book," 45–47.

In July 1828, Betsey Stockton's initial successes were memories as the Philadelphia summer swept into the lives of teacher and students at Gaskill Street. Without running water or indoor sanitation, crowded with the average attendance of between eighty and ninety, contagion was inevitable. Despite the school's requirement of "certificates of freedom from whooping cough, measles or any contagious disease," certified by the school's Dr. Walton, measles broke out among the "little learners." Deaths from disease were reported as "another infant was carried off from time to eternity."[32]

Stockton herself was sick during July 1828. "In consequence of Betsey Stockton's indisposition, the improvement of the pupils has not been as rapid during the last month as has been anticipated." What happened next at the school underlined Betsey Stockton's and Rebecca Call's skills and could be considered humorous, if you were not the substitute teacher:

> Some members of the committee endeavored to supply her place, by attending alternately, and instructing the children, but their exertions effected but little. At the end of a week, the brother of Rebecca Call, the assistant died, and being thus deprived of her services also, the committee thought it most efficient to dismiss the school until the teachers should be able to resume their duties.[33]

In addition to her teaching duties, Principal Stockton dealt with the solicitation for a coal stove to warm the classroom and for cast-off clothing—almost certainly shoes as well—to enable children to come to school. She must have overseen the proscribed cutting of children's hair as a health measure, perhaps performed by her assistant teacher, Rebecca Call.

Her scholars numbered one hundred by the time of the Quarterly Examination in December 1828. "The Committee for Coloured School report that the school continues to flourish," as some of the members had "visited among the children."[34]

After only one year, in May 1829, with the school attendance averaging over one hundred, "the Committee reported that Betsey Stockton has left the school for a few months to establish schools in the wilds of Canada and that they have engaged Mrs. Williams to supply the place during her absence."[35]

This was a two-month hiatus from the Gaskill Street school, during which Betsey Stockton travelled along the Erie/Barge Canal to Grape Island

32. "Rules for Attendance," Sept. 4, 1827, in Infant School Society of Philadelphia, "Record Book," 19.

33. Infant School Society of Philadelphia, "Record Book," 53.

34. Infant School Society of Philadelphia, "Record Book," 57.

35. Infant School Society of Philadelphia, "Record Book," 72–74.

Mission with Methodist missionaries. There she taught Ojibwa children before returning to Cooperstown.

In September 1829, the school's record book noted: "B Stockton was to return [from the wilds of Canada] to her charge on the first [of September]."[36] In October,

> the committee approving of Mrs. Williams and Miss Stockton as teachers, it was resolved to sanction the engagement with Mrs. Williams and also to engage Miss Stockton with the provision that if at anytime they should think proper to leave the service of the society, they must give three months notice of their intention.[37]

By this time, "the school [was] in good order and great improvement observable in several branches."[38] In December, the attendance, reaching one hundred and forty children, was so stable that the organizers of the school resolved that "three cents a week or twenty-five cents quarterly, be exacted from the children in all the schools, whenever they are able to pay, etc." It was followed by the resolution "that by way of experiment the teachers be requested to devote every afternoon of the present month to instruction in reading."[39] And, just to inform any visitors to the school of the moral tenor of the place, it was resolved "that a card be put up in each school with these words—'NO *whipping or shaking permitted in this school*.'"[40]

Civic-minded citizens of Philadelphians were again taking notice of the progress of the colored school and coming to its aid financially. For example, "one hundred books [were] received from Mr. [Caspar] Wistar [and are] to be sold for the benefit of the schools [and are] appropriated to the coloured school."[41] Wistar, one of Philadelphia's first citizens, a rich physician and publisher, recognized the value of Stockton's school because of its organization and excellence for teaching the city's African American children.

By November 1830, several infant schools for colored children had been established in Philadelphia. A "set of rules for the government of the schools" allows readers a view into the functioning of one of Wilderspin's American schools:

36. Infant School Society of Philadelphia, "Record Book," 81.
37. Infant School Society of Philadelphia, "Record Book," 81.
38. Infant School Society of Philadelphia, "Record Book," 93.
39. Infant School Society of Philadelphia, "Record Book," 95.
40. Infant School Society of Philadelphia, "Record Book," 95.
41. Infant School Society of Philadelphia, "Record Book," 97.

At 8:30, teachers arrived at the schools.

By 9:00, teaching of "scholars commenced." Prayers and religious exercises followed for half an hour.

Next, spelling, reading, and instruction of the alphabet class continued for one hour.

Then, direct instruction was broken up with marching and playing, separately, for half an hour.

From eleven to twelve o'clock, arithmetic, geography, natural history, and Scripture lessons, with particular attention to religious instruction on Mondays and Saturdays.

Displays and singing at twelve o'clock.

Assemble at two o'clock. Miscellaneous lessons for one hour.

March and play separately for half an hour. Lessons at the teacher's discretion for the remainder of the afternoon, only every child in the school must say a lesson once a day to one of the teachers.

Dismiss with short prayer at half past four in the winter and five in the summer.

Finally, "the teacher must in rotation remain with the children between school hours until they are called for in the afternoon,"[42]

presumably between morning and afternoon classes.

Additional rules for the several schools now included the statement that "one of the teachers must be at the school at eight in the summer, commencing with the 1st of April and at half past eight in the winter, Monday and Thursday [for] particular religious instruction."[43]

As of July 1831, school number three, location unclear, responded with 102 attending, and the "School in good order. They appear delighted with the new method of instruction in circular classes, additional pupils are received, almost every week."[44]

In summary, this very detailed chapter revealed Betsey Stockton's extraordinary role as first principal and first main teacher for the Infant School for the Coloured at No. 60 Gaskill Street, Philadelphia, in 1828 and beyond. Her grasp of the new and recommended teaching method exemplified by specialized teaching equipment and staging of the classroom

42. "Schedule," November 1830, in Infant School Society of Philadelphia, "Record Book," 117.

43. Infant School Society of Philadelphia, "Record Book," 117.

44. Infant School Society of Philadelphia, "Record Book," 117.

was a testament to her executive functioning—advanced organization skills—first shown by Stockton's written responses to lessons at Princeton Theological Seminary eight years earlier.

That a thirty-something young woman of color rallied support from Philadelphia's African American community and its wealthy elite is a second testament—this time to her vision of freedom through education. Most importantly, African Americans supported Stockton's school by their contribution of time and talent. That school was endorsed and probably visited by John Brown Russwurm, then a noted abolitionist newspaper editor, whose office acted as a conduit of information and materials between infant schools in New York City and Philadelphia in the 1820s.

In 1847, a list of schools available to Black children in Philadelphia included "Public Grammar School in Lombard Street, Abolition Society's Infant School in Lombard Street, Public Primary School in Gaskill Street of which the majority of the students came from Center City."[45]

The primary sources of Betsey Stockton's Philadelphia Infant School for Coloured Children corrected the oft-repeated—and erroneous—phrase that she taught at an "infant school for boys" in Philadelphia. Stockton's legacy of 1828 established another school for African American children on Gaskill Street and a second public school using the infant school method, before her move to Princeton, where she became the matriarch of the Witherspoon-Jackson neighborhood of free African Americans there.

The sign posted in each infant school classroom prohibiting "any whipping or shaking" in the school poses the clearest contrast to Charles Dickens's exposure and ridicule of so many schoolmasters in the early schools in England and America.

Stockton's principalship and her role as master teacher bring the reader a unique understanding of the application of Londoner Samuel Wilderspin's international system of the infant school method, influenced by Swiss educational philosopher Johann Pestalozzi. Stockton's was judged to be an excellent school, a harbinger of her later efforts to establish schools in Canada and Princeton.

In the decades of the 1830s and 1840s, other schools in America and England were imagined and organized. They followed the decline of the infant school movement in the United States and elsewhere, supplanted by other educational schemes.[46] One of these ideas, called the Ragged School Movement in London, was seen very clearly as a vehicle for salvaging individual children's lives, as well as an alternative to increasing societal costs of inmates of prisons, of populations in poorhouses, of "Ignorance

45. Society of Friends, *Statistical Inquiry*, 19.
46. Society of Friends, *Statistical Inquiry*, 19.

and Want" personified, as Charles Dickens wrote in his December 1843 *Christmas Carol*.

As with so many early schools, the London ragged schools met with uneven success. The educational and social needs of urban children, of chil- dre living in one of the most densely populated cities in the world, would require decades before schools met those needs.[47] Still, the Ragged School Museum at 46–50 Copperfield Road, Mile End, London, exhibits the ex- pected classroom equipment of a chalkboard and desks in wooden rows, for teaching repetitive, mind-numbing lessons.

The Field Lane Ragged School was a very different setting—the first floor of a dilapidated house among the alleys of Saffron Hill, London—than what Wilderspin had envisioned. Dickens visited it at the request of a friend. He found the children there were steeped in profound ignorance and perfect barbarism, "a sickening atmosphere, in the midst of the taint and dirt and all the pestilence: with all the deadly sins let loose, howling and shrieking at the doors." He commented to a friend, "I have very rarely seen in all the strange and dreadful things I have seen in London and elsewhere, anything so shock- ing as the dire neglect of soul and body exhibited in these children." Angered though he was at the plight of these children at the Field Lane Ragged School, Dickens remained an author, not an educational theorist.[48]

Contrast this with the infant schools that Samuel Wilderspin, Joanna Bethune, or Betsey Stockton sought and used as airy and spacious class- rooms, there to teach the youngest, poorest, and least literate of children in the urban settings of Quaker Street, Green Street, or Gaskill Street.

Although the Museum of the City of London houses some artifacts from pre-Victorian classroom settings, the model school of Samuel Wilder- spin on Quaker Street, Spitalfields, was demolished at the end of the nine- teenth century.[49] When this author walked Quaker Street and visited the museum in 2000, curators there were unsure of the actual location or of any details about Wilderspin's early school.

Betsey Stockton's warm and knowledgeable teaching style would in- deed "set forward Wilderspin and set back Fagin [the kidnapper of orphans in Charles Dickens's *Oliver Twist*]." In May 1847, as the popularity of the infant school system was fading, Dickens spoke on behalf of the system and sent "such a nice letter" to Wilderspin and three pounds, three pence" to a retirement fund for London's innovative school founder.[50]

---

47. Lascarides and Hinitz, *History of Early Childhood Education*, 80.
48. Ackroyd, *Dickens*, 404, 405, 406.
49. McCann and Young, *Samuel Wilderspin*, 284.
50. McCann and Young, *Samuel Wilderspin*, 283.

Chapter 9: **To Grape Island, Canada, and the Ojibwa School, Summer 1829**

Clues to the Mission

BETSEY STOCKTON'S FLEETING PRESENCE in Grape Island, Canada, was materialized in Charles Seaforth Stewart's letter of October 1899. Stewart wrote to a relative:

> Betsey after her return [from the Sandwich Islands] was sent to Canada to establish a school or schools among indians [lowercase in original] there. On the way back in the summer or autumn of 1829 . . . she stopped to see us bringing me a birch bark canoe some 3 or 4 feet long.[1]

Seriously ill mother Harriet had been joined by Charles, Hattie, and Martha at New Haven, Connecticut, for a year's stay. Stockton visited them there, bearing the souvenir miniature canoe. The lovely image of Stockton's joyful reunion with her missionary family belies the certain hardships of her journeys to and from the Canadian wilderness. But Stewart's letter, written exactly seventy years after the visit, was an important source of Stockton's whereabouts during her hiatus from Philadelphia to Princeton. It was a starting point for reconnecting the dots about Stockton's missionary work in Canada and the history of the Grape Island mission itself.

That Stockton was sent emphasizes her role as a Christian emissary for an extant arm of the church. Which one—and why Stockton? Who paid her expense? Why did she leave the now renowned Philadelphia "Infant School for the Coloured" at Gaskill Street, where she had proved herself so invaluable, to teach Indians in the wilds of Canada? Clearly a Christian calling rallied Stockton to her wildest—and most challenging—teaching post. Specifically, Stockton's teaching expertise using the Wilderspin/Pestalozzi method recommended her as a uniquely qualified teacher at the Methodist mission of Ojibwa children at Grape Island in 1829. Being a woman of color

---

1. C. Seaforth Stewart, "Letter to Martha Chamberlain."

and a linguist were other reasons Stockton was called by noted missionaries to teach at the mission school there.

In the late 1820s, two Methodist missionaries, Massachusetts native Rev. William Case (1780–1855) and Rev. Peter Jones (1802–1856) led performances of their conversions in the persons of Ojibwa youths who spoke, read, and sang Bible verses or hymns in English and Ojibwa. Jones, whose Ojibwa name meant Sacred Waving Feathers, was the son of an Ojibwa mother, Tuhbenahneequay, and a Welsh surveyor father, Augustus Jones. As he was both bilingual and bicultural, Case knew that his friend Jones could be a living bridge to North American Methodists on their spring 1829 fundraising and proselytizing tour. They traveled through Boston, Newport, Baltimore, New York, and Philadelphia. Both these men belonged to the cadre of Christian emissaries of the Methodist-Episcopal church on both sides of the Canadian border.

During 1828 and 1829, Jones had also begun to translate, print, and publish hymnbooks and Scripture in Ojibwa and English. In the early 1800s, Case and Jones's missionary work among indigenous peoples in Canada was published in *The Christian Advocate and Zion's Herald* in New York City, an arm of the Methodist-Episcopal Church.

Case and Jones were following a pattern of offering written language acquisition to indigenous peoples through Christianity. Native leaders who asked for help to acquire languages did so to hold onto ancestral lands and to convert these lands to farms. Schools to teach bilingualism were requested by the Ojibwa as a tool to minimize cheating by Anglo fur traders. They showed their "eagerness for schools by making contributions in both money and labour," as had the African American parents at Gaskill Street.[2] Also in Case and Jones's favor was the Christian Protestant Methodists' advocacy of abstinence from alcohol. This policy made Methodist missionaries' message especially attractive to Ojibwa leaders who had witnessed the drug's debilitating effects on their indigenous population.

From the Methodists-Episcopalians, not the Presbyterians, came a rare specific reference to Betsey Stockton's teaching at Grape Island. Curtly stated:

> Paid traveling expenses etc. to Miss Stockton, who was employed to use the Pestalozzian system of instruction in the school at Grape Island 17 L, 10 s' on July 30, 1829 at the mission school.[3]

---

2. May et al., *Empire*, 165.

3. May et al., "Fifth Annual Report," as cited in May et al., in *Empire*, 163.

That Stockton was paid by the Methodist church in British currency—seventeen pounds, ten shillings—clearly not American money—is noteworthy, as they were working within the currency of the Imperial Canadian Government.

So Jones's preaching to his people in their given tongue meant ever greater acceptance of Christianity. Convergence of cultural ideas, such as the diversity shown in nature by the Great Spirit, meant that "surely such a Creator would accept more than just one religion . . . . And so we [Ojibwa] listened to the missionaries and many converts were made."[4] Human diversity and dignity were ever in the minds of such Ojibwa speakers as Rev. Peter Jones. Before leaving the city of Baltimore, Jones gave a moving "short discourse to the Africans in Sharp Street Church" and wrote in his journal "may the Gospel soon make them *free indeed*."[5]

One of Jones's converts, whose English name was Peter Jacobs, poetically recorded his first impressions of Christianity:

> I first said, "No, that is the white man's God, and white man's religion and that God would not have anything to do with the Indians" . . . . I thought God could only understand English. . . . I then met Peter Jones, who was converted a few months before me, and, to my surprise, I heard him return thanks, at meal, in Ojibwa. This was quite enough for me. I now saw that God could understand me in my Ojibwa, and therefore went into the forest and prayed, in the Ojibwa tongue.[6]

According to Jones's *Journal*, as Case and Jones entered Philadelphia on April 15, 1829, they gave exhibitions and prayer meetings at several venues. On April 16, the pair were speakers at the Philadelphia Conference of the Annual Missionary Meeting in the Philadelphia Academy. That date and place was the most likely occasion for Betsey Stockton's recruitment as a teaching missionary at the Grape Island Ojibwa mission.[7]

Alternatively, Stockton may have been approached by Case and/or Jones at other known Philadelphia venues. These included the Ebenezer Church, "Dr. Skinner's" or "Dr. Eley's" Presbyterian churches, or possibly at two Sunday Schools, locations unspecified.

By April 20, Case and Jones had left Philadelphia on a steamer for New York City, starting for their home in Canada. The night before they began

---

4. MacClean, "Positive Experiment," 35.

5. P. Jones, *Life and Journals*, 211.

6. MacClean, "Positive Experiment," 35.

7. P. Jones, *Life and Journals*, 211.

their journey, Rev. William Case was married to Miss Hetty Hubbard, "the school teacher from Grape Island."[8]

The probability is that Stockton left Philadelphia with Case and Jones at that time. Her absence from the Gaskill Street school was noted, with longing, at that time. The committee members for the colored school noted in their record book on May 4, 1829: "Committee for the Coloured School report that Betsey Stockton has left them for a few months to establish schools in the wilds of Canada."[9]

Stockton and Company Travel on the Barge Canal

During that very cold April and May journey, Stockton's traveling partnership with bilingual Jones, recruiter Case, and Hetty Hubbard Case, his school teacher bride, enabled her to learn—en route—the indigenous Ojibwa language. Jones and Case could tell her the condition of the Grape Island school. Just as Stockton had acquired the Hawaiian language from three indigenous speakers on board the whaleship *Thames*, she must have acquired at least rudimentary Ojibwa from Sacred Waving Feathers, the Rev. Peter Jones, in 1829.

Peter Jones's *Journal* offers an eyewitness account of their chilly journey. The missionary group traveled by packet boat on the Erie Canal, then called the "Barge Canal," stopping at major settlements. By May 10, they had reached Utica, where they attended the quarterly meeting of a Methodist church. By Tuesday, the group arrived at Syracuse, and on Wednesday, they left for Oswego by the "Oswego canal," a tributary of the Barge/Erie. On May 13, Jones wrote:

> Our course was northward. Packet boat traveling is pleasant but rather dangerous, on account of the numerous bridges under which [we] had to pass, at which every body, whether Yankee or European or Indian has to *bow or* have his head knocked off . . . . Our boat was drawn by two and sometimes three horses, and travelled at the rate of three or four miles per hour . . . . Arrived at the village of Oswego, on the banks of Lake Ontario at 6 P.M.[10]

The next day, May 14, the missionary party took passage on a schooner, a small sailing vessel, for the settlement of Kingston in Prince Edward

8. P. Jones, *Life and Journals*, 217.

9. Infant School Society of Philadelphia, "Record Book," 81.

10. P. Jones, *Life and Journals*, 219.

County. There they stayed the night with the editor of the *Religious Advocate and Kingston Gazette* and no doubt told him of their tour, their mission, and other news. And on Monday, May 18, the party "went on board the steam boat *Toronto* for Grape Island."[11]

Almost immediately after their monthlong northern trek, the newly arrived residents of Grape Island mission began planting corn and potatoes. But the long-term goal of the mission, teaching bilingualism to the Ojibwa to enable them to read religious texts, was the primary goal of the mission. Jones wrote, "Again visited the school and gave them some good advice." The infant school at the mission opened on June 2, 1829.[12]

Betsey Stockton Teaches at the Ojibwa School at Grape Island

What would Stockton have seen once she had arrived at the Grape Island mission? Information from the National Archives of Canada sheds light on the condition and progress at Stockton's future pioneer mission school:

> **1826. At Grape Island (Mississauga Indian Mission).**
> Grape Island and Huff's Island were leased [from the Ojibwa?] for a period of 999 years, for a sum of five shillings. Fifteen Indians signed the indenture, which was dated Belleville, October 10th, 1826. The above islands comprise some sixty-one acres, and upon Grape Island, the smaller of the two, a village was projected and constructed. The first winter many Indians camped at Grape Island, since the dwellings were not yet up . . . . The tribe numbered some 130 person, ninety of them adults . . . . A school and meetinghouse was erected in July 1827, 30 feet long by 25 feet in width. . . . The Report of the Methodist Episcopal Missionary Society of the United States for 1829 says that "Fifty children were taught in the schools." This would imply that another school was added to the mission. Lorenzo Dow [a noted divine], visiting there in 1829, writes under July 29th regarding the good conduct of the children.[13]

Based on her experienced teaching of the infant school system, Betsey Stockton helped to reorganize the existing Grape Island school. With Stockton's arrival at Grape Island, changes were made to accommodate the methods of American infant schools. The original school building was enlarged,

11. P. Jones, *Life and Journals*, 219.

12. P. Jones, *Life and Journals*, 219.

13. Eames, *Pioneer Schools*, 101–2.

... [to] measure 30 feet by 25 feet and had separate "apartments" for male and female students. A gallery was built in to one end. There is no record of a playground. The overall enrolment was about sixty children and youth: about two-thirds of all school-aged children at the mission in 1830. Of these number, 34 were reading, 25 writing, and 15 doing arithmetic, while the "smaller ones" were learning their "ABC's and spelling." Apparently, students across a wide range of ages were admitted to the school.[14]

As Stockton had taught at Gaskill Street, picture cards were used as a starting point for lessons and recitations at the Grape Island school.

> After a recess, all students were assembled in the gallery, where they were taught on the infant plan, the elements of arithmetic, geography, astronomy, geometry, English grammar, and natural and sacred history," according to John Benham, another teacher at the school.[15]

Additional equipment for the spacious school room were number frames, a world map, a globe, a blackboard, and forms with which to teach geometry.

> "We hope the plan of the infant school will do well for teaching the Indian children English, and that we shall be able to extend the influence of religion and education more generally," noted William Case.[16]

This infant school system was based on East Londoner Samuel Wilderspin's school model, which was, in turn, influenced by the teaching materials and methods of Swiss theorist Johann Pestalozzi. Remarkably, Stockton had now expanded the system's reach into the "wilds of Canada."

In July 1829, after Betsey Stockton's arrival, William Case reported in *The Christian Advocate and Zion's Herald*:

> Grape Island, Upper Canada: All our missions and schools appear to continue in a good way. The Scriptures, hymns &c. lately printed in the Indian [Ojibwa] languages in New-York, are of great value. They give a new impulse to spiritual and literary improvement, and afford the missionaries and teachers a further influence for improving the Indian congregations in civilized life. The school here, on the infant system, answers every

---

14. May et al., *Empire*, 170, 173.

15. May et al., *Empire*, 173.

16. May et al., *Empire*, 173.

expectation. We witness, with a pleasing surprise, the improvement of the children, effected in 31 days.[17]

The Christan Advocate and Zion's Herald publishes "A Survey . . ."

Possibly meant to augment William Case's July 1829 report, "A Survey of the Infant School System" was carried in the February 1830 issue of *The Christian Advocate and Zion's Herald*. It was written anonymously, but carried the byline "communicated by an experienced teacher," possibly Stockton or Joanna Bethune. The article was an in-depth examination of the Wilderspin/Pezztalozzian system, in an effort to educate the newspaper's Christian readership.

Its topicality informed and justified the newly international education system. The article supported the ongoing work of teachers in remote areas, such as Betsey Stockton, as well as urban practicitioners like Bethune, who was teaching in Five Points, a Manhattan hell-hole.

> This system in not inaptly called the system of *mental development*, as the moral physical and intellectual powers are gradually urged to unfold themselves, and every progressive step is not so much gained by the aid of the teacher, as by the mental effort of the pupil, who may, in a sense, be said to *instruct himself*, being left almost to his own resources . . . and the pupil is made to derive his knowledge by immediate feeling, or through the *senses*.

> But to proceed to a survey of this system: it may be said to comprise four general principles: first by sensible objects to communicate knowledge through the medium of our feelings; second, any subject thus presented to the mind is analyzed, and thus rendered more obvious; third, by the agreeable manner in which it is presented (amusement being blended with instruction), an excitement is produced that tends to make the mind more impressible, when every idea acquired is retained with greater strength of understanding; fourth, every lesson is made to comprise some moral point, and the suitable reflections with which each lesson is closed, leaves on the pupil's mind the fullest impressions of the utility and high purposes of this education . . . . This system . . . while it develops the mind . . . it at the same

---

17. Case and Waugh, "What Christian Missions."

time disciplines and trains the body, rendering it strong and healthy by cheerful and well regulated exercise and recreation.

In the infant schools in our own city [New York], which embrace children from eighteen months to seven years of age we may see with our eyes and hear with our ears, the demonstration of its truth [of the system's success]. We may see children at every age within these limits who are acquiring all the elements of reading writing, arithmetic, grammar, geography, natural history, astronomy &c, &c, and all of these at one and the same time, without books, and almost without effort, certainly without any painful effort, either of body or mind. Instead of enforcing silence upon their tongues, and fixity upon their limbs, both of which are odious restraints to their minds, and pernicious to their health, a noisy cheerfulness is encouraged, their tongues and limbs are kept in a playful perpetual motion, highly conclusive to health of body and vigor of mind. Their smiling countenances and sparkling eyes attest to enjoyment that they realize, and almost without knowing that they are learning any lesson whatsoever, even their innocent gambols are made subservient to the expansion of their minds, and the acquirement of the most valuable knowledge in literature, morals and religion.

It may be inquired, How is all this accomplished? We can only answer, It is by teaching the ideas rather than words, encouraging them to think rather than to talk and to study men and things rather than books. And instead of tying them to a bench, poring over a slate or a primer; they are kept in motion by marching and counter-marching, singing as they go the very lesson which they are about to learn. And their lessons are taught them by sensible objects, images, pictures and other simple and appropriate machinery, the adaptation of which to their fancy and simplicity blends amusement with instruction. It is thought this is childish, we admit it, and allege that is appropriately so. It is "becoming all things to all men," and therefore all things to all infants. The pupils are children, and not until they are men should they "put away childish things." Our fatal mistake was, we were treated in our education as men while we were children, and hence now that we are men, so many of us in knowledge are found children still. To reverse the order is to follow nature, and hence according to the dictates of reason, philosophy and religion, this system proceeds to turn things "upside down," for nothing less than a thorough and radical change in the plans of education is contemplated by the proposed reform which this system introduces to our adoption.[18]

Here was an explanation of the child-centered system for readers in a nutshell.

Grape Island's remote location and Harriet Stewart's grave illness were reasons for Stockton to reassess her calling to teach at the infant school at the Methodist mission on Grape Island, Canada. The mission on Grape Island and its school were closed in 1830, but the infant school system introduced by Betsey Stockton was "later developed by teachers at nearby Credit River and Rice Island schools."[19]

As fleeting as Stockton's presence was, a single ephemeral drawing recorded the location of the mission station on the western edge of an 1835 map of Grape Island. On a later rendition of the same map, no such mission station was drawn. It had ceased to exist.[20]

Ojibwa efforts to preserve their ancestral land, their integrity as a people, and their language in the face of increased intrusion by Whites were all supported through Methodist missionary contact, including Betsey Stockton. Biligual teachers and preachers like lifelong leader Rev. Peter Jones left a legacy of literacy and cultural stability. Eight years after Stockton's teaching at Grape Island, another bilingual tool was printed. *The Speller and Translater in Indian and English for the Use of the Mission Schools, and Such as May Desire to Obtain a Knowledge of the Objiwa Tongue* was written by James Evans, another Methodist preacher. This speller and translator was published in New York City in 1837.[21]

As Helen May's brilliant article explains,

> The response of the Objibwa to the day schools demonstrates that [they] . . . were not opposed to their children obtaining schooling. On the contrary, they were willing and able to support schooling which met Native objectives and which they perceived as a positive experience.[22]

Betsey Stockton approached her post among indigenous peoples as an invited mixed-race ambassador. She brought the tool of literacy through bilingualism. Her Ojibwa students' success was a direct result of her teaching expertise and her ability to partner with Rev. Peter Jones and

18. "Survey of Infant School System."

19. May et al., *Empire*, 159.

20. May et al., *Empire*, 151, 153.

21. Evans, *Speller and Interpreter.*

22. May et al., *Empire*, 57.

Rev. William Case. She was a force for learning, a catalyst for literacy at Lahaina, at Gaskill Street, and at Grape Island.

In 1997, Stockton's bilingual Ojibwa teacher, Kahkewaguonaby, a.k.a. Rev. Peter Jones, was declared by Canada a Person of National Historic Significance. A historic plaque detailing Jones's life was erected at Echo Villa, his final residence, by the Ontario Archaeological and Historic Sites Board. Eliza Field Jones, his British-born wife, posthumously published his *Life and Journals* in 1860 and *History of the Ojebway Indians* in 1861.[23]

Charles Seaforth Stewart's recollection of Stockton's visit with the souvenir gift of the birchbark canoe tells its own story. The power of that lost artifact reveals Stockton's use of the Wilderspin/Pestalozzian system of learning through objects, as she had recently practiced it at Grape Island. The adaptability of Stockton's mind, coupled with her increased understanding of the infant school method, enabled her to seek out teachable materials and methods from her own life experiences.

23. "Peter Jones (Missionary)."

Chapter 10: Betsey Stockton Keeps Princeton Township District School No. Six and a Night School

IN THE EARLY 1830s, Betsey Stockton returned to her birthplace, Princeton. During her recent past, she had founded, been principal, and taught in schools at Lahaina, Maui; Grape Island, Canada; and Gaskill Street, Philadelphia.

During her years as a teen in Princeton, Stockton taught African American children, remembered Ashbel Green and Michael Osborn of Princeton Theological Seminary. Both men wrote of her early teaching; now her avowed vocation was to blossom into her most permanent schools.

Then in her early thirties, Stockton's use of bilingualism, the infant school system, and her personal charisma made her a master teacher, a force for learning. She created the first publicly funded school for African Americans in New Jersey—perhaps unique in the North. Born a slave, she now wielded power unique to her birth status, gender, and education: the unfolding story of literacy for African Americans, writ large.

Three decades before the Civil War, teaching African American adults and children to read and write was considered illegal and was sometimes fatal to both teacher and student, even in the North. Yet a not previously noted 1788 New Jersey law stated that "all Owners of any Negro or Mulatto Slave or Slaves . . . must be taught and instructed to read, while under the Age of Twenty-one Years" or be fined five pounds.[1]

Both Stockton, held as the child slave of Ashbel Green, and Marcus Marsh, owned since infancy by the Stocktons of Morven, benefitted from their owners' teaching Stockton and March to read and write. Stockton became the founder of four schools, while Marsh became an invaluable medical apprentice to the Stocktons' son-in-law Dr. Benjamin Rush in Philadelphia.

Supported by rich Presbyterian Anthony Simmons, Betsey began teaching informally in the two-story Presbyterian Session House on

1. Nov. 26, 1788, in New Jersey General Assembly, *Acts of Thirteenth General Assembly.*

Spring Street, around the corner from Witherspoon Street, around 1833. But, by 1847, she formally became the principal and head teacher at Princeton Township District (Common) School No. 6 for Colored Children on Witherspoon Street. Remembered by the township school superintendent as a convenient rectangular wooden building, today it is known only through contemporary references.

Accompanied by the Stewart children—Charles Seaforth, ten; Harriet, eight; and Martha, five—Stockton began her life as a surrogate single parent while shouldering professional duties at her groundbreaking school. Their mother was in her grave at Cooperstown, New York, and their father was at sea as chaplain aboard the *US Vincennes*. Stockton sent Charlie to the 1829 Edgehill (Preparatory) School for Boys. She had financial help from the Stewarts' friend, physician Dr. George B. McClennan. By raising their children as her own, Stockton honored her promise to their parents.[2]

The earliest formal record of Stockton as a Princeton resident was the 1840 Federal Census, which listed Betsey Stockton under "free colored persons," "females," between the ages of "36 and 55."[3] Her household embraced her surrogate family; Charles, whom she delivered in April 1823, mid-Pacific, spent his boyhood with Stockton. He was to place first, academically, in the famous 1846 class at West Point Military Academy. No evidence of the schooling for his sisters in Princeton has come to light.

Who were Stockton's pupils, called scholars? According to the United States 1850 Federal Census, 534 (free) African Americans lived in Princeton, or about twenty-percent of its total population.[4] Most of this population had been born in New Jersey. The 1850 census shows that Stockton was teaching a stable population of free children, most of whose parents owned businesses and houses. Some of these African American parents, women and men, were employed as skilled tradespeople, laborers, or cooks; some were employed in the professions as ministers and teachers, one of whom was Stockton herself. In the 1850 Federal Census, her occupation was listed as teacher and her race as Mulatto.[5]

The 1850 Federal Census lists "colored" and "free inhabitants"; in these categories are included twenty-four girls and twenty-five boys, with their ages and race, who "attended school," thus identifying the first complete roster of Stockton's scholars. By given and family name, the 1850 list augments the 1840 Federal Census of African Americans in Princeton Township.

2. Woodhull and Mudge, "Betsey Stockton," Apr. 7, 1906.
3. "Betsey Stockton," in "Manuscript Population Schedule" (1840).
4. Hayden, "With Promptness, Efficiency and Exactness," 23.
5. "Betsey Stockton," in "Manuscript Population Schedule" (1850).

As any experienced teacher knows, teaching families with many children goes with the job, for better or worse. In Stockton's case, the three Montgomery children—William, nine; Anna, seven; and Catherine, four— joined the families of the Gordons, Craigs, Scudders, Lanes, Van Hornes, Voorhees, and Tituses, all of whom sent multiple children to Stockton's District School No. 6, Princeton Township.[6] These were among the "large and highly respected families" referred to by African American historian Anna Bustill-Smith.[7] In this cohort, Stockton's students ranged from two- to three-year-old toddlers, while the oldest scholars were in their teens. Forty-seven children were listed as Black by the census taker, with two—William L. Gordon, five, and his sister Virginia, eight—listed as Mulatto.

Fifteen years after Stockton's return to Princeton, April 1847, marked the first written record of Betsey Stockton's public school for African American children on Witherspoon Street. Kept in a bound ledger by O. H. Bartine as the "Town Superintendent's Common School Register," this holograph manuscript book gives us details of Stockton's District School No. 6 in Princeton Township.[8] Notes in this ledger seem to indicate that Bartine was continuing a register previously begun by John Maclean, his predecessor. That first register is now lost. Could that book have documented an even earlier school kept by Betsey Stockton in the same location?

Named a "common school," because young children attended it in common with others in a public place, Stockton was both principal and head teacher at the wooden school building on Witherspoon Street, the first Witherspoon School for Colored Children, known now only through the superintendent's register. Stockton's first wooden school on Witherspoon Street burned in 1870, as the second school, a much larger Victorian building, was finished. While the first school was in use, from at least 1847 to Stockton's death in 1865, we may imagine the portly figure of Betsey Stockton, walking like a Hawaiian queen, turbaned headpiece in place, unlocking the door of her wooden school house, followed by her neighbors' children, beginning another school day. "April 8, 1847, Betsey Stockton, teacher, in District School #6 was paid $36.00," while "Miss Lockwood, teacher, ditto [District #6] was paid $42.00." Miss Lockwood was presumably White and was paid on the same date for an unspecified amount of time, probably as part of a yearly wage.[9]

6. See "Manuscript Population Schedule" (1850), for "Free Inhabitants" by name, age, race, and "Attended School."

7. Bustil-Smith, *Reminiscences of Colored People*, 5.

8. See, for example, Apr. 8, 1847, in Bartine, "Town Superintendent's Common School Register."

9. Bartine, "Town Superintendent's Common School Register," 31.

These well-paid jobs, whose prestige and stability were guaranteed by tax monies, became a key to the success of Stockton's school. Owning her own house was another factor in Stockton's life in Princeton. The earliest documented proof that Betsey Stockton was living in her own residence, probably rented, was in the holograph manuscript book "Minutes of the Common Council of the Borough of Princeton," on June 4, 1849, where the following entry appears in a list of appeals to the council: "The following appeals were heard—of Betsey Stockton—property tax remitted."[10] Like so many other freed slaves, paid work and her own house propelled Betsey Stockton's agency—her energy—into education for her people.

Besides tax monies, Stockton's school received financial support from bachelor Professor John Maclean, her personal friend at the college.

On June 7, 1850, Superintendent Bartine made note of a huge contribution to the funds for Princeton Township schools by the tax collector James O.(?) Leigh, Esq. [lawyer] of $467.79 of which $74.48 were allocated to District School No. 6, while $53.20 was allocated for District School No. 6 "for Coloured" at that same time.[11]

On April 20, 1850, Bartine wrote:

No. 6. District school for the whites . . . $46.52.

Ditto for Coloured . . . $20.00, from Princeton Township.[12]

This entry remains a specific example of how literacy for African Americans was economically hobbled and might have been eliminated, but for the power of one woman: Betsey Stockton.

In July 1851, Bartine wrote extensively of progress under Stockton's purview:

Visited the [school] taught by Betsey Stockton in the school house in Witherspoon Street. Examined the children & found them quite proficient, school one of the best in the Township. Good government, average number of scholars, 40, branches taught, reading, wrighting [sic], geography, arithematic [sic] & grammar.[13]

The number of forty scholars on average—out of forty-nine possible attendees—meant that her classes were well attended. Stockton's experience, her firm and steady discipline, and—most importantly—her continuity

10. "Minutes of the Common Council," June 4, 1849, unpaginated.
11. Bartine, "Town Superintendent's Common School Register," 8.
12. Bartine, "Town Superintendent's Common School Register," 8.
13. Bartine, "Town Superintendent's Common School Register," 57.

with each student's progress in a child-centered classroom, insured that each scholar would learn at her or his own pace, no matter age, gender, or previous schooling.

Six years later, on August 1, 1857, Stockton's school was described in even greater detail. The superintendent noted the entire range of schools for all children in Princeton at that time:

> Owing to a want of a united effort it has been difficult if not impossible to maintain a large district school in this district suited to the wants of all classes. A parochial school has therefore been established by the 1st Presbyterian Church under the care of Mr. A. Vanduyn (38 scholars) and Miss Lockwood (39) and another by the Episcopal Church under the care of Miss Downing (29). The only district school is for colored children under the care of Betsey Stockton an excellent teacher (formerly a Missionary to the Sandwich Islands.) She has taught 26 years—in this school 10 years—compensation $1.50 per week exclusive of public money. No. of pupils on register 45—average no. 30—in Alpht. [alphabet] 7—spelling 20—reading 15—learning to define words 2—in Arithmetic not beyond simple sums—3—Geography 10. School house of wood—rectangular neat and Convenient—discipline parental—an excellent school.[14]

This entry dates Stockton's formal teaching at the first Witherspoon Street School from the year 1847.

Bartine then continued to make notes on this single page, now entirely devoted to notes about Stockton's "Dist. No. 6" school. The school taught by Betsey Stockton for colored children remained the only public school run consistently and successfully—for children of any race—in mid-nineteenth-century Princeton.

> Oct.—visited the school and found it doing well. Average no. of scholars 33.

> Sep. 18—A district school for white children was established at this date under the charge of Mr. Stewart, a young man well-qualified for the situation. Compensation $100 per quarter/ Gave a license.

> Dec. 2—No. of scholars 23. School increasing & well conducted. Visited Betsey Stockton's school—school prosperous.

> March 2—Visited the school under Mr. Stewart's care. No. of scholars 21. Eng. Gr. 2, Reading 21, Writing 18, Spelling 21,

14. Bartine, "Town Superintendent's Common School Register," 56–57.

Arith. 11. A good school. Teacher's age 23 has taught here 6 mos. elsewhere 6 mos.

June 25—Visited the colored school still under the care of Betsey Stockton & found it as usual admirably well conducted. White School not in operation.

April 6 1851—Renewed Betsey Stockton's [teaching] license for one year.

April 10 [1862]—Renewed Betsey Stockton's license for one year.[15]

That Betsey Stockon's expertise was licensed by the Princeton Township superintendent of schools, an eyewitness to the excellence of her school management and teaching, marks her as the single African American woman to be recognized as a paid professional school principal and teacher.

A year later, in April 1852, the writer of the register notes: "District No. 6 (Princeton) White & Colr [colored]" on top of page 61 of the ledger. Below this heading appears "Betsey Stockton is the teacher for the colr [colored] scholars in this district. Licensed by the late Supe [Superintendent, i.e., O. H. Bartine]. Average number attending about forty-five. Report of the number of children from the District recd [received].

July 13—Visited the above school & found it in an Excellent Condition. Thirty in writing & 20 in geography

Sept 8—The school still flourishing & in good order

The white school in this district taught by Mr. P. M. Schenck, a tolerably good teacher, but the school not in very good order.

1853 [Jan.?] An I. Stewart having been licensed as teacher for the above school, visited it & found it in a better condition & more orderly and think [it is] improving.[16]

Once again, Stockton proved herself superior to the transient White teachers of Princeton Township's public White schools, because of her methods, her consistency, and her reputation as a brilliant teacher in Princeton, as evidenced by entries in the superintendent's ledger.

That Stockton was licensed to teach by White superintendents marks another first in the history of education for African Americans. For four consecutive years, March 1853 to March 1856, T. (or F.?) N. Manning, the Princeton Township superintendent of common schools, licensed

15. Bartine, "Town Superintendent's Common School Register," 61.
16. Bartine, "Superintendent's Common School Register," 61.

Betsey Stockton to teach at the colored school. By comparison, only once in March 1856, did he license a person named Jan D'gue (?) to teach at the White school. To put her recognition in perspective, educational pioneer Stockton's licenses predate the first ones earned from Trenton State Normal College (then changed to New Jersey State Normal School and now called College of New Jersey), to accredit/certify young women as professional teachers in 1855.

Documents tell the story of Stockton's teaching in Princeton. What is omitted from the historical record by mistake or by design reveals attitudes of the creators of those documents. In 1858, the first publicly published and funded report on the Princeton schools was printed. Were the twenty previous years of Betsey Stockton's principalship and teaching at the Witherspoon Street School for Colored Children acknowledged as those of a professionally licensed teacher? No.

In 1858, three years before the outbreak of the Civil War, Princeton's "First Annual Report" of the public schools in Princeton omitted the name of Betsey Stockton in the list of the "Teachers of the Public Schools" on the second page of the published report.[17]

In 1857, the Supreme Court had issued the Dred Scott decision, an act that legally denied freedom, even to those who, like former slave Dred Scott, had lived as free individuals in states where slavery had been declared illegal.[18] At the time, both the college and the seminary were known to have strong financial ties with the South.

Perhaps the 1847 pages of the superintendent's ledger were never consulted to document the history of Stockton's school by those who wrote the "First Annual Report" with reorganization of the township's schools. The ledger certainly would have revealed consecutive superintendents' paid assessment of Stockton's teaching excellence. The comparison to the disorganization and "tolerable" teachers of White children in the same township would have been obvious. More to the point, misguided racist attitudes suppressed—purposely or otherwise—Stockton's hard-won expertise and faithful work in "District School No. 6 for Colored Children."

Instead, debts of former districts no. 6 and 7 amounting to $140 and "to the School for colored children . . . $175.00" were listed just above a notice "to the Public Schools of the District, previous to the establishment of the Graded Public School."[19] The report confirmed that "the School was organized on the 21st day of September, in the old session house in

17. Board of Education of Princeton, New Jersey, "First Annual Report," 2.

18. *Dred Scott v. Sandford*, 60 U.S. (19 How.) 393 (1857).

19. Bartine, "Superintendent's Common School Register," 61.

Witherspoon Street, under Mr. H. Farrand as Principal, and an assistant female teacher," unnamed.[20] Betsey Stockton's name and her decades of excellent teaching were purposely omitted during the reorganization of the public schools of Princeton Township.

Two questions arise. First, what building was the "old session house" (of the Presbyterian Church?) on Witherspoon Street? Might it have been the building in which Stockton's morning and afternoon Sabbath schools had met for years? Was it the building now occupied by Anthony Simmons, whose store was next to the Princeton Bank?—according to Anna Bustill-Smith's 1913 *Reminiscences of Colored People of Princeton, N.J.*[21] Second, was the assistant female teacher Stockton, and, if so, why was her name omitted from this official report? The record shows that she was no assistant teacher. Her status as matriarch with ongoing schools and a flourishing church mark this published report as blatant racism and gender exclusion.

While omitting Stockton by name, the 1858 writers did include details of her school, including an amount for teachers' salaries there. For "estimated expenses for supporting the schools of the District for the coming year, without further enlargement of school accommodations, is as follows: . . . For Salaries of teachers, janitor, fuel and other incidentals . . . for the Colored School, $175."[22] The compilers of the "First Annual Report" of the Board of Education of Princeton Township paid Betsey Stockton to meet their legal obligation but did not name her, which would have acknowledged her written record of teaching excellence—the lone master teacher in Princeton's public schools for several decades.

Tellingly, on the final page of the 1858 "First Annual Report," comes this culturally jaded note:

> The colored school for the past year, has been under the charge of the same efficient teacher who has for some years conducted it with such gratifying success. The number of pupils throughout the year has been about 50—the average attendance about 30. Notwithstanding [that] considerable irregularity in the attendance has been unavoidable, the progress of the pupils has been such as to secure the highest confidence of the Board in its present management.[23]

20. Board of Education of Princeton, New Jersey, "First Annual Report," 2.

21. Bustill-Smith, *Reminiscences of Colored People*, 5.

22. Board of Education of Princeton, New Jersey, "First Annual Report," 9.

23. Board of Education of Princeton, New Jersey, "First Annual Report," 12.

The 1860 United States Federal Population Census, in the Schedule of Free Inhabitants in Princeton Township, Co. of Mercer, listed twenty-eight boys and thirty-nine girls who "attended school within the year." Stockton's scholars were listed by name, age, gender and race, either Black or Mulatto. Betsey Stockton herself was listed as teacher, Mulatto, age sixty, whose personal estate was worth $400.[24]

While the numbers of Stockton's scholars attending her Witherspoon Street School had increased since the 1850 census, the names of David Comfort, age fifty-two, and Andrew B. Chambers, age thirty-nine, both of whose occupation was listed as teacher in Princeton, had been hired by the Board of Education under the 1858 reorganization of the Princeton public schools.[25]

The most salient feature of the names of Stockton's students in 1860 was their school attendance by family. The Scudder, Stryker, Lane, Golden, Conover, Shenck, Craig, Voohees, Van Horne, Van Dyke, Simpson, and Clifton families of Princeton sent their progeny to the Witherspoon Street School during the year.

Ranging in age from five years old to teens of fifteen and sixteen, Stockton's scholars' names were listed with Stockton. 1860 Princeton residents included ordained Presbyterian ministers and the Rev. John Maclean, Stockton's school benefactor, now college president. Many of the parents of Stockton's students were hostlers, stone cutters, washer and ironers, farm owners . . . and Anthony Simmons, an African American businessman and Stockton's early educational supporter, whose worth was listed as $10,000.[26]

The 1860 map of Princeton with its business directory shows a building marked "school" two plots south of the African Methodist Episcopal Church, founded in 1838. This school was located between Maclean and Quarry Streets and faced Witherspoon Street. It may very well have been Stockton's early schoolhouse, which stood near the current location of several storefronts.[27]

24. "Betsey Stockton," listed in "Schedule of Free Inhabitants of Princeton Township, County of Mercer, State of New Jersey, 15th of June 1860" in the 1860 Federal Census. With an Ancestry Library subscription, this content may be viewed online at http://content.ancestrylibrary.com/Browse/view.aspx?dbid=7667&path=New+Jersey.Mercer.html.

25. "Andrew B. Chambers" and "David Comfort," listed as "Teachers" in "Schedule of Free Inhabitants of Princeton Township, County of Mercer, State of New Jersey, 15th of June 1860" in the 1860 Federal Census.

26. "Anthony Simmons," listed as "Confectioner" in "Schedule of Free Inhabitants of Princeton Township, County of Mercer, State of New Jersey, 15th of June 1860" in the 1860 Federal Census.

27. "Princeton, Mercer Co. with Business Directory."

To date, there are no images or plans of Betsey Stockton's "rectangular wooden school building," referred to in the 1847 school superintendent's report. A beautiful, ghostly, partially blurred photograph has recently been published as "The Original Witherspoon School for Colored Children," the current building on the corner of Witherspoon and Maclean Streets, in the *Princeton Magazine* of September 2019.[28] That building has since been correctly identified as the *second* Witherspoon School for Colored Children.

Details of the construction, builder, and cost of the existing building on the site, now a residence, were documented in several *Princeton Press* articles of 1873 and 1874.

On April 26, 1873, the *Press* reported:

> On the 14th day of October last [1872], at a special meeting of the taxable inhabitants of the district duly called to consider the propriety of purchasing a lot and erecting a School House for the colored children of the district, the following resolution was unanimously passed: to purchase a lot . . . not to exceed $2,500, and to raise by taxation such a sum of money . . . . The Board of Education borrow the sum . . . in addition of the collection of the tax of 1873. [The board then invited several sealed bids for the proposal and] entered into a contract with Mr. J. W. Wright for the erection of the building upon a lot on the corner of Witherspoon and Maclean streets, purchased of Patrick Kallerson. . . . The site is believed to be the most eligible that could be secured for the purpose and the building which is fast approaching completion . . . . At the colored school there were registered during the year 106 and the daily average attendance was 24.[29]

On June 21, 1873, the *Princeton Press* reported:

> At 3 ½ o'clock Monday morning, an alarm of fire was sounded, which brought the three fire companies out, and it was found that the old two-story frame building used as a public school for the colored children was in flames. No water could be obtained, and the house, which was of little value, was destroyed. The upper story was used as a lodge room for the Odd Fellows and their regalia, books, & etc. [sic] were all destroyed. The fire was undoubtedly the work of an incendiary. The new school-house, a tasteful structure, has just been finished by Mr. J. W. Wright, on the corner below the A. M. E. Church."

28. Gilpin, "Preserving History," 56.
29. MacDonald and Wright, "On the Fourteenth Day . . ."

From this newspaper description, it is impossible to tell whether the incendiary was a fire-causing device or a person. Great news, though, that the new, tasteful building was finished and that the fire did not damage it![30]

The Victorian schoolhouse built by Joseph Wright was not Betsey Stockton's school, but the successor to her "old two-story wooden frame building" located behind or very near it. Today, the building on the corner of Witherspoon and Maclean Street is a much-altered private dwelling.

The following year, on April 25, 1874, the *Princeton Press* reported:

> The annual meeting of the tax payers of the Princeton Borough school district was held at the Model School: . . . At the Witherspoon Street Colored School there have been registered 124, average term attendance 59. It is estimated that about 175 children in the district are educated at private school and by private tutors; and that about 150 between the ages of 5 and 18 receive no instruction at all. Notice of the new building for colored children completed last Spring is made; and the benefits in an increased attendance of scholars is pointed out.[31]

Betsey Stockton's Night School for African American Adults

Perhaps drawing on her knowledge of adult night schools for African Americans in Philadelphia and New York City, Betsey Stockton saw the need for a school where her scholars could engage in advanced subjects in Princeton at a night school. This school was another application of Stockton's brilliant innovations in Princeton. She may have gleaned this idea from her work with Joanne Bethune and from reports of those in New York City as early as 1828, in *Freedom's Journal*, edited by abolitionist John Brown Russwurm, provider of imported classroom supplies to Stockton at her Infant School for the Coloured on Gaskill Street, Philadelphia.

"She [Stockton] was deeply interested in the higher education of her people," wrote Rev. Lewis B. Mudge, a personal friend of Stockton and the superintendent of the Sabbath schools at the First Presbyterian Church for the Colored. To further her former students' education, Stockton requested Mudge, then a Princeton Theological Seminary student, to organize this adult night school. In keeping with their lifelong scholarly interests, Stockton

---

30. "At Three-and-a-Half O'Clock . . ."
31. "The Annual Meeting of the Tax Payers . . ."

and Mudge enjoyed mutual Latin readings of Julius Caesar's *Commentaries on the Gallic Wars*, keeping their linguistic abilities honed.[32]

The adult school was held in the Presbyterian Church parsonage, possibly at 110 Witherspoon Street.

> It was very well attended, and the College and the Seminary teachers, who gave their time and pains to this enterprise included a number who have been or are distinguished ministers of the gospel . . . not only ordinary branches of learning but such subjects as history, English Literature, Algebra and Latin were taken with success and profit by the [adult] pupils.[33]

Stockton never taught these advanced subjects in Hawaii, as has been erroneously reported. In Princeton, Stockton organized this school as an agent for change between town and gown, further educating free African American adult women and men to attend classes in the hours following their working day.

What became of Stockton's pupils who graduated from these two Princeton secular schools? A tentative list of Stockton's young scholars, compiled from the names in the 1850 and 1860 Federal Censuses, is a place to begin searching for them. In Chester County, Pennsylvania, the 1854 Asthmun Institute, later renamed Lincoln University, conferred the first higher degrees on African Americans. Their student rolls yield several former Stockton scholars.[34]

In 1870, Mary Scudder, residing in Princeton, was listed in the New Jersey State Normal School's *Seventeenth Annual Report* for the year ending 1871.[35] Having trained as a teacher, she may have succeeded Betsey Stockton in the second Witherspoon Street School for the Colored.

One of Stockton's most famous pupils, Mahlon Van Horne, enrolled at Lincoln University at age nineteen and graduated in 1868.[36] He had begun lessons with Stockton at the Witherspoon Street School in 1850, when he was ten years old. His father was Mathias Van Horne, a laborer, and his mother was Diana Oakham Van Horne. In 1867, during Reconstruction, as schools for newly freed African Americans opened in the South, Mahlon Van Horne was appointed principal of the Zion School for Colored Children

---

32. Woodhull and Mudge, "Betsey Stockton," Apr. 7, 1906.

33. Woodhull and Mudge, "Betsey Stockton," Apr. 7, 1906.

34. When names are compared to Stockton's probable students from the 1850 census.

35. Board of Trustees of the New Jersey State Normal School, *Seventeenth Annual Report*, 17.

36. Lincoln University, *Catalogue of Lincoln University*, 28.

in Charleston, South Carolina, which boasted eighteen faculty members and nine hundred students. Later, Van Horne was elected as a representative to the Rhode Island General Assembly—the first African American to sit in that legislative body. In 1896, US President William McKinley appointed Van Horne as American Consul to the then Danish-held island of St. Thomas. Van Horne was an ordained minister and held a pastorate in Rhode Island. Like Stockton, he became a missionary to Antigua, the West Indies, where he died in 1910.[37] His grave is the Lawrenceville, New Jersey, Presbyterian Churchyard.

Another Stockton pupil, Thomas L. Schenck, fourteen years old in 1860 at Stockton's school, graduated from Lincoln University in the class of 1869.[38] Ananias H. Clifton, thirteen, attended the Witherspoon Street School in 1860 and may have furthered his education at Lincoln University as well.

Cecilia Van Tyne, one of the first women teachers at the Witherspoon Street Presbyterian Church Sabbath School, travelled to Rio de Janeiro in 1848 as a missionary. Stockton's scholar Sarah Stockton possibly attended Trenton State Normal School, although their records are incomplete.

George Harris, listed as "coloured," served as a sailor in the North, during the Civil War; received a disfiguring wound to his face; and was discharged from duty. He was living in Princeton in 1885.

S. William Gordon, born 1841 (five feet, four inches tall; "Mulatto"), enlisted December 1863 in Philadelphia in the US naval forces as a landsman and served on the vessel *Conemaugh* as an African American Civil War sailor. He attended Stockton's Witherspoon Street School for the Colored in 1850, at age five, as William L. Gordon, with his sister Virginia Gordon, who was eight that year.

Frances Craig, a co-teacher friend of the author at Princeton's Community Park Elementary School, during the 1990s, is a direct descendant of Francis [sic] E. Craig, a little girl of eleven years old, who was one of Betsey Stockton's scholars in June, 1860. She was the daughter of Henry A. Craig. The Craig family sent many children to the school, beginning with W. H. Craig, seven, who attended Stockton's school in 1850. What a legacy!

Albert Einstein, a Princeton resident, was an indirect recipient of Betsey Stockton's pioneering work, using the Wilderspin/Pestalozzi child-centered method of instruction. "Pestalozzi's Method was used by the cantonal school in Aarau that Albert Einstein attended, which has been credited with fostering Einstein's process of visualizing problems and his use of 'thought

---

37. Christensen, "Mahlon Van Horne."
38. Lincoln University, *Catalogue of Lincoln University*, 29.

experiments.' Einstein said of his education at Aarau: 'It made me clearly realize how much superior an education faced on free action and personal responsibility is to one relying on outward authority."[39]

Nota bene: O. H. Bartine, school superintendent and keeper of the bound manuscript of the "Town Superintendent's Common School Register" for Princeton was listed as a physician in the business directory on the 1860 map of Princeton, Mercer County.[40] His large property bordering Moore Street, beyond the current location of Princeton High School, was also shown on this map.

39. "Legacy," in "Johann Heinrich Pestalozzi."
40. "Princeton, Mercer Co. with Business Directory."

Chapter 11: Betsey Stockton Founds the Witherspoon Street Church for the Colored[1]

GLORIOUSLY POINTING ITS WHITE spire into the Princeton sky, the Witherspoon Presbyterian Church is a palimpsest—a historical slate—of 180 years of the town's history. Boasting an 1840 Greek Revival facade, Betsey Stockton's Christian church is still the most visible icon of her work in Princeton. It was always a Black church; it was never a poor church. It had originally been named the First Presbyterian Witherspoon Street Church of Color in Princeton. In 1845, led by Stockton and its pious elders, it reported to the New Brunswick General Assembly as the Witherspoon Street Presbyterian Church.[2] Today, the church continues Betsey Stockton's mission of social responsibility in the Jackson-Witherspoon Historic District and beyond.

The Witherspoon Church's congregation was gathered in 1836 and continued to flourish until the close of the Civil War in 1865, a bulwark during the three most volatile decades in American History. In 1844, its African American membership was strengthened by the return to the fold of two of the church's own: missionaries Aunt Betsey Stockton from the Sandwich Islands and Aunt Cecilia Ann Van Tyne from Liberia.[3] These two church pillars who equated reading with personal freedom were examples of the power of Black church women who shaped the fabric of their society—a safety net—during decades of Jim Crow. Manumission from slavery by White male owners was a first step. The safety net of a sisterhood of literacy was freedom's forward guarantee.

In 1835, a second devastating fire in the First (Nassau Street) Presbyterian Church began an impetus for segregation of its White and African American communicants in Princeton.[4] Closely aligned with the College

---

1. Portions of this chapter previously appeared in Escher, "She Calls Herself Betsey Stockton."

2. "Names of the Coloured Members of the Princeton Presbyterian Church," Mar. 10, 1846, in "Register of the Presbyterian Church of Princeton," unpaginated.

3. Yocum, "Cecilia Ann (Vantyne) Vantine."

4. Greiff et al., *Princeton Architecture*, 123.

of New Jersey, the early church had originally welcomed African American slaves and newly freed individuals, such as Stockton, as communicants there. Stockton was baptized and joined on September 20, 1816, where she was listed as "Betsey Stockton—a coloured woman living in the family of the Revd. Dr. Green, [who] applied for admission to the Lord's table . . ." and was received into membership.[5] She had been manumitted by this time from former owner and Elizabeth Stockton Green, now deceased, and Rev. Ashbel Green, her manumitter. No doubt in part due to Stockton's "experimental acquaintance with religion and her good conduct,"[6] Green supported his surrogate daughter and her church throughout his lifetime.

The fire led Stockton and other African Americans "to worship apart, in a little place of their own." By 1836 or 1837, Presbyterian African Americans consisted of eighty men and women, free and slave,[7] "who [have] been by custom seated separately in the upstairs gallery of the Old First Church."[8] At that time, some members of the First Church, like many other White Princeton residents, held racist views toward their African American sisters and brethren. During those years, architecture separated Christians by race, just as it had in many churches in the South.

On September 4, 1840, "Col John Lowery, elder of the First Church, on behalf of the colored people, requested permission from the New Brunswick session to have a separation communion in their own church, [which] before that time had been built for them in Witherspoon Street." Apparently "through the efforts of Dr. John Breckinridge, who received from James Lenox, of New York, $500 toward paying off the debt for the building," the church was erected.[9]

Betsey Stockton's name headed the list of ninety living communicants—one hundred thirty-one names—"dimissed" from the First Presbyterian Church on Nassau Street, to form a parallel institution to the Nassau Street Church.[10] The position of Stockton's name signified her unique status as a former missionary and spiritual leader of the new church. The church's dignified founding and Stockton's leadership of it was the genesis of the flowering of education in Princeton's African American community of families.

5. "List of Communicants" in Presbyterian Church of Princeton, "Minutes of the Session," unpaginated.

6. J. Jones, *Life of Ashbel Green*, 364.

7. Witherspoon Street Presbyterian Church, "One Hundredth Anniversary Program," unpaginated.

8. James W. Alexander in Link, *First Presbyterian Church*, 33, 35.

9. Hageman, *History of Princeton*, 2:209.

10. "Names of the Coloured Members of the Princeton Presbyterian Church," Mar. 10, 1846, in "Register of the Presbyterian Church of Princeton," unpaginated.

Stockton's intelligence and experience legitimized trust in the future of this church for both her African American neighbors and her White friends at the college and theological seminary.

In 1836, Anthony Simmons, a successful entrepreneur, was the first superintendent of Stockton's two schools, organized under the wings of the nascent church on Witherspoon Street. By great good fortune, a primary source exists, which offers a rare, detailed view of Stockton's direct influence on the religious education of her townsfolk. "Records of the Morning Sabbath School, 1852–1865" allows us a firsthand understanding of an institution of religious education in the Middle States during three decades of enormous change in educational theory and practice.

Chronological entries were made by each of the successive school superintendents, who were White male students at the theological seminary. The earliest organization was as follows:

> Previous to 1848, [the management of the Sabbath school] was altogether in the hands of the colored people. Mr. Anthony Simmons had conducted it for 13 years [i.e., from 1836]. During that time or a portion of it his assistant teachers were Mrs. Flora Scudder, Mrs. Charlotte Gordon, Mrs. Caroline Thompson, Miss Cicelia [sic] Van Tyne, Miss Betsey Stockton & Miss Flora Van Tyne. Mrs. Samuel Scudder was librarian.[11]

Regular sessions of the Sabbath school, really two schools in one, were held mornings and afternoons before regular services for the whole congregation, throughout the calendar year. The students, or scholars, ranged in age from the infant class of toddlers to teens and senior adults. Opening with a unison recitation of the Ten Commandments, the service moved through readings of the Holy Scripture and hymn singing, while an offering of pennies concluded the group exercises.

Afterward, the teachers met in various classes to hear catechism readings and to answer questions that were recited as well as written. All students were grouped into three classes or divisions, according to their abilities and, in the case of the youngest scholars, by gender. Stockton's extensive teaching in Hawaii, Upper Canada, and Philadelphia led her to organize and to direct these Sabbath Schools.

Most importantly, Stockton employed Londoner Samuel Wilderspin's infant school methods, which she had used with marked success at the Gaskill Street, Philadelphia, "Infant School for Coloured Children." Using these innovative methods and materials was a patently progressive plan,

11. First Presbyterian Church for the Colored, "Records of Morning Sabbath School," 44.

marking Stockton's flexibility in adapting this forward-looking educational philosophy to different localities. School attendance by children less than two years old, continuous learning in the same setting, group student recitations, oral and written responses to lessons, active listening to spoken texts, singing and play under "parental discipline" were copied from her experience at the Gaskill Street school. Division into progressively more challenging classes—unheard of in most American schools of the time— were the hallmarks of Stockton's child-centered teaching.

Stockton's school organization predated the Public Graded School plan of 1858 in Princeton by at least fifteen or more years. Her materials can only be described as a brilliant use of teaching reading, with exciting texts suited to the learning audience.

Augmenting her weekday teaching in Princeton Township District School No. 6, Stockton turned her talents to directing that cohort of women teachers, among them Cecilia Ann Van Tyne, returning to Princeton from missionary work as a teacher in 1844, first in Brazil with Rev. J. C. Fletcher, later in Liberia. Van Tyne also taught an infant class in the church school.[12]

How was the teaching corps trained? Stockton borrowed from her previous teaching experiences as newly literate adult students became teachers. In 1853, for example, the highest class of the superintendent Mr. Lorenzo Westcott "was broken up. Its scholars are now teachers."[13]

Frequent teachers' meetings, often at Aunt Betsey's house on Quarry Street, were usually well attended. These occasions allowed the school's administrators to plan curricula, to hear talks about Scripture by the various ordained ministers or theological student superintendents, and to check teachers' class rolls of scholars, as well as to discuss the general mission of the school. Separate prayer meetings for teachers were held each Saturday night at Aunt Betsey's house for many years. Here was where Stockton held educational court, within her own Quarry Street residence. Those meetings were filled with discussions, with reading, thinking, and planning. Sabbath school scholars benefitted enormously from the rigorous and regular intellectual symposiums that a Stockton-trained teacher could pass on. One is reminded of the Monthly Prayer Concerts observed by Stockton's missionary family on board the *Thames* whaler in the middle of the Atlantic and Pacific Oceans in 1822–1823. Through piety came learning.

What were they reading? In addition to the Bible and catechism questions, scholars at the Sabbath school were required to enlarge their literacy.

12. First Presbyterian Church for the Colored, "Records of Morning Sabbath School," 44.

13. First Presbyterian Church for the Colored, "Records of Morning Sabbath School," 73.

Copies of the *Youth's Penny Gazette*, a semi-monthly newspaper-like reader published by the Sunday School Union in Philadelphia, New York City, and Boston, were distributed to each church family for home reading, the first known homework.[14] Her choice of texts showcased a brilliant use of teaching reading with exciting texts; ones suited to her learning audience. Cosmopolitan in content, *The Youth's Penny Gazette* opened windows on a wider world for first readers within a supportive family circle.

Entertainment as well as Christian precepts were featured in the *Gazette*. For example, the front page of the December 3, 1845, issue boasted lithographed prints of "The Kangaroo" followed by an encyclopedia article about the animal. The lead article on the next page may have been written by Stockton herself. Entitled "Newspapers in the Sandwich Islands," the editors continued in a chatty narrative:

> We suppose readers of the *Youth's Penny Gazette* know . . . that it is but twenty-five or thirty years since the natives of these Islands were wild and cruel savages . . . without any written language. In consequence of the blessing of God upon the labours of Christian missionaries they now have a language written and printed, flourishing churches and schools . . . and five newspapers published at one of the Islands! Who has ever heard the like of any other community on the face of the earth?[15]

The paper copies of the *Gazette* were augmented by a well-established church library of religious books, each carefully charged out against a Sabbath school teacher's name by the school's librarian.

But the finest example of Betsey Stockton's gifted organization was the all-church entertainment of November 5, 1852. An October outbreak of smallpox prohibited "the usual fall Sabbath school picnic in the woods to gratify the scholars and give a spring to the school."[16] Instead, the school's leadership proposed "an exhibition at the church when Aunt Betsey's scholars will speak and afterwards a refreshment table [will be] spread in the hall over the school room." All teachers and students of both morning and afternoon Sabbath schools were to be invited, as well as former superintendents, some of whom were seminary students, and teachers of the schools.

Although the evening of November 5, 1852, proved rainy and muddy, a good attendance at the school showed that Aunt Betsey's entertainment

14. First Presbyterian Church for the Colored, "Records of Morning Sabbath School," 15, 17.

15. *Youth's Penny Gazette*, Dec. 3, 1845.

16. First Presbyterian Church for the Colored, "Records of Morning Sabbath School," 29.

consisted of the irresistible chance for parents and relatives to view their progeny performing on a public stage.

> At the church the performances surprised everyone. The speaking of Aunt Betsey's scholars greatly surpassed my expectations and their singing was excellent. Two of the girls (Sarah Jane Craig and Ellen Huston) sang very sweetly a most delightful duet. Prizes were given to the best three speakers: "A Pilgrim's Progress" [by John Bunyan, also read by the March sisters in *Little Women* by Louisa May Alcott] and two Testaments and Psalms (awarded to Thomas Little and Theodore Scudder). Speaking over we proceeded to the School house where a handsome repast was spread with credible taste. The "grown folk" partook and after the children who until then remained below in [the] schoolroom. When their turn came they *did enjoy* it as only children can. Everything was admirably got up and very well served. Six ladies of the Afternoon School were present and a full term of the Gentlemen of both schools.
>
> The whole affair passed off pleasantly and harmoniously in a way highly creditable to Aunt Betsey's efficiency as a teacher and the management and good taste of our teachers.[17]

Two weeks later, a superintendent noted "an encouraging increase in the number of scholars, fifteen teachers and sixty-one scholars—the entertainment of the 5th touched them [sic] in the right quarter."[18]

The success of Stockton's November 1852 exhibition gave impetus to achieve a long-term goal: improvement to the physical plant. Formerly, after 1849, the Sabbath schools had been meeting in Princeton Township District School No. 6, Stockton's "neat and convenient wooden" building on Witherspoon Street. Now was the moment for the Sabbath schools to build their own place.

In the following year, in April 1853, three plans to provide for a larger and better ventilated space (Victorians believed that disease was spread by bad vapors or miasmas) were discussed by Sabbath School elders. Would it be better for the church to "purchase a piece of ground and erect a building . . . [or] enlarge the present building or make a basement under the church?"[19] Dr. John Maclean, Stockton's friend and later a President of

17. First Presbyterian Church for the Colored, "Records of Morning Sabbath School," 27.

18. First Presbyterian Church for the Colored, "Records of Morning Sabbath School," 28.

19. First Presbyterian Church for the Colored, "Records of Morning Sabbath School," 15.

the College, preferred the basement plan, he told the school superintendents. But Maclean was overruled. After a year and a half of "interesting
teachers' meetings,"[20] often at Aunt Betsey's house, a new school building
was opened on October 21, 1854.

> Held our first meeting this afternoon at 3 o'clock in the building
> erected for the use of the Sabbath Schools connected with The
> Witherspoon Presbyterian Church. . . . The building is forty feet
> in length and [blank] in breadth, affording room for the acco-
> modation of the schools. It is a plain edifice and including the
> lot has been erected at a cost of somewhat over $900.[21]

Ever the Christian gentleman, John Maclean offered the concluding
prayer. Cash gifts for the building from all parts of the community left only
a small debt, soon to be eradicated by the committee of the past, the school
superintendent and "the coloured teachers [who] have secured and collected the subscription by which the building has been erected."[22]

Betsey Stockton and the cohort of Sabbath school female teachers
flexed their architectural muscle. Their efforts built the "African Ch[urch]
School" which was labeled and appeared on an interior lot on Maclean
Street, on the 1860 Princeton, Mercer County, map. The building is no
longer extant.[23]

At Stockton's Sabbath schools, the message was religion and the
method was literacy—just as it had been in Lahaina. Stockton's teacher
training, graded classes with written lessons, oral recitation, reading materials sent home for families, and student-generated activities, all attest
to her use of the Wilderspin/Pestalozzi Infant School System. Years later,
the school Albert Einstein attended in Arrau, Switzerland, adapted this
system. Today, Maria Montesorri and Wilberforce schools have inherited
this child-centered method of teaching students.

In 1913, Anna Bustill-Smith, an African American genealogist and
writer, noted,

> The Witherspoon Presbyterian Church is the most flourishing
> [of all the African American churches in Princeton]. . . . It has a

---

20. First Presbyterian Church for the Colored, "Records of Morning Sabbath
School," 17.

21. First Presbyterian Church for the Colored, "Records of Morning Sabbath
School," 58, 97.

22. First Presbyterian Church for the Colored, "Records of Morning Sabbath
School," 97.

23. "Princeton, Mercer Co. with Business Directory."

large auditorium and a parish house and several properties, all in good condition. They are valued at $37,000.[24]

More than 180 years after Betsey Stockton founded the church, Presyberian Historical Society member Shirley Satterfield continues Stockton's legacy of vibrant outreach and service at the Witherspoon Presbyterian Church.

24. Bustill-Smith, *Reminiscences of Colored People*, 14.

Chapter 12: **Matriarchy**

Jesus said unto them, a Prophet is not without honor, save in his own country.—Matthew 13:57 KJV

Among her people, she moved a queen and her word was law.—Dr. Lewis W. Mudge, DD[1]

Matriarch

BY ANY MEASURE ONE choses, Betsey Stockton's apotheosis from slave to community matriarch stands as a triumph over adversity.

Spurred in 1898 by the pending annexation of Hawaii as a US territory, retired Civil War surgeon General Alfred A. Woodhull joined Rev. Lewis W. Mudge in a series of *Princeton Press* articles publicly soliciting ideas and funds for a permanent memorial to Betsey Stockton.[2] With great humility, they remembered their years of Stockton's friendship, 1859–1865, during their time as teachers at her African American adult school in Princeton. Their goal: that most Edwardian of emblems, the bronze tablet, to be dedicated, as soon as sufficient funds were donated.

Woodhull and Mudge outlined their plan to honor this "excellent woman"[3] on the front pages of the *Press* on May 27, 1899; November 21,

---

1. Woodhull and Mudge, "Betsey Stockton," Apr. 7, 1906. Dr. Alfred Alexander Woodhull Jr. (1837–1921) graduated from the College of New Jersey (now Princeton University) in 1856 and the University of Pennyslvania in 1859. In 1899, during his efforts toward a Stockton memorial, he was chief surgeon of the Department of the Pacific (Philippines) and was promoted to brigadier general in 1904. In 1906, as he wrote "Betsey Stockton" for the *Princeton Press*, he was a lecturer at Princeton University, his alma mater, on hygiene and sanitation (see "Dr Alfred Alexander Woodhull Jr." for more information). As he began his written memorial of Betsey Stockton, Reverend Lewis Ward Mudge (1839–1914), a graduate of Princeton Theological Seminary in 1861, enjoyed great success as a published author of numerous collections of church music, including "Carmina for the Sunday School" in 1899. Betsey Stockton earned the devotion of this Princeton University lecturer and ordained Presbyterian scholar, both of whom worked relentlessly to publish their accolade to her social contributions in 1906. The town of Princeton was ready to celebrate one of its own.

2. Woodhull and Mudge, "Betsey Stockton," Apr. 7, 1906.

3. Woodhull and Mudge, "Betsey Stockton," Apr. 7, 1906.

1903; and April 7, 1906. For seven years, Stockton's former colleagues championed her past, undeterred by time, distance, human frailty, or their professional duties. They were visible examples of Stockton's ability to inspire lasting friendships born of mutual trust, respect, and affection. As a catalyst, Stockton mobilized a network of individuals to contribute time and money to the education of her community.

The two colleagues turned first to Stockton's surrogate son, Brigadier General Charles Seaforth Stewart, the infant she had delivered in April 1823 aboard the whaler *Thames*, mid-Pacific Ocean. Woodhull and Mudge hoped for suggestions from him.

In October 1899, in response to their request, Stewart wrote to his cousin, Martha Chamberlain: "This year it has been suggested in Princeton, that a tablet to her services and memory be cast and sent to the islands & placed there." Stewart enclosed "photographs of my father and from a portrait of my mother . . . also a photograph of Betsey Stockton."[4] Stewart gave his support for the plan, but added no specifics to Woodhull and Mudge.

In May 1899, Lt. Col. (as he was then) Woodhull turned his thoughts to a memorial for Stockton in Hawaii: "Its proper situation would be the Kawaiahoa [Kawaihoa] School in Honolulu. It is a flourishing institution, for teaching domestic and mechanical art as well as letters on the original mission site."[5] Lewis Mudge added, money had already been collected for Stockton's plaque. "Princeton being an educational centre and strictly a university town, . . . such a historical connection with the beginnings of education in one of our new national possessions should be appropriately worked."[6]

By November 20, 1903, Woodhull's ideal plan had changed: "It is desired by some of her friends to place in a church in Lahaina, Island of Maui, Hawaii, where her missionary work was done." Woodhull then published the proposed inscription, adding that it might not cost more than $200. Again, he opened the solicitation for funds, adding, "Should there be a surplus it will be used in connection with the Witherspoon Street Church, to which Aunt Betsey was much attached."[7]

The conclusion of Woodhull and Mudge's quest had come full circle. In 1906, the two friends published the Witherspoon Street Presbyterian Church service describing the dedication of the bronze plague to Stockton. Their biographical sketch authenticated dates and details of Stockton's extraordinary circumnavigation around the world. But soulmates Woodhull

4. C. Seaforth Stewart, "Letter to Martha Chamberlain."
5. Woodhull and Mudge, "Betsey Stockton and Hawaiian Schools."
6. Woodhull and Mudge, "Betsey Stockton," May 27, 1899.
7. Woodhull and Mudge, "Betsey Stockton," Nov. 21, 1903.

and Mudge emphasized Betsey Stockton's early activism for education in Princeton:

BETSEY STOCKTON

A very interesting exercise was held on Sunday afternoon, April first in the Witherspoon Street Presbyterian Church on the occasion of unveiling a memorial tablet in commemoration of the career of Betsey Stockton, a colored native of this town whose life was devoted to good works. This tablet, to secure which attention has been drawn in the *Press* several times within the past few years, it was originally hoped to set up at Lahaina, Maui, in a large school on the site of her original labors in Hawaii. Circumstances rendered that impractical and the plan was modified, it appears very much for the better, so to place the memorial within this church of which she was so long a member about a hundred yards from her home and her successful school. The memorial is a heavy, polished, brass plate, very legibly inscribed with black capital letters and surrounded by a heavy oaken frame. The brass is twenty-five inches and the frame is two and a half inches wide, so that the whole is twenty by thirty in size. It was artistically executed by the Church Glass and Decorating Company of New York, and is worthy of position in any church edifice in the country.

The inscription runs:

BETSEY STOCKTON,

THROUGH HER DESIRE TO SERVE THE CAUSE OF CHRIST, ACCOMPANIED THE FIRST AMERICAN MISSIONARIES TO HAWAII AND OPENED A SCHOOL FOR THE COMMONALTY AT LAHAINA, MAUI, IN 1823. AFTER HER RETURN TO THE UNITED STATES SHE WAS FOR MANY YEARS A VAUABLE MEMBER OF THIS CONGREGATION, A TEACHER OF ITS YOUTH AND A POWERFUL INFLUENCE FOR GOOD IN THE COMMUNITY. THIS MEMORIAL IS SET UP IN RECOGNITION OF HER FAITHFUL CHRISTIAN CHARACTER AND MOST USEFUL LIFE BY FRIENDS WHO HONORED HER AND LOVED HER. SHE WAS BORN IN PRINCETON IN 1798 AND DIED THERE OCTOBER 24, 1865. HER BODY LIES IN COOPERSTOWN, NEW YORK.

There was a full and interesting congregation, a special section of it being nearly all of Aunt Betsey's surviving resident scholars. The introductory service consisted of prayer, praise and the reading of the Bible, the music and the Scriptures having been selected with special relevance of the occasion. The pastor, the Rev. G. S. Stark, very admirably set forth an account of this excellent member of the church as he had gathered it from her remaining acquaintances and from local traditions, and emphasized the moral obligation of those who had been under her initiative to follow her religious leadership, notwithstanding that they might fall behind her in mental activity.

Gen. [Alexander] Woodhull representing the donors then thanked the church authorities for their perseverance to place the tablet on the wall, and spoke substantially as follows:

"Betsey, as she was known in her later years, and always within my own memory as Aunt Betsey, was a light woman of color, born in 1798, it is believed in the family of Robert Stockton, Esq. of Princeton, a kinsman of the Stocktons of Morven in that mild servitude which then existed in New Jersey. The Rev. Ashbel Green, then President of the College [1812 to 1821] married Mr. Stockton's eldest daughter, and Betsey became a part of his household at a time which cannot now be determined. She became a thoroughly trained domestic nurse, accomplished cook, acquiring an invaluable [amount] of education so that she could do skillfully anything that was assigned her. It is understood that Dr. Green did not favor educating his servants in books, but she was so desirous to learn that his sons, who appreciated her natural intelligence and her merit, helped her in her studies. Mr. Charles S.[amuel] Stewart, afterward a Doctor of Divinity, and long the Senior Chaplain in the United States Navy, was ordained from the College in 1815, a graduate student in 1816, was in the Th[eological] Seminary 1818–'21. During all of his Princeton residence he was an intimate in Dr. Green's family and thus had the opportunity of learning Betsey's character. She had become a devoted Christian early in life and when Mr. Stewart, who had been accepted as a missionary, took his bride to Princeton to meet his old friend, Betsey saw her and expressed her desire to accompany them to their foreign field. 'Finally an arrangement was made with Dr. Green (by Mr. Stewart) which enabled her to go.' It does not appear what this arrangement was, but possibly it involved a pecuniary element. The party of twenty or more, the first American missionaries for the Hawaiian Islands, sailed in November 1822 and Mrs. Stewart and Betsey landed at Honolulu 16th May 1823. Mr. Stewart was assigned to form a mission to Lahaina, island of Maui, which they reached on 31st May 1823. It was there, as Aunt Betsey herself told me, that she opened a school for the common people,

which was certainly the first of its kind in Maui and probably
the first in all Hawaii; for at the beginning the missionaries were
chiefly engaged in the instruction of the chiefs and their families. This school work was concurrent with and additional to her
domestic service. It shows that a sincere desire to accomplish a
good purpose need not be thwarted by other necessary engage-
ments. However humble or exacting. Mrs. Stewart's health soon
become so infirm that to save her life the family was compelled
to return in the autumn of 1825, reaching New York by way of
England 18th August 1826. After Mrs. Stewart and the children
were safe at home in Cooperstown, N.Y., Betsey went to Philadelphia where she conducted an infant school for children. This
was in 1827 and in part of 1828; and while there Dr. George B.
McClellan, an eminent member of the medical profession, the
father of the famous general and the grandfather of the present
Mayor of New York was very kind and always cared for her. She
returned to Mrs. Stewart in 1828, but the next year was sent to
Canada and there organized schools among the Indians. This
suggests that she might still have some connection with a Mission Board. In 1830 she again joined Mrs. Stewart; now a help-
less invalid who died the same year. Betsey, who had promised
to care for the children, did so most faithfully for the next five
years. In 1833, Mr. Stewart himself, who had become a Naval
Chaplain, being at sea, she brought the children to Princeton
among their father's old friends, and Mr. Stewart's son went to
school at Edgehill.

"After 1835 Betsey appeared to have no direct connection
with Mrs. Stewart's family and she probably took up her inde-
pendent resident here then. But the affectionate gratitude of the
Stewarts was always extended to her and to the end of her days
she was regarded by them as 'her children.' The son graduated
from West Point, became an officer of Engineers in the United
States Army, dying not long since as a Brigadier-General on the
retired list. He was actively interested in the memorial as indeed
is his son, also an officer in the army. Not long before his death,
General Stewart wrote that Betsey had probably saved his life as
a child by her courage and adroitness when threatened by a wild
bull, and added that although disposed to be nervous and sometimes excitable in her early life she was always cool and rose to
the occasion in emergencies. Whenever possible Col. Stewart
called at Princeton on her account and the last time he saw her
was during the Civil War . . . when, going North from illness
contracted in the field, he spent a day or two in Princeton. While
here his wife and children stayed at a friend's, but he went to

Betsey's cottage, where, in his own words, 'she cared for me and nursed me as she had done when I was a child.' Where such affectionate confidence is shown by a distinguished soldier all his life, it certainly rested upon good grounds.

"At her death in 1865, her remains were taken to Cooperstown and were buried in the Stewart family plot. The inscription upon her tomb-stone reads:

The grave of

BETSEY STOCKTON

a native of Princeton, NJ.

Where she died

Oct. 24, 1865

Aged 67 YEARS

Of African blood and born in

Slavery, she became fitted by

Education and divine grace,

For a life of great usefulness,

For many years, she was a

Valued missionary at the

Sandwich Islands in the

Family of Rev. C. S. Stewart,

And afterwards till her

Death, a popular and able

Principal of Public Schools

In Philadelphia & Princeton

Honored and beloved by a

Large circle of Christian

Friends.[8]

"Aunt Betsey's school must have been established about 1835, and for the next thirty years she was an active agent for good in this borough. Although respected and welcomed among the better white families and frequently yielding them needed service of a higher grade, her daily work was that of a teacher of the colored youth and her example and counsel were efficient

8. For a photo of the tombstone itself, see the website under "Betsey 'Betsy' Stockton" in the bibliography.

among the colored adults as well. In my youth I knew that Aunt Betsey had the respect and regard of the whole town, smaller and more homogenous and of longer-settled families than now. She lived in a one-story white cottage on a lot near the corner of Green and Witherspoon, now built upon. The grounds and building were always neat and attractive and the interior of the house was a model of cleanliness and order."

The Rev. Lewis W. Mudge, D.D., prevented by his pastoral duties from being present, contributed this sketch:

"The period of time from which I knew 'Aunt Betsey,' as she was familiarly called, extended from about 1859 to 1865. In those days the interests of the Witherspoon Street Church were in the hands of the College Faculty. The pulpit was supplied by Dr. [George Musgrave] Giger, the professor of Latin, and the superintendent of the Sunday School was selected by the faculty. At their request I became superintendent in my Sophomore year, and was not only Superintendent but virtually pastor, with charges of the prayer meetings and the pastoral visitation, until the close of my tutorship in the college. In this way, I was thrown into intimate acquaintance with Betsey Stockton, who was the most instrumental person in the colored community. In those days there were many colored families in Princeton who were honored and respected, and worthily so. They were intelligent and of high morals and religious character. Generally they owned their own homes and were industrious and frugal. Among such families were the Stocktons, Van Tynes, Craigs, Simmones, Hustins, Gordons and others. And among them all none was so highly regarded as Aunt Betsey. Among her people, she moved a queen and her word was law. I still have her picture, given to me by herself, with her turban, as she always wore it, her strong but placid face and her portly form. Her manner was dignified and deliberate and by the colored people she was both loved and feared. Among the older people her influence was supreme. The colored people are almost proverbially suspicious and jealous, but everybody trusted Aunt Betsey. Her opinion was sought on all matters of personal and family concerns and her judgment always thoughtfully given and with great dignity, was regarded with the greatest respect. Her daily employment was the charge of a school for colored children, the school which for many years under her instruction took the place of the present Witherspoon Street Colored School. And the scholars were well taught. Her faithfulness and her success as a teacher were manifest in the Sunday School where reading of the Bible and the spoken words of the scholars in the lessons would compare favorably with any white school. Aunt Betsey was never satisfied with her own attainments. She had scholarly instincts and I had the pleasure of taking her through considerable portions of Caesar's Commentaries. She was very deeply interested in the higher education of her people, and at her solicitation I started a night school for the young men and women. This school was held in the house now owned and occupied as the Presbyterian parsonage. It was very well attended and the College and Seminary teachers, who gave their time and pains to this enterprise, included a number who have been or are distinguished ministers of the Gospel. Among them I may name the Rev. Drs. Butler, Holliday, Burkhalter, Kellogg, Knox and the Wylie Brothers and the Rev. Mr. Coale. Perhaps no better illustration can be given of the intelligence of the Princeton colored community of those days than the statement that not only ordinary branches of learning but subjects as History, English Literature, Algebra and Latin were taken with success and profit by some of the pupils. One at least of the scholars became a minister, and two of them, wives of two prominent colored ministers. It is but giving due acknowledgment to say that the success of this night school was due in large measure to the preparation obtained under Aunt Betsey's tuition. At that time the women teachers of the Sunday School were colored, the male teachers and officers being students. Aunt Betsey taught a large class of boys. Here and in the church her influence was as marked, her counsel as wise, as in her secular affairs. She was a most devoted Christian. Her piety was of the devotional type. She was constant in her attendances at service and took large part in caring for the temporal interests of the church. With the other colored teachers she saw to the needs of the poorer scholars, securing clothing for them from the benevolent ladies of the Presbyterian Church. Her daily life was one of manifest communication with her Savior. She walked with God, and her death was but a speedy passing from earthly fellowship to the beatific vision of heaven."

Gen. Woodhull added that the life which has just been reviewed, and of which the tablet would always be a reminder, showed that adverse circumstances should never prevent one religiously inspired from carrying on a good work. There are none present, certainly none of the young people, who have infinitely better opportunities for education and for Christian service if they choose to use them, and the memory which this brass would always reflect should be a perpetual inspiration.

The tablet was then unveiled by Alexander Webber, of Trenton, one of her old pupils and it was formally turned over to the church as a memorial gift. A small photograph of Aunt Betsey in her characteristic turban, belonging to Dr. Mudge, was exhibited at the same time. The audience, which had listened with close attention, and lively interest to all that had been done, thanked the speaker as representing the donors for the performance and beautiful record of this good woman and after singing another hymn, the service closed with a benediction.

There are few in any church whose Christian activities covered so wide and practical a range, and there are few congregations privileged to enjoy a memorial service that so closely represented a daily life of service for themselves and their children.

General A. Alexander Woodhull and Dr. Lewis W. Mudge, D.D.[9]

Coda: Betsey Stockton, the Scholar

"Family is who we live with" is a current phrase describing the shared households of African Americans in the face of the formidable racism in America during the decades before the Civil War. Betsey Stockton formed several such families, beginning with her surrogate, possibly natural, father Rev. Ashbel Green.

Through him, she found sister, brother, and children with Harriet and Rev. Charles Samuel Stewart, and an even larger family in the parents of children she taught, in the church she founded in Princeton.

Her early reading ability brought with it many linguistic gifts. Colleague Lewis W. Mudge mentioned reading a specific Latin text with her: "It was my pleasure while connected with the Witherspoon Street Sunday School to review her Caesar with her in Latin."[10] He remembered, "She had scholarly instincts and I had the pleasure of taking her through considerable portions of Caesar's Commentaries [on the Gallic Wars]."[11]

What was the significance of these shared readings in such a scholarly and "dead" language?

Almost by chance, an answer suggested itself. It was a gentle scholarly rebuke—an inside joke—that Stockton and Mudge might have enjoyed during their time together. Could it have involved the South Carolina Senator John C. Calhoun (1782–1850), one of slavery's most virulent apologists?

9. Woodhull and Mudge, "Betsey Stockton," Apr. 7, 1906.

10. Woodhull and Mudge. "Betsey Stockton and Hawaiian Schools."

11. Woodhull and Mudge, "Betsey Stockton," Apr. 7, 1906.

While I was researching Betsey Stockton's connection to John Brown Russwurm, who, like Stockton, was born of a mother of color and a White father, and sometime editor of the abolitionist newspaper *Freedom's Journal*, I came across a 1932 key to this puzzle. "The abolitionists supported the colored leaders in their programs for the higher education of the Negro youths, though at the time it was very impracticable."[12] But were there other reasons for Stockton and Mudge's literary pastime?

Apparently a long-lost conversation between African American educator Alexander Crummell (1819–1898) and John C. Calhoun added significance to their reading:

> A knowledge of Greek and Latin helped to vindicate the manhood of the race. Alexander Crummell, while working in the office of the Anti-Slavery Society in 1833 [in New York City?], overhead a conversation concerning Calhoun's statement to the effect that "if he could find [a] Negro capable of mastering Greek syntax, he would then believe that the Negro was a human being, and had a soul." This sentiment was quite prevalent and led many to advocate the learning of Greek and Latin at any cost.[13]

Calhoun's racist belief was shattered by the existence of Stockton's African American scholars, who possessed both Christian souls and excellent minds.

Still another reason suggested itself for Stockton and Mudge's brushing up on their Latin. New Jersey historian John M. Murrin noted:

> Upon entrance [to the College of New Jersey, now Princeton University] a student was expected to be able to translate passages from Sallust, Caesar's *Commentaries*, and Virgil; convert a standard English text into grammatical Latin; and translate portions of the Greek Gospels into English and analyze the Greek grammar.[14]

In her adult school, Betsey Stockton and Lewis Mudge were preparing African American adults for further education at institutions of higher learning. They included Latin and algebra in the school's curricula. Lifelong learners themselves, these friends held themselves to the highest standards of scholarship—exemplifying goals to pass on to their scholars.

---

12. Gross, "*Freedom's Journal*," 245.

13. Crummel, *Attitude of the American Mind toward the Negro Intellect*, 10–11; as cited in Gross, "*Freedom's Journal*," 245.

14. Murrin, "Christianity, Enlightenment, and Revolution," 227.

Appendix A: **Princeton's Presbyterian African Americans**[1]

The Coloured members of this church were dismissed to the number of ninety to form a church under the name of the First Presbyterian Church of Colour of Princeton; and the church was organized by B. H. Rice, Jno [John] Maclean, & Jos [Joseph] H. Davis, a committee of the Presbytery of New Brunswick (recorded): Names of Coloured Members of the Princeton Presbyterian Church, March 10, 1846, [to further their own church,] were:

> 1. Betsey Stockton, 2. Margaret Scudder, 3. Peter Voohees, 4. Flora Scudder, 5. Jane Oppie, 6. Flora Scudder, 7. Clarisa Voohees, 8. Margaret Schenck, 9. Catherine Titus, 10. Lydia Ditmas . . . lives near Hightown or Cranbury, 11. Flora Jennings, 12. Jane Hunt, 13. Peter Scudder Jr., 14. Phyllis Scudder, 15. Joseph Scott, 16. Margaret Long, 17. Judith Roberts, 18. Celia Hoagland, 19. John Skillman, 20. Thomas Stockton, 21. Anthony Simmons, 22. Caroline Simpson, 23. Jemima Little, 24. Rachael Stockton, 25. Cao Mosiez, 26. Hetty Mosiez, 27. Violet Peterson, 28. York Van Voitwick [sp?], 29. Isaac Hoagland, 30. Julia Gholson, 31. David Little, 32. Ellen Scudder, 33. Charles Hendrickson, 34. Hagar Hendrickson, 35. Grace Johnson, 36. Martha Nevious, 37. Julia Ann S. Bonny, 38. Thomas Bonny, 39. Anthony Voorhees, 41. Horace Scudder, 42. Peter Lane, 43. Hannah Lane, 44. May Ann Hawkins, 45. Catherine Curtis, 46. Eve Duryee, 47. Clara Hendrickson, 48. Flora Voohees, 49. David VanTyne, 50. Flora VanTyne, 51. Cicelia [sic] Vantyne, Missionary to Africa, Returned 1844, 52. Caroline Oppie, 53. Sarah Vroom, 54. Amy Duryee, [55.—missing], 56. Thomas Cuberly, 57. Betsy Van Horn, 58. Anthony Johnson, 59. Mary Matthews, 60. Peter Miller, Jun., 61. Matthias Van Horn, 62. Charlotte Gordon, 63. Sarah Craig, 64. Fanny Nevius, 65. Rosanna Beekman, 66. Ellen Beekman, 67. Mary Jane Stives, 68. Sarah Sydam, 69. Mary Mosier [70. Jane Hunt—crossed out], 70.

1. Link, *First Presbyterian Church*, 35–36; cf. Hageman, *History of Princeton*, 2:209. This is the most complete list of Princeton's Presbyterian African Americans, Stockton's flock of ardent Christians.

Peter Scudder Sr., 71. Margaret Craig, 72. Cartherine Nevius, 73. Henry Stryker, 74. Mary Simpson, 75. Cecelia Roberts, 76. Ann Little, 77. James Tusus, 78. Phillis Nevius, 79. Charlotte Murray [80. Sarah Van Arnsius?—crossed out], 80. Samuel Scudder, 81. Lewis Stryker, 82. Julia Moors, 83. Eliza Van Dyke, 84. Edward Erwin, 85. Hetty Mannus, 86. Charles Bickner, 87. Jemima Bickner, 88. Caroline E. Salter, 89. Bina Centurion, 91. Jeffry Hampton, 92. Spencer Henry, 93. Mary Ann Henry, 94. Deanna Carman, 95. Deanna Van Horn, 96. Primus Beekman, 97. Susanna Elizabeth Van Horn, 98. Isaac Stockton, 99. Mary Ann Stockton, 100. Elenor Boyles, 101. Margaret Gholson, 102. William Thompson, 103. Cornelia W. Ditmus, 104. Catherine Ann Hawkison, 105. Elenor Cudjo, 106. Henry Harrison, 107. Henry Thompson, 108. Mary Clawson, 109. Emily Davis, 110. Mahlon Van Horn, 111. Catherine Parker, 112. Rachel Titus, 113. Rachel Ten Eyck, 114. Thomas Ten Eyck, 115. Garret Oppie, 116. Susan Simmons, 117. Caroline Simpson, 118. Dianna Scudder, 119. Susan S. Scudder, 120. Jane Dill, 121. Joseph Stryker, 122. Elisha Glocester, 123. Deanna Holcomb, 124. Thoda Bergen, 125. Catherine Van Cleve, 126. Thomas Stockton, 127. Ann Innis, 128. John Voorhees, 129. Alfred Martin, 130. Joseph Innis, 131. Abram Van Tromf, 132. Penny? or Perry [both spellings with question mark in original]Thompson.

Appendix B: **Essential Chronology of Betsey Stockton's Life**

c. 1798 Betsey Stockton is born to African American slave mother Sealy and White father at Constitution Hill, residence of Robert Stockton, Princeton, NJ. Betsey Stockton lives with Ashbel Green at the Philadelphia manse of the Presbyterian Church.

June 1813: Three years of Stockton's time sold to Nathaniel Todd, Woodbury, NJ.

1815: Charles Samuel Stewart graduates from the College of New Jersey.

June 1816: Stockton returns to live with Ashbel Green at the President's House, College of New Jersey, Princeton.

Sept. 20, 1816: Church session minutes: "Betsey Stockton—a coloured woman living in the family of the Revd. Dr. Green, applied for admission to the Lord's table. Session being satisfied as to the evidence of her experimental acquaintance with religion, and her good conduct—agreed to receive her" into the congregation at Nassau Presbyterian Church.

1820: Stockton has brief residence in Philadelphia, listed as "in the household of Rev. Dr. Green" on residence inventory.

1820+: Stockton is educated through tutorials at Princeton Theological Seminary by Osborn and responds in writing to catechisms after studying required texts assigned by her tutors there.

July 23, 1820: Quaker Street Infant School, Spitalfields, central London, opened by Samuel Wilderspin as a model school for his infant school system. The school was closed and torn down, late nineteenth century. Museum of the City of London curators could not establish its location in 2000.

Nov. 20, 1820: Nantucket whaler *Essex* is stove in by a whale near the equator.

Feb. 23, 1821: Captain George Pollard Jr. and Charles Ramsdell of Nantucket are rescued by whaler *Dauphin* off coast of Chile.

June 11, 1821: Charles Ramsdell arrives at Nantucket Island on the *Eagle* with Captain William H. Coffin.

June 1821: News of *Essex* disaster reaches Nantucket Island via newspaper accounts.

Sept. 1821: Letters between Ashbel Green and the American Board of Commissioners for Foreign Missions (ABCFM) in Boston plan for Stockton's missionary work. Letters from Princeton Theological Seminary students attest to Stockton's ability to read and write about ancient texts.

Sept. 18, 1822: Contract made between Stockton and the ABCFM in New Haven, Connecticut, ensuring "an humble friend" was a freed slave and not a runaway fugitive slave at sea. Her role was to be that an "assistant Missionary" and a teacher in the Sandwich Islands, and she was not to do more than her stated share of common duties. She is bound in that capacity to the ABCFM. Contract signed by Green, Stewart, Stockton, Evarts.

Nov. 19/20, 1822: Stockton, Charles Samuel Stewart, and wife, Harriet Bradford Tiffany Stewart (pregnant), sailed on American whaler *Thames*, out of New Haven, Connecticut, with Captain Reuben Clasby of Nantucket and Charles Ramsdell, boatsteerer, crew member. Five-month voyage to Honolulu.

Apr. 11, 1823: Shipboard birth of Charles Clasby (later Seaforth) Stewart, a son, to Charles Samuel Stewart and Harriet. Stockton, midwife, assisted by Rev. Stewart.

Apr. 27, 1823: *Thames* arrives at Honolulu, voyage of 158 days, rounding the Horn twice. Stockton and Stewarts assigned to Lahaina, Maui, mission.

1823/24: Stockton and Stewarts board royal Hawaiian yacht *Cleopatra's Barge* (*Hilo*), recently purchased by King Kamehameha II purchased for 8,000 piculs of sandalwood, worth $80,000 at the time, as his royal transport among the Sandwich Islands. Stockton and the Stewarts sail on this ocean-going yacht, built in Salem, MA, by the Crowninshield family.

June 29, 1823: Betsey Stockton establishes the first school for non-royal Hawaiians, the *maka ainina*, at Lahaina mission station.

Sept. 8, 1824: *HMS Blonde*, 46 guns, lying at Woolwich, receives bodies of king and queen of Sandwich Islands that had been resting in a vault under the church of St. Martin-in-the-Fields, London.

Sept. 20, 1824: Stockton establishes the second school for the other non-royal Hawaiians in Lahaina.

Sept. 28, 1824: Departure of the *Blonde* from Spithead, London, with queen's and king's bodies in triple coffins of mahogany, oak, and lead.

Feb. 12, 1825: News of the death of Queen Kahamanu and King Kamehameha II, friends of Stockton and the Stewarts, in London, reaches Lahaina.

Apr. 30, 1825: Harriet Bradford Stewart is born at Lahaina mission station, with Stockton, "an humble friend," assisting the family.

May 6, 1825: Pilot ship from Maui announces the frigate *HMS Blonde* anchored at Lahaina, where Stockton is residing with son and daughter of Stewarts. Commodore George Anson, Lord Byron, carrying the bodies of King Kamehameha II and Queen Kahamanu for Christian burial at Lahaina.

May or June, 1825: Charles and Harriet Stewart take a month-long cruise on the *Blonde* for Mrs. Stewart's health, as she has to be carried in a chair to the *Blonde*. Stockton remains with missionary families in Honolulu, as a nurse for toddler Charlie and infant Harriet Stewart.

Oct. 17, 1825: Stockton sails from Honolulu on British ship *Fawn*, Captain Charles Dale, out of London, with four Stewarts.

Nov. 1825: The *Fawn* passes Tahiti on voyage toward tip of Africa.

Apr. 4, 1826: The *Fawn* arrives in London at (New) London Docks, which were finished 1808. Stockton and Stewarts remain in London for three months.

Apr./May/June, 1826: Stockton and family reside at the Adam(s) family of Marshgate at Homerton, a northern suburb of the city, now Hackney. "This is one of the household into which myself and the [missionary] family were received with all Christian hospitality, on our arrival in London from the Sandwich Islands, 1826" (C. Samuel Stewart, *Sketches of Society*, 1:29). Stewart arrives in London, just as Chaplain Bloxom of the *Blonde* leaves via Portsmouth. Lord Byron addresses the slander against the American missionaries in the Sandwich Island.

May 1826: C. Samuel Stewart addresses meeting of the British and Foreign Bible Society, London. He addresses the charges against the American missionaries.

Aug. 4, 1826: Stockton and Stewarts arrive New York aboard British ship *Richmond.*

Aug. 18, 1826: At NYC dockyards, ship *Clis* carries Stockton, Harriet Stewart, and children up Hudson River to Cooperstown, NY (Stockton's hometown), while Rev. Charles Stewart departs to begin a missionary tour of the South with a member of the ABCFM.

1827–1830: Stockton is hired by Committee of Eight women as school principal and head teacher at the Infant School for Coloured Children, 60 Gaskill Street, Philadelphia. Stockton uses Wilderspin's methods.

Apr. 21, 1828: Stockton arrives in Philadelphia after visiting Joanna Bethune at NYC infant school at Five Points, Manhattan: First Infant School at Green Street, basement of Canal Street Presbyterian Church. John B. Russwum, editor of *Freedom's Journal,* sends set of colored lithographs to Philadelphia school.

May 4, 1829: Stockton leaves Philadelphia Infant School.

July 30, 1829: Stockton is sent traveling expenses, teaches at Ojibwa mission school, Grape Island, (Belleville) Ontario, Canada. Uses Pestalozzi method and some materials similar to Wilderspin (see "Map of Prince Edward District, Upper Canada," 151, especially fig. 4.1).

Oct 5/14, 1830 "Betsey Stockton has resigned her [post] owing to private duties. Her place [at the Gaskill Street school] has not yet been permanantly supplied."

Jan. 25, 1829: Rev. C. Samuel Stewart departs from Washington, DC, and arrives on US ship *Guerriere,* Hampton Roads, Virginia, on Jan. 30, 1829.

1830: Stockton presumed to have moved back to Princeton, after death of Harriet Stewart with surrogate children Charles "Charlie" Seaforth Stewart and daughter Harriet "Hattie" Stewart. Rev. C. Samuel Stewart is now US naval chaplain. Betsey Stockton enrolls Charlie in Edgehill School for Boys on Edgehill Street, Princeton, supported by the McClellan family. Aided by Anthony Simmons, an African American entrepreneur, Stockton holds classes on the second floor of the Presbyterian Church session house, now Kopps' Cycle Shop, near Princeton Public Library.

1837: "Scene at the Sandwich Islands: Stewart" in *The Eclectic Fourth Reader* by William H. McGuffy, 10–14 (Cincinnati: Truman and Smith, 1837). "The Whale Ship" a narrative of the loss of the *Essex*, 31–33; and "The Character of Wilberforce," 8off, are in the same volume.

Nov. 14, 1838: Princeton's first school is kept by Betsey Stockton. "There are now kept in Princeton to my knowledge no less than 6 schools namely … one by Betsey Stockton & lastly one by G. Yaffe—the last two for negroes" (Richard Stockton, "Letter to Joseph Addison Alexander").

Oct. 1841: Founding of the Witherspoon Street Church for the Colored, Princeton, NJ, with Stockton on the list of ninety-two communicants who applied for membership there from the New Brunswick Presbytery. These individuals are dismissed by the Presbyterian Church in Princeton, with dates of dismissal, to form their own church.

April 1847: Entry about Stockton's District School #6, forty-five scholars, in "Town Superintendent's Common School Register." This rectangular wooden school, facing Witherspoon Street, between Maclean and Quarry Streets, no longer exists.

Nov. 5, 1852: Evening exercises by "Aunt Betsey's scholars" for students, parents, and the public who afterwards pass to the public school house.

Oct. 21, 1854: New wooden building erected on Witherspoon Street for morning and afternoon sessions of the Witherspoon Street Presbyterian Church.

Nov. 1, 1860: Captain Charles Seaforth Stewart (whom Stockton delivered on shipboard of the whaler *Thames*) buys a house on Witherspoon Street and leases it to Stockton "for her natural life, for one dollar a year" (*Mercer County Book of Deeds*, bk 49, p. 34, and bk Sp. A, p. 12; recorded Mar. 1, 1861).

1860: Stockton's niece Evelina Brazier, "Mulatto," is living with her, according to the 1860 Princeton census.

1860: "Captain Pease, otherwise unidentified, met Stockton at the depot on the NY Central RR. She was returning from Cooperstown, NY, to attend the burial of Charles Stewart's youngest daughter, Martha Stewart Wilson (1828–1860)" (*Sailors' Magazine and Seamen's Friend* 51 [1913] 100–101).

May/June, 1863: Three daguerreotype portraits of Betsey Stockton, Frederick Douglass, and Rev. Charles Samuel Stewart are taken at Augustus Moran's Brooklyn, NY, studio, as marked on back of Stewart's portrait.

Oct. 25, 1865: Stockton dies at Princeton. Her obituary is published in the *Freeman's Journal and New York Observer*, **Nov. 9, 1865**. Burial in Cooperstown, NY, in Stewart family plot, beside Harriet Stewart, as Stockton requested. A fitting epitaph, drawn from Ashbel Green's published early sermon on *The Christian Duty of Christian Women*, would be "She Hath Done What She Could."

Feb. 23, 1866: House formerly occupied by Stockton published as for sale in *Princeton Standard*.

1902: Charles Seaforth Stewart dies at his house at Siasconset, Nantucket, MA. He had graduated from Valley Forge Military Academy, Class of 1846, valedictorian, and served in the Civil War. He had mentioned Stockton nursing him during the Civil War. In her will, Stockton had returned to him the house he had bought for her on Witherspoon Street, Princeton. He had become a civil naval engineer and chief designer of bridges in San Francisco.

1906: A. A. Woodhull (Civil War physician) and Rev. Lewis Mudge conduct a service of commemoration of Stockton in Witherspoon Street Presbyterian Church, placing a bronze plaque on the wall. This is possibly the time at which the stained glass window was placed as well.

Nota bene. From Ashbel Green's will: Green thought he would "destroy his journal," the secret journal that he wrote in cryptographic holograph, as there were aspects that he did not want to be revealed after his death.

Reading Group Guide
Questions and Topics for Discussion

1. Who might have fathered Betsey Stockton, assuming that Sealy or Celia, an African slave at Constitution Hill, was her mother?

2. What role did Reverend Ashbel Green play in her early education? In her later education?

3. Remembering the possibilities of education for girls in the early nineteenth century, why do you think Ashbel Green sent Betsey Stockton to live with Nathaniel Todd for three years when she was in her teens?

4. What life skills that Betsey Stockton learned at the Todds' were later essential for her physical health, as well as that of her "mission family"?

5. Where did Stockton's "missionary brother," Rev. Charles Samuel Stewart, gain his knowledge of the law and his familiarity with medicine? How was his knowledge of law and medicine useful to Betsey Stockton in the Sandwich Islands? In Princeton?

6. From the excerpts included here, how would you characterize the authors of the three *Thames* whaleship journals of Betsey Stockton, Charles Samuel Stewart, and Louisa Everest Ely?

7. In what ways was Betsey Stockton's "Jounal" aboard the *Thames* a precursor of Herman Melville's masterpiece *Moby Dick*?

8. What was/were the cause(s) of the poor health of many of the missionary wives and the early death of their young children in the Sandwich Islands, perceived as a paradise? Upon what elements from early nineteenth-century New England was their perception based?

9. Why did mother Harriet Bradford Stewart and father Rev. Charles Stewart entrust Betsey Stockton with the extended care of their year-and-a-half year old son Charles and three-month-old infant Harriet Stewart during their three-month cruise on Lord Byron's *HMS Blonde* in 1825?

10. What factors contributed to the primitive shelter and meager diet of Betsey Stockton, the Stewarts, and their two young chilcren at Lahaina, Maui, 1822 to 1825?

11. How did Betsey Stockton's bilingualism, teaching expertise, and/or organization benefit the scholars' in each of the following schools?

   a. Princeton, "apt to teach colored children," 1818?

   b. Lahaina, Maui, *maka aninima*, eight commoners, school in the yard of the mission house, June, 1823, her first school there

   c. Lahaina, Maui, teaching English to thirty Sandwich Islanders with other mission wives, 1824/25

   d. Infant School for Coloured Children, 60 Gaskill Street, Philadelphia, 1828/29

   e. Grape Island Ojibwa Mission School, Summer 1829

   f. Tutoring Charles Seaforth Stewart, Princeton 1830s

   g. District School #6, Princeton 1847–1865

   h. Morning and afternoon Sabbath School, First Presbyterian Church for the Colored, Witherspoon Street, after 1842 until 1865

Bibliography

Primary Sources

American Board of Commissioners for Foreign Missions. *Report of the American Board of Commissioners for Foreign Missions. Fourteenth Meeting.* Boston: Crocker and Brewster, 1823.

"American Missionaries at the Sandwich Islands." *North American Review* 26, no. 58 (Jan. 1828) 59–111. https://www.jstor.org/stable/25102686?refreqid=excelsior%3 A497557652de2f5f294e9416853e9bc88&seq=1#metadata_info_tab_contents.

"The Annual Meeting of the Tax Payers . . ." *Princeton Press,* Apr. 25, 1874.

"At Three-and-a-Half O'Clock . . ." *Princeton Press,* June 21, 1873.

Bangs, Nathaniel, and Beverley Waugh, eds. *Christian Advocate and Zion's Herald* (June 1829; July 11, 1829; Feb 5, 1830; Feb. 19, 1830).

Bartine, O. H. "Town Superintendent's Common School Register of the Township of Princeton, County of Mercer. 1847–1860s." Holograph manuscript. Collection of the Historical Society of Princeton, NJ.

Bethune, George. *Memoirs of Mrs. Joanna Bethune by Her Son, with an Appendix Containing Extracts of Some of Her Writings.* New York: Harper, 1863.

Bingham, Hiram. *A Residence of Twenty-One Years in the Sandwich Islands; of the Civil, Religious, and Political History of Those Islands.* 3rd ed. Reprint, New York: Praeger, 1969.

Board of Education of Princeton, New Jersey. "First Annual Report." Apr. 19, 1858. PB 1184.7353. Princeton University Library, Princeton, NJ.

Board of Trustees of the New Jersey State Normal School. *Seventeenth Annual Report of the Board of Trustees of the New Jersey State Normal School and Accompanying Documents, for the Year Ending October 31, 1871.* Trenton: State Gazette Office, 1872. College of New Jersey, Ewing, NJ.

Bustill-Smith, Anna. *Reminiscences of Colored People of Princeton, N.J., 1800–1900.* Philadelphia: Baugh, 1913.

Byron, George Anson. *Voyage of H.M.S. Blonde to the Sandwich Islands in the Years 1824–1825.* Edited by Maria Graham Callcott. London: Murray, 1826.

Case, William, and Nathaniel Waugh. "What Christian Missions Have Done." *Christian Advocate and Zion's Herald* 2, no. 44 (July 2, 1829) 173–74.

Chase, Owen, et al. *Narratives of the Wreck of the Whaleship Essex.* Reprint, New York: Dover, 1989.

Clasby, Reuben. "List of Persons Composing the Crew of the Ship *Thames* of New Haven whereof Is Master Reuben Clasby Bound for the Pacific Ocean." Manuscript, signed Oct. 8, 1822. E791, box 16, National Archives and Records Administration, Northeast Region (Boston).

———. "Report and Manifest of the Cargo Laden on Board the Ship *Thames* of New Haven, Manifest Dated November 10, 1825. 'Nineteen Hundred Barrels of Sperm

Oil in Casks of Different Sizes.'" Manuscript, signed Oct. 29, 1825, Reuben Clasby.
E774, box 85 (New Haven, Inward Foreign Manifests), National Archives and
Records Administration, Northeast Region (Boston).

Davidson, Amelia. "Letter to John Brown Russwurm." Apr. 1, 1828. In "Letterbook of
the Coloured School Committee." Box 1, file (Phi), 1665. Historical Society of
Pennsylvania, Philadelphia.

———. "Letter to John Brown Russwurm." Apr. 24–28, 1828. In "Letterbook of
the Coloured School Committee." Box 1, file (Phi), 1665. Historical Society of
Pennsylvania, Philadelphia.

———. "Letter to Betsey Stockton." Apr. 1, 1828. In "Letterbook of the Coloured
School Committee." Box 1, file (Phi), 1665. Historical Society of Pennsylvania,
Philadelphia.

Ellis, William. *An Examination of Charges against the American Missionaries of the
Sandwich Islands, as Alleged in the Voyage of the Ship* Blonde *and in the* London
Quarterly Review. Cambridge, UK: Hilliard, Metcalf, 1827. https://archive.org/
details/examinationofchaooelli.

———. *A Journal of a Tour around Hawaii the Largest of the Sandwich Islands by a
Deputation of the Mission on Those Islands.* New York: Haven, 1825.

———. *Polynesian Researches: Being a Resident of Nearly Eight Years in the Society and
Sandwich Islands.* Vol 4. 2nd ed. London: Fisher, Son & Jackson, 1832.

Ely, Louisa Everett. *Diary of Missionary Voyage from New Haven Connecticut via
Cape Horn to the Sandwich Islands on Ship Thames, 1822–1823.* Ms. 77547 at the
Connecticut Historical Society, Hartford, CT.

Evans, James. *The Speller and Interpreter in Indian and English, for the Use of the Mission
Schools, and Such as May Desire to Obtain Knowledge of the Ojibway Tongue.* New
York: Fanshaw, 1830.

Evarts, Jeremiah. "Contract between Betsey Stockton and the American Board of
Commissioners for Foreign Missions." Holograph copy, Nov. 18, 1822. Bank 3,
drawer A, Missionary Letters (1816–1900) Collection, Hawaiian Mission Houses
Site and Archives, Honolulu.

First Presbyterian Church for the Colored. "Records of the Morning Sabbath School,
1852–1865." First Presbyterian Church for the Colored, Princeton. Gen. Mss
bound. Ms 1184-738. Princeton University Library, Princeton, NJ.

Green, Ashbel. "Sandwich Islands." *Christian Advocate* 3 (May 1825) 234–36.

———. *The Christian Duty of Christian Women: A Discourse Delivered in the Church at
Princeton, New Jersey, August 23, 1825, before the Female Society for the Support of
a Female School in India.* Princeton, NJ: Borrenstein, 1825.

———. *Diaries, 1792–1848.* Bound typescript volumes with pagination. 4000 pages.
Papers of Ashbel Green, Princeton University Library, Princeton, NJ.

———. "Letter to Jeremiah Evarts." Sept. 3, 1821. A. B. C. F. M. Collection. Houghton
Library, Harvard University, Cambridge, MA.

———. "Last Will and Testament." Sept. 14, 1848. Philadelphia, PA, County File 226.
Will Book 21, 81–88.

———. *Proceedings of the Bible Society at Nassau Hall.* Trenton, NJ: George Sherman,
1814.

———, ed. "Religious Intelligence." *Christian Advocate* 2 (May 1824) 232–35.

Infant School Society of Philadelphia. "Account Book of the Infant School Society of Philadelphia." Md. Bd. 1828–1832. Historical Society of Pennsylvania, Philadelphia.

———. "Constitution and By-Laws of the Infant-School Society of Philadelphia." Philadelphia: Stavely, 1833.

———. *The First Annual Report of the Infant School Society of Philadelphia.* Philadelphia: Lydia R. Bailey, 1828.

———. *The Fourth Annual Report of the Infant School Society of Philadelphia.* Philadelphia: Geddes, 1831.

———. "Letterbook of the Coloured School Committee." 1828. Box 1, file (Phi), 1665. Historical Society of Pennsylvania, Philadelphia.

———. "Record Book of the Infant School Society of Philadelphia, 1827–1885." Ms. Bd, Am 1665. Historical Society of Pennsylvania, Philadelphia.

———. *The Second Annual Report of the Infant School Society of Philadelphia.* Philadelphia: Geddes, 1829.

Jones, Joseph H. *The Life of Ashbel Green, V.D.M., Which Was to Be Written by Himself in His Eighty-Second Year and Continued until His Eighty-Fourth.* New York: Carter, 1849.

Jones, Peter. *Life and Journals of Kah-Ke-Wa-Quo-Na-By (Rev. Peter Jones).* Toronto: Green, 1860.

Lincoln University. *Catalogue of Lincoln University, Chester County, Pennsylvania, for the Academical Year 1877–78.* Philadelphia: Ashmead, 1878. https://www.lincoln.edu/sites/default/files/library/specialcollections/CATALOGUES/1877-78.pdf.

Loomis, Albertine. *Grapes of Canaan.* New York: Dodd, Mead, 1950.

Loomis, Elisha. *Copy of the Journal of E. Loomis, 1824–1826.* Compiled by William D. Westervelt. Honolulu: University of Hawaii, 1937.

MacDonald, James, and Thomas Wright Jr. "On the Fourteenth Day . . ." *Princeton Press,* Apr. 26, 1873.

"Manuscript Population Schedule, Princeton Township, Mercer County, NJ." In 6th US Census (1840). National Archives, Washington, DC.

"Manuscript Population Schedule, Princeton Township, Mercer County, NJ." In 7th US Census (1850). National Archives, Washington, DC.

"Map of Prince Edward District, Upper Canada." Carto N-4012. F0005309. Archives of Ontario, Canada.

McGuffey, William H. *The Eclectic Fourth Reader: Containing Elegant Extracts in Prose and Poetry, from the Best American and English Writers, etc.* Cincinnati: Truman and Smith, 1837.

Mercer County Book of Deeds. Mercer County Clerk's Office, Trenton, NJ.

"Minutes of the Common Council of the Borough of Princeton, 1848—." Holograph manuscript. Princeton Municipal Building, Witherspoon Street, Princeton, NJ.

New Jersey General Assembly. *Acts of Thirteenth General Assembly of the State of New Jersey October 1788.* Trenton, NJ: Collins, 1788.

"New York Passenger Lists, 1820–1957." For the ship *Richmond*; port of departure: London; arrival on Aug. 4, 1826, New York. Microfilm serial M237, microfilm roll M237_8, list number 451. Ancestry Library. http://search.ancestrylibrary.com/cgi-bin/sse.dll?+nypl%2c&rank=0&tips=0&gsfn=Charles&gsl.

Nickerson, Thomas. *The Loss of the Ship,* Essex, *Sunk by a Whale and the Ordeal of the Crew in Open Boats.* Nantucket, MA: Nantucket Historical Association, 1984.

———. "The Ship *Two Brothers*." Unpublished holograph manuscript, 1881. Collection 106, folder 3½. Nantucket Historical Association Collection, Nantucket, MA.

"Obituary [of Betsey Stockton]." *New York Observer*, Nov. 9, 1865.

"Obituary [of Betsey Stockton]." *Freeman's Journal* (Cooperstown, NY), Nov. 3, 1865.

Orme, William. *A Defense of the Missions in the South Sea and Sandwich Islands.* London: Holdsworth, 1827.

Osborn, Michael. "Letter to Jeremiah Evarts." Sept. 3, 1821. A. B. C. F. M. Collection, Houghton Library, Harvard University, Cambridge, MA.

Pomeroy, Ann. "Letter to Harriet Stewart." July 2, 1822. Cooperstown Female Missionary Society. New York State Historical Association, Cooperstown, NY.

Presbyterian Church of Princeton. "The Minutes of the Session of the Presbyterian Church of Princeton, NJ, 1792–1822." In *The Church Book, 1792–1822,* unpaginated. Speer Library, Princeton Theological Seminary, Princeton, NJ.

———. "Register of the Presbyterian Church of Princeton, Prefaced by the Session, in Obedience to the Order of the Presbytery, at the Meeting in Cranberry, Oct. 1841." Speer Library, Princeton Theological Seminary, Princeton, NJ.

"Princeton, Mercer Co. with Business Directory." Circa 1860. Map Division, Firestone Library, Princeton University, Princeton, NJ.

Registers of Vessels Arriving at the Port of New York from Foreign Ports, 1789–1919. Micropublication M237, rolls 1–95. Washington, DC: National Archives and Records Administration.

Rush, Benjamin. "Letter to Julia Rush." Sept. 22, 1793. In *Letters of Benjamin Rush,* vol. 2, 1793–1813. Princeton, NJ: Princeton University Press, 1951.

———. "Observations Intended to Favour a Supposition that the Black Color (as It Is Called) of the Negroes Is Derived from the Leprosy." Read at a special meeting, July 14, 1792. In *Transactions of the American Philosophical Society* 35, 288–97. Philadelphia: American Philosophical Society, 1799.

Russwurm, John Brown, ed. *Freedom's Journal.* New York: Mar. 1827–Mar. 1829.

Society of Friends. *Statistical Inquiry into the Condition of the People of Colour, of the City and Districts of Philadelphia.* Philadelphia: Kite & Walton, 1849. https://www.loc.gov/item/12014690/.

Stewart, Charles Seaforth. "Letter to Martha Chamberlain." Oct. 27, 1899. Hawaiian Children's Mission Society, Honolulu.

Stewart, Charles Samuel. *A Private Journal of a Voyage to the Pacific Ocean and Residence at the Sandwich Islands, in the Years 1822, 1823, 1824, and 1825, Including Descriptions of the Natural Scenery, and Remarks on the Manners and Customs of the Inhabitants; an Account of Lord Byon's Visit in the British Frigate* Blonde, *and an Excursion to the Great Volcano of Kirauea in Hawaii.* 3rd ed., corrected and enlarged with an introduction and notes by Rev. William Ellis. New York: Haven, 1828.

———. *A Residence in the Sandwich Islands.* Boston: Weeks, 1839.

———. *Sketches of Society in Great Britain and Ireland.* 2 vols. Philadelphia: Carey, Lea and Blancard, 1834.

———. *A Visit to the South Seas, in the U.S. Ship Vincennes, during the Years 1829 and 1839; with Scenes in Brazil, Peru, Manilla, the Cape of Good Hope, and St. Helena.* Edited by William Ellis. 2 vols. New York: Haven, 1831.

Stewart, Harriet Bradford Tiffany. "Letter to Her Mother." Oct. 24, 1824. Reverend Charles Stewart Papers (collection 263), New York State Historical Association, Cooperstown, NY.

————. "Letter to Miss Olivia Murray." July 3, 1822. Reverend Charles Stewart Papers (collection 263), New York State Historical Association, Cooperstown, NY.

————. "Letter to My Very Dear Friend" [Miss Olivia Murray]. Mar. 21, 1827. Reverend Charles Stewart Papers (collection 263), New York State Historical Association, Cooperstown, NY.

————. "Letter to Unnamed Recipient." Dec. 19, 1828. Reverend Charles Stewart Papers (collection 263), New York State Historical Association, Cooperstown, NY.

Stockton, Betsey. "Holograph Last Will and Testament of Betsey Stockton, Single Woman." Nov. 22, 1862. Book D, folio 389, 8–11. Wills of Mercer County, NJ, Archives, Trenton, NJ.

————. "Journal." *Christian Advocate* 1 (Feb. 1823) 88–89, (Sept. 1823) 423–26; 2 (May 1824) 232–35, (Dec. 1824) 563–66; 3 (Jan. 1825) 36–40, (Apr. 1825) 187–89.

————. "Letter to Levi Chamberlain." Dec. 5, 1824. Hawaiian Mission Children's Society Archives, Honolulu.

————. "Letters to Reverend Charles S. Stewart." Oct. 20, 1845, and Jan. 6, 1846. Papers of C. S. Stewart, New York Historical Association, Cooperstown, NY.

Stockton, Richard. "Letter to Joseph Addison Alexander." Nov. 14, 1848. Letters and Journal of Joseph Addison Alexander, Princeton 1837–1851. Mss bd. CO 199. Princeton University Library, Princeton, NJ.

Stockton, Robert. "Letter to Ashbel Green." Apr. 24, 1797. Ashbel Green Collection, box 2, folder 48, CO 257. Princeton University Library, Princeton, NJ.

"A Survey of the Infant School System." *Christian Advocate and Religious Intelligence* 4, no. 23 (Feb. 5, 1830) 1.

Wilderspin, Samuel. *A System for the Education of the Youth, Applied to All the Faculties; Founded on the Immense Experiences of Many Thousands of Children.* London: n.p., 1840.

Witherspoon Street Presbyterian Church. "One Hundredth Anniversary Program of the Witherspoon Street Presbyterian Church of Princeton, New Jersey, Sunday, October 20th, to Monday, October 28th." 1940. Unpaginated. Program in author's possession.

Woodhull, A. A., and Lewis W. Mudge. "Betsey Stockton and the Hawaiian Schools." *Princeton Press*, May 27, 1899.

————. "Betsey Stockton." *Princeton Press*, Nov. 21, 1903.

————. "Betsey Stockton." *Princeton Press*, Apr. 7, 1906.

Youth's Penny Gazette 3, no. 25 (Dec. 3, 1845). New York: American Sunday School Union.

———— 16, no. 4 (Feb. 17, 1858). New York: American Sunday School Union.

Secondary Sources

Ackroyd, Peter. *Dickins.* London: Harper Collins, 1990.

Altenbaugh, Richard J., ed. *Historical Dictionary of American Education.* Westport, CT: Greenwood, 1999.

Annan, Kofi. "Secretary-General Stresses Need for Political Will and Resources to Meet Challenge of Fight against Illiteracy." United Nations Meetings Coverage and Press Releases, Sept. 4, 1997. https://www.un.org/press/en/1997/19970904. SGSM6316.html.

Aymar, Brant. *A Pictorial Treasury of the Marine Museums of the World.* New York: Crown, 1967.

Bacon, Jacqueline. "'Acting as Freemen': Rhetoric, Race, and Reform in the Debate over Colonization in *Freedom's Journal,* 1827–1828." *Quarterly Journal of Speech* 98, no. 1 (2007) 58–83.

———. *Freedom's Journal: The First African-American Newspaper.* New York: Lexington, 2007.

Barbash, Ilisa, et al., eds. *To Make Their Own Way in the World: The Enduring Legacy of the Zealy Daguerreotypes.* Cambridge, MA: Peabody Museum, 2020.

Barclay, W. C. *Part One: Early American Methodism 1769–1844.* Missionary Motivation and Expansion 1. New York: Board of Missions and Church Extension of the Methodist Church, 1949.

Beatty, Barbara. *Preschool Education in America: The Culture of Young Children from the Colonia Era to the Present.* New Haven, CT: Yale University Press, 1995.

Bernier, Celeste. "Frederick Douglass the Destination." *New York Times,* Dec 1, 2019, 20.

"Betsey 'Betsy' Stockton." Find a Grave. https://www.findagrave.com/memorial/143939357/betsey-stockton.

Biographical Catalogue of the Princeton Theological Seminary, 1815–1932. Princeton, NJ: Princeton Theological Seminary, 1933.

Birchenough, Charles. *History of Elementary Education in England and Wales from 1800 to the Present Day.* London: Clive, 1925.

Blight, David W. *Frederick Douglass: Prophet of Freedom.* New York: Simon & Schuster, 2018.

Brennan, Lawrence. "Chaplain Charles S. Stewart, 1795–1870, and a 158-year-old Cover." *New Jersey Philatelist History* 43, no. 3 (Aug. 2015) 134–40.

Brown, Lesley. *The New Oxford Shorter English Dictionary.* 2 vols. Oxford, UK: Clarendon, 1993.

Buckley, J. M. *A History of Methodists in the United States.* New York: Christian Literature, 1846.

Calhoun, David B. *Princeton Seminary: Faith and Learning, 1812–1868.* Carlyle, PA: Banner of Truth Trust, 1994.

Carmelich, Julie P. "Witherspoon Street School for Colored Children." Introduction in "National Register for Historic Places Registration Form," 8. Submitted to National Historic Sites Registry, Washington, DC, Jan. 6, 2005.

Christensen, Nate. "Mahlon Van Horne (1840–1910)." Black Past, June 3, 2011. https://www.blackpast.org/african-american-history/van-horne-mahlon-1840-1910/.

Cushing, Thos, and Charles E. Sheppard. *History of the Counties of Gloucester, Salem, and Cumberland New Jersey.* Philadelphia: Everts and Peck, 1883.

Demos, John. *The Heathen School: A Story of Hope and Betrayal in the Age of the Early Republic.* New York: Knopf, 2014.

Dowling, David O. *Surviving the Essex: The Aftermath of America's Most Storied Shipwreck.* Lebanon, NH: University Press of New England, 2016.

Delaney, John. *Strait Through: Magellan to Cook and the Pacific: An Illustrated History.* Princeton, NJ: Princeton University Library, 2010.

"Dr Alfred Alexander Woodhull Jr." Find a Grave. https://www.findagrave.com/memorial/19344483/alfred-alexander-woodhull.

Duryee, H. B. "Public Sale of House and Lot, Formerly Occupied by Betsy (sic) Stockton, Dec'd . . . " *Princeton Standard,* Feb. 23, 1866.

Dye, Ira. "Early American Merchant Seafarers." *Proceedings of the American Philosophical Society* 120, no. 5 (Oct. 15, 1976) 331–60. Philadelphia: American Philosophical Society, 1976.

Eames, Frank. *Pioneer Schools of Upper Canada: Grape Island.* Papers and Records 17. Ontario Historical Society. Toronto: Archives of Canada, 1920.

Escher, Constance K. *Being Themselves: Four Stars of Princeton: The Children's Museum Exhibit Guide.* Princeton, NJ: Historical Society of Princeton, 1984.

———. "Betsey Stockton." In *Past and Promise: Lives of New Jersey Women,* edited by Joan N. Burstyn, 87–89. Metuchen, NJ: Scarecrow, 1990.

———. "A Force for Learning." *Princeton Alumni Weekly,* July 13, 2018.

———. "Rachel Boudinot Bradford." In *Past and Promise: Lives of New Jersey Women,* edited by Joan N. Burstyn, 10–12. Metuchen, NJ: Scarecrow, 1990.

———. "She Calls Herself Betsey Stockton." *Princeton History: The Journal of the Historical Society of Princeton* 10 (1991) 71–101.

———, and Carolyn DeSwarte Gifford. "Jarena Lee." In *Past and Promise: Lives of New Jersey Women,* edited by Joan N. Burstyn, 77–79. Metuchen, NJ: Scarecrow, 1990.

Fishman, William J. *The Streets of East London.* London: BAS, 1979.

Frank, Stuart M. *Herman Melville's Picture Gallery: Sources and Types of the 'Pictorial' Chapters of Moby Dick.* Fairhaven, MA: Lefkowitz, 1986.

Frear, Walter F. "Anti-Missionary Criticism with Reference to Hawaii." Paper read at the Honolulu Social Science Association, Jan. 7, 1935. Honolulu: Advertiser, 1935.

French, Thomas. *The Missionary Whaleship.* New York: Vantage, 1963.

Gates, Henry Louis, Jr. "The Face and Voice of Blackness." In *Facing History: The Black Image in American Art 1710-1940,* by Guy C. McElroy, edited by Christopher C. French, xxix–xliv. Washington, DC: Corcoran Gallery, 1990.

Gibson, Arrell Morgan. *Yankees in Paradise: The Pacific Basin Frontier.* Albuquerque: University of New Mexico Press, 1993.

Gilpin, Donald. "Preserving History: The Witherspoon-Jackson Heritage Tour." *Princeton Magazine* (Sept. 2019) 55–61.

Greiff, Constance M., and Wanda S. Gunning, eds. *Morven: Memory, Myth and Reality.* Princeton, NJ: Historic Morven, 2004.

Greiff, Constance M., et al. *Princeton Architecture: A Pictorial History of Town and Campus.* Princeton, NJ: Princeton University Press, 1967.

Grimshaw, Patricia. *Paths of Duty: American Missionary Wives in Nineteenth-Century Hawaii.* Honolulu: University of Hawaii, 1989.

Gross, Bella. "*Freedom's Journal* and the Rights of All." *Journal of Negro History* 17, no. 3 (July 1933) 241–86.

Hageman, J. F. *History of Princeton and Its Institutions.* 2 vols. New York: Lippincott, 1879.

Hamm, Theodore, ed. *Frederick Douglass in Brooklyn.* New York: Akashic, 2017.

"Harriet Bradford Tiffany Stewart." https://en.wikipedia.org/wiki/Harriet_Bradford_Tiffany_Stewart.

Hayden, Philip A. "With Promptness, Effciency and Exactness: Princeton and the 1850 Census." *Princeton History* 9 (1990) 18–29.

Hefferman, Thomas Farel. "Miffinburg Academy." In *History of That Part of the Susquehanna and Juniata Valleys, Embraced in the Counties of Mifflin, Juniata, Perry, Union and Snyder, in the Commonwealth of Pennsylvania,* edited by F. Ellis and A. N. Hungerford, 2:1367. Philadelphia: Everts, Peck and Richards, 1886.

————. *Stove By a Whale: Oven Chase and the Essex.* Middletown, CT: Wesleyan University Press, 1993.

"History of Slavery in New Jersey." Wikipedia, last edited Nov. 2, 2021. https://en.wikipedia.org/wiki/An_Act_for_the_Gradual_Abolition_of_Slavery.

Jackson, Kenneth R. *The Encyclopedia of New York City.* New Haven, CT: Yale University Press, 1995.

"Johann Heinrich Pestalozzi." https://en.wikipedia.org/wiki/Johann_Heinrich_Pestalozzi.

Johnston, Paul Forsythe. "A Million Pounds of Sandalwood: *Cleopatra's Barge* in Hawaii." *American Neptune* 62, no. 1 (2002) 1–41.

————. *Shipwrecked in Paradise: History of Cleopatra's Barge in Hawai'i.* Washington, DC: Smithsonian Institution, 2015.

Judd, Bernice. "Voyages to Hawaii before 1860." Honolulu: University Press of Hawaii, 1960.

Judd, Beatrice, et al. *Missionary Album: Portraits and Biographical Sketches of the American Protestant Missionaries to the Hawaiian Island.* Honolulu: Hawaiian Mission Children's Society, 1969.

Kaestle, Carl F. *Pillars of the Republic: Common Schools and the American Society, 1780–1860.* New York: Hill and Want, 1983.

Karttunen, Frances Ruley. *The Other Islanders: People Who Pulled Nantucket's Oars.* New Bedford, MA: Spinner, 2005.

Lascarides, V. Celia, and Blyanthe F. Hinitz. *History of Early Childhood Education.* London: Falmer, 2000.

Link, Arthur S., ed. *The First Presbyterian Church of Princeton: Two Centuries of History.* Princeton, NJ: Princeton University Press, 1967.

Little, Stephen, and Peter Ruthenberg, eds. *Life in the Pacific of the 1700's, Exhibition Guide.* Honolulu: Honolulu Academy of Arts, 2006.

MacDonald and Wright. "On the Fourteenth Day." Princeton Press, April 26, 1873. Front page.

MacLean, Hope. "A Positive Experiment in Aboriginal Education: The Methodist Ojibwa Day Schools in Upper Canada, 1824–1833." *Canadian Journal of Native Studies* 22, no. 1 (2002) 23–63. http://www3.brandonu.ca/cjns/22.1/cjnsv.22no.1_pg23-63.pdf.

Macy, Obed. *The History of Nantucket . . . and Whale Fisheries.* 2 vols. Boston: Hilliard, Gray, 1835.

May, Helen. "'Nurseries of Discipline': Infant School Experiments in Britain." *Journal of the History of Childhood and Youth* 8, no. 2 (2015) 71–110.

May, Helen, et al. "'The Blessings of Civilization': Nineteenth-Century Missionary Infant Schools for Young Native Children in Three Colonial settings—India, Canada and New Zealand 1820's–1840's." *Paedagogica Historica* 45, nos. 1–2 (Feb.–Apr., 2009) 83–102.

————. *Empire, Education, and Indigenous Childhoods: Nineteenth-Century Missionary Infant Schools in Three British Colonies.* Ashgate Studies in Childhood, 1700 to the Present. Surrey, UK: Ashgate, 2014.

McCann, Phillip, and Francis A. Young. *Samuel Wilderspin and the Infant School Movement.* London: Croon Helm, 1982.

McElroy, Guy C. *Facing History: The Black Image in American Art, 1710–1940.* Washington, DC: Corcoran Gallery, 1990.

McKissack, Patricia C., and Frederick M. McKissack. *Black Hands, White Sails: The Story of African-American Whalers*. New York: Scholastic, 1999.

McLachlan, James. "Ashbel Green, A. B. 1783." In *Princetonians: 1776-1783: A Biographical Dictionary*, edited by Richard A. Harrison, 404-20. Princeton Legacy Library. Princeton, NJ: Princeton University Press, 1981.

Melville, Herman. *Moby-Dick; or, The Whale*. New York: Penguin, 1992.

Mitros, David. "Jacob Green and the Slavery Debate in Revolutionary Morris County, New Jersey." Morristown, NJ: Morris County Heritage Commisssion,1993.

Mitter, Siddhartta. "Looking for Frederick Douglass in Savannah." *New York Times*, Nov. 29, 2019.

Moffett, Elaine, and John Andrews. "Betsey Stockton: Stranger and in a Strange Land." In *Profiles of African-American Missionaries*, edited by Robert J. Stevens and Brian Johnson, 157-66. Pasadena, CA: William Carey Library, 1995.

Montague, C. J. *Sixty Years in Waifdom; or, The Ragged School Movement in English History*. New York: Kelley, 1969.

Moorhead, James H. "'The Restless Spirit of Radicalism': Old School Fears and the Schism of 1837." *Journal of Presbyterian History* 78, no. 1 (1997) 19-33.

Morales, R. Isabela. "A Great Physician Had Help from a Freed Slave." *Princeton Alumni Weekly* 119, no.10 (Apr. 10, 2019) 51.

Murrin, John. "Christianity, Enlightenment and Revolution: Hard Choices at the College of New Jersey after Independence." *Princeton Library Chronicle* 50, no. 3 (Spring 1989) 220-61.

Newhall, Beamont. *The History of Photography: From 1839 to the Present*. Rev. ed. New York: Museum of Modern Art, 1982.

Obeyesekere, Gananath. *Cannibal Talk: The Man-Eating Myth and Human Sacrifice in the South Seas*. Berkeley, CA: University of California Press, 2005.

Ott, Alice T. "The 'Peculiar Case' of Betsey Stockton: Gender, Race and the Role of an Assistant Missionary to the Sandwich Islands (1822-1825)." *Studies in World Christianity* 21, no. 1 (2015) 4-19.

"Peter Jones (Missionary)." https://en.wikipedia.org/wiki/Peter_Jones_(missionary).

Philbrick, Nathaniel. *In the Heart of the Sea: The Tragedy of the Whaleship* Essex. New York: Penguin, 2000.

Reeds, Karen. "Come into a New World: Linnaeus and America: An Exhibition to Commemorate the Three Hundredth Birthday of the Great Swedish Scientist Carolus Linnaeus." Philadelphia: American Historical Swedish Museum, 2007.

Richards, Rhys. *Honolulu: Centre of Trans-Pacific Trade: Shipping Arrivals and Departures, 1820 to 1840*. Honolulu: Pacific Manuscripts Bureau and the Hawaiian Historical Society, 2000.

Roper, Caitlin, ed. "The New York Times Magazine 1619 Project." *New York Times Magazine*, Aug. 18, 2019.

Rothstein, Edward. "When Slavery and Its Foes Thrived in Brooklyn." *New York Times*, Jan. 17, 2014.

S., David. "A Reckoning In Princeton." Presbyterian Historical Society, Feb. 18, 2016. https://www.history.pcusa.org/blog/2016/02/reckoning-princeton.

Satterfield, Shirley A. *Witherspoon School Reunion: 1848-1948*. Princeton, NJ: Booklet Committee of the Witherspoon School Reunion Committee, 1996.

Savage, Henry Littleton. *Nassau Hall, 1756-1956*. Princeton, NJ: Princeton University Press, 1956.

Schneider, Paul. *The Enduring Shore: A History of Cape Cod, Martha's Vineyard, and Nantucket.* New York: Holt, 2000.

Shanahan, Ed. "New Jersey Seminary Pledges $27 Million in Reparations for Slavery." *New York Times,* Oct. 23, 2019.

Smith, Bernard. *European Vision and the South Pacific.* New Haven, CT: Yale University Press, 1985.

Smylie, James H. *American Presbyterians: A Pictorial History.* Philadelphia: Presbyerian Historical Society, 1985.

Sprague, William B. "William Case." In *Annals of the American Pulpit,* 7:425–27. New York: Carter, 1859.

Stackpole, Edouard A. *Sea-Hunters: The New England Whalemen during Two Centuries, 1635–1835.* Philadelphia: Lippincott, 1953.

Starbuck, Alexander. *The History of Nantucket County, Island and Town, including Genealogies of First Families.* Rutland, VT: Goodspeed, 1969.

Strasser, Susan. *Never Done: A History of American Housework.* New York: Pantheon, 1982.

Stauffer, John, et al. *Picturing Frederick Douglass: An Illustrated Biography of the Nineteenth Century's Most Photographed American.* New York: Norton, 2015.

Van Doren Honeyman, Abraham. *Somerset County Historical Quarterly* 1 (1912). Raritan, NJ: Somerset Historical Publications Reprint, 1977. https://dspace.njstatelib.org/xmlui/handle/10929/46268.

Wagner-Wright, Susan. *The Structure of the Missionary Call to the Sandwich Islands 1790–1830: Sojourners Among Strangers.* San Francisco: Mellon Research University Press, 1990.

Washington, Jack. *The Long Journey Home: A Bicentennial History of the Black Community of Princeton, New Jersey, 1776–1976.* Trenton, NJ: Africa World, 2005.

Waugh, John C. *The Class of 1846: From West Point to Appomattox: Stonewall Jackson, George McClennan, and Their Brothers.* New York: Random House, 1994.

Webb, Vivian, et al. *Les Sauvages de la Mer Pacificque: Manufactured by Joseph Dufour et Cie 1804–05 after a Design by Jean-Gabriel Charvet.* Australian Collection Focus 7. Sydney: Art Gallery of New South Wales, 2000.

Wilder, Craig Steven. *Ebony and Ivy: Race, Slavery, and the Troubled History of America's Universities.* New York: Bloomsbury, 2013.

Wilentz, Sean. "Princeton and the Controversies over Slavery." *Journal of Presbyterian History* 85, no. 2 (Fall/Winter 2007) 102–11.

Wilson, Joseph H. "Nathaniel Todd." In *Presbyterian Historical Almanac and Annual Remembrancer of the Church for 1868,* 10:152–53. Philadelphia: Wilson, 1868.

Wright, Giles R. *African Americans in New Jersey: A Short History.* Trenton, NJ: New Jersey Historical Commission, 1988.

———. "Stockton, Betsey. (c. 1798–1865) in Biographical Index of Missionaries— Sandwich Islands, Hawaii." Presbyterian Heritage Center. https://www.phcmontreat.org/bios/Bios-Missionaries-Hawaii.htm.

———. "Trustees Name Garden for Betsey Stockton, Arch for James Collins Johnson." *Princeton University Bulletin* 107, no. 4 (May 3, 2018).

Yocum, Cari. "Cecilia Ann (Vantyne) Vantine (1813–1886)." WikiTree, Nov. 8, 2019; modified Dec. 14, 2020. https//www.wikitree.com/wiki/Vantyne-17.

American Offshore Whaling Voyages

1. Voyages with Reuben Clasby at command. Six entries: beginning with ship *John and James* out of Nantucket, MA, departed c. 1811, arrived c. 1813; ending with ship *Thames*, out of New Haven, CT, departed Nov. 1822 for the Pacific, arrived New Haven, CT, Nov. 4, 1825. (Stackpole notes that Clasby rounded the horn five times.)

2. Voyages with Charles Ramsdell at command. Two entries: ship *Lydia* departed from Salem, MA, 1835, arrived Nov. 1837 from South Atlantic; ship *Lydia* departed from Salem, MA, Dec. 1837, arrived home Mar. 1840. See http://integratedstatistics.com/ejosephs/v2pages.

"American Offshore Whaling Voyages: A Database." National Maritime Digital Library. https://nmdl.org/projects/aowv/aowv/.

Burns, Ric. *Into the Deep: America, Whaling and the World*. Boston: WGBH Educational Foundation and Steeplechase Films, 2010. DVD.

CPSIA information can be obtained
at www.ICGtesting.com
Printed in the USA
LVHW010007281122
734125LV00009B/356

9 781725 275447